Study Guide Contents

Introduction to the Study Guide and Computer Workbook

This Study Guide is designed to help you learn the material in the text by providing summaries of chapter contents and by providing self-tests at the end of each chapter consisting of

- completion items based on the Key Terms defined in the chapter,
- multiple-choice items to test your knowledge of important terms and concepts presented in the chapter, and
- practice problems to test your ability to perform the calculations presented in the chapter.

Responses to the practice problems in the Key for each chapter follow the computational format in the text and are intended to be sufficiently complete to help you identify any mistakes you may make. These responses also follow the five-step hypothesis-testing process used throughout the text where appropriate. Chapters presenting analyses that can be conducted using a computer conclude with a section providing additional practice using SPSS.

Please note that no data were collected from any person, and although the studies are based on the author's research experience, no studies like those used as examples, to the author's knowledge, have actually been conducted. All data in the text examples and the practice problems were contrived to illustrate specific points, and the topics of the studies were designed to reflect studies that a behavioral scientist might conduct. I hope you find that the contexts of these hypothetical studies hold your interest and provide additional insight into behavioral science research. I also hope the data clearly reflected the instructional points made by the authors of the text.

Acknowledgments: The guidance of the text authors was very helpful in providing focus for this Study Guide, and special thanks are due to freelance editor, Erin K. L. Grelak, for providing information and answering questions in an amazingly short time. Thanks are also due to my students, who have contributed to the validity of the exercises by pointing out all my errors and lack of clarity.

Chapter 1
Displaying the Order in a Group of Numbers Using Tables and Graphs

Learning Objectives
After studying this chapter, you should:
- Know the differences among statistics, descriptive, and inferential statistics.
- Be able to use the terms *variable*, *value*, and *score* correctly.
- Be able to explain the concept of levels of measurement and know the different levels at which variables may be measured.
- Be able to construct frequency tables, grouped frequency tables, and histograms.
- Know the differences among unimodal, bimodal, and multimodal frequency distributions.
- Know the differences between symmetrical and skewed frequency distributions.
- Know what floor and ceiling effects are.
- Be able to distinguish normal, heavy-tailed, and light-tailed distributions.
- Know the ways that frequency tables and graphs are used in research articles.

Statistics and the Two Branches of Statistical Methods
Statistics is the branch of mathematics that focuses on the organization, analysis, and interpretation of groups of numbers, or data.

Descriptive statistics are used to summarize and make groups of numbers understandable.

Inferential statistics are used to draw conclusions based on the numbers actually collected during a research study, but going beyond these numbers.

Variables, Values, and Scores
A **variable** is a condition or characteristic that can have different values.

A **value** is a number or category that can result from the measurement of a variable.

A **score** is the value obtained by a particular person when a variable is measured.

Levels of Measurement
Numeric variables are also called *quantitative* variables. The three types of numeric variables are:

1. **Equal-interval variables** are numeric variables in which the numbers represent equal amounts of the condition or characteristic being measured. The intervals between the numbers that represent the amount of the variable a person has are equal so that the distance between scores of 10 and 12 is the same as the distance between 22 and 24 or 43 and 45.
2. **Rank-order variables** are numeric variables in which numbers correspond only to the relative position of the person on the condition or characteristic being measured (that is, the person's rank as first, second, and so on). The distances between ranks, however, may be equal. Rank-order variables are also called *ordinal* variables. An example of an ordinal scale would be ranking a group of people on a scale using markers like "severely depressed," "moderately depressed," "somewhat depressed," and "not significantly depressed."
3. **Nominal variables** are also called *categorical variables* because the values represent names or categories. A person's gender or diagnoses of anxiety or depression are examples of nominal variables.

Thus, **levels of measurement** reflect the types of underlying numerical information provided by a measure.

Frequency Tables
Frequency tables show how frequently each score occurs and are used to make the pattern of numbers clear at a glance.

How to Make a Frequency Table
1. Make a list of each possible value down the left side of a page, starting from the lowest and ending with the highest.
2. Go one by one through the group of scores, making a mark for each next to its value on your list.
3. Make a table showing how many times each value on your list was used.
4. Figure the percentage of scores for each value.

Frequency tables can also be made for nominal variables, for example, like the numbers of men and women in a study.

Grouped Frequency Tables

Grouped frequency tables are used when there are so many possible values that a frequency table would be too large to give a simple account of the information. The intent is to create groups of values, called intervals, so that after entering all the scores that fall within a certain interval, the pattern is easier to see at a glance.

How to Make a Grouped Frequency Table

Computers are used to create grouped frequency tables. However, the steps are the same as those for making a frequency table except that **intervals** replace the listing of possible values in Step 1 for making a frequency table. When determining the interval size, use a whole number that will result in 5–15 intervals. The lower limit of each interval should be a multiple of the interval size. For example, intervals including three values might look like this:

0–2
3–5
6–8
9–11
12–14

Histograms

A **histogram** is a bar chart used to display the information in a frequency table graphically. The bars are put next to each other with no space between them, and the height of each bar corresponds to the frequency of each value in the frequency table or in each interval of a grouped frequency table.

How to Make a Histogram from a Frequency Table

1. Make a frequency table (or a grouped frequency table).
2. Put the values along the bottom of the page (from left to right and lowest to highest).
3. Make a scale of frequencies along the left edge of the page (that extends from 0 at the bottom to the highest frequency observed for any value).
4. Make a bar for each value (that is as high as the frequency of the value it represents, making sure the middle of the bar is above its value on the horizontal axis).

Shapes of Frequency Distributions

A frequency table, histogram, or frequency polygon describes a **frequency distribution**, the pattern or shape of frequencies are spread out or "distributed."

Unimodal and Bimodal Frequency Distributions

- A distribution with a single high peak is a **unimodal distribution**.
- A distribution with two fairly high, equal peaks is a **bimodal distribution**.
- A distribution with two or more peaks is a **multimodal distribution**.
- A distribution in which all the values have about the same frequency is a **rectangular distribution**.

Symmetrical and Skewed Distributions

A distribution with approximately equal numbers of cases on both sides of the middle is a **symmetrical distribution**.

A distribution that clearly is not symmetrical is a **skewed distribution**. The side of the distribution that has fewer scores is considered the direction of the skew. That is, the direction of skew is the side with the long tail. A distribution that is *skewed to the right*—the positive side of the distribution—is also called *positively skewed*. A distribution *skewed to the left*—the negative side of the distribution—is also called *negatively skewed*. In practice, highly skewed distributions in psychology are seen primarily when the variable being measured has an upper or lower limit.

The situation in which many scores pile up at the low end because it is impossible to have any lower score is called a **floor effect**. The situation in which many scores pile up at the high end because it is impossible to have any higher score is called a **ceiling effect**.

Normal, Heavy-Tailed, and Light-Tailed Distributions

Distributions also may be described in terms of whether their tails are "heavy," with many scores in them, or "light" or "thin," with few scores in them. The former are called **heavy-tailed distributions** and latter **light-tailed distributions**. This aspect of a distribution is called *kurtosis*. The standard of comparison is a bell-shaped curve, called the **normal curve**, that is widely approximated in psychological research and in nature generally.

Frequency Tables and Histograms in Research Articles

Because researchers mainly use frequency tables and histograms as a step in more elaborate statistical analyses, they are not usually included in research articles. The shapes of distributions are occasionally described in words. Frequency tables are used to summarize the characteristics of people in studies, especially demographic variables like age or gender.

Chapter Self-Tests

The practice test items that follow are based on the following scenario. A group of behavioral scientists plans to administer an inventory designed to measure the self-esteem reported by students in a statistics course. The inventory asks students to indicate which of 40 statements about their chances to succeed in the course are true for them. True responses are scored as 1 and false responses as 0, so that scores can range from 0 to 40.

Understanding Key Terms in Chapter 1
Directions: Using the word bank that follows, complete each statement.
Word Bank: bimodal distribution / ceiling effect / descriptive statistics / equal-interval variables / floor effect / frequency distribution / frequency table / grouped frequency table / histogram / inferential statistics / kurtosis / levels of measurement / multimodal distribution / nominal variables / normal curve / numeric variable / rank-order variables / rectangular distribution / score / skewed distribution / statistics / symmetrical distribution / unimodal distribution / values / variable

In order to organize, analyze, and interpret the data they collect, the behavioral scientists will use the branch of science known as **(1)** _____. If the behavioral scientists want to make a statement about the self-esteem reported by students in general, the behavioral scientists will calculate **(2)** _____. If the behavioral scientists compute the percentages of male and female students who report various levels of self-esteem, the behavioral scientists are computing **(3)** _____. Self-esteem is the measured **(4)** _____, and can assume **(5)** _____ between 0 and 40. If the sum of a student's responses is 20, the student's **(6)** _____ is 20.

As the behavioral scientists plan the statistical analyses they will conduct as they collect data, they consider the level at which they will measure the variables in the study. Since numbers will reflect the amount of the construct being measured, the behavioral scientists are using **(7)** _____. If a student who has a score of 20 on the self-esteem inventory is reporting twice as much self-esteem as a student with a score of 10, self-esteem is an **(8)** _____. If the differences between self-esteem scores of 10 and 20 and 20 and 30 are not equal, allowing the behavioral scientists only to say that the three people are reporting different amounts of self-esteem, self-esteem is being measured as a **(9)** _____. If the behavioral scientists say that people in the top half of the distribution have "high" self-esteem and people in the bottom half have "low" self-esteem, self-esteem is being measured as a **(10)** _____. The three types of variables are based on different **(11)** _____.

As a first step in analyzing their data, the behavioral scientists tally the number and percentage of times each self-esteem score occurred. The resulting table is a **(12)** _____. Because they have measured the self-esteem of so many people, the behavioral scientists then decide to combine values into groups of five values and report the number of people whose scores fall in each group. The resulting table is a **(13)** _____. If the behavioral scientists create a graph using their data consisting of bars with no spaces between them, the graph is a **(14)** _____. If the behavioral scientists create a graph that shows the pattern or shape of the spread of self-esteem scores, they have created a **(15)** _____. If this graph shows only one high point in the data, it depicts a **(16)** _____. If the graph shows that the distribution of self-esteem scores has two fairly equal high points, it depicts a **(17)** _____. Any distribution that has two or more fairly equal high points is a **(18)** _____. If two students have scores of 0, two students have scores of 1, two students have scores of 2, two students have scores of 3, and so on, the graph will depict a **(19)** _____.

If the behavioral scientists examine a graph of the self-esteem scores and find that there are equal numbers of scores on either side of the middle, the scores form a **(20)** _____. If the graph shows that there are more low self-esteem scores than high self-esteem scores, the graph is depicting a **(21)** _____. Since scores on the self-esteem inventory cannot be lower than zero, the inventory has a **(22)** _____. If the 40 statements do not permit students to express the true extent of their self-esteem, scores may pile up at the high end of the distribution, demonstrating a **(23)** _____. If the curve of self-esteem scores is bell-shaped, the curve is a **(24)** _____. If a curve has many scores in its tails, the curve is said to be **(25)** _____. On the other hand, if the curve has few scores in its tails, the curve is said to be **(26)** _____.

Multiple-Choice Items

1. If the behavioral scientists use statistics like frequency tables to summarize the numbers collected in their study, they are reporting
   A. inferential statistics.
   B. descriptive statistics.
   C. intuitive statistics.
   D. abstract statistics.

2. If the behavioral scientists use the numbers collected in their study to make generalizations about the self-esteem levels of students throughout the United States, they will calculate
   A. inferential statistics.
   B. descriptive statistics.
   C. intuitive statistics.
   D. abstract statistics.

3. If the behavioral scientists also study the amount of anxiety students experience before a test, anxiety is a
   A. score.
   B. descriptive statistic.
   C. value.
   D. variable.

4. Since a student can make a score between 0 and 40, 0–40 are
   A. ranks.
   B. intervals.
   C. variables.
   D. values.

5. A student's score on the self-esteem inventory is an example of a
   A. numeric variable.
   B. qualitative variable.
   C. confounding variable.
   D. independent variable.

6. If a student who has a score of 18 on the self-esteem inventory is reporting two times as much self-esteem as a student who has a score of 9, self-esteem is
   A. a nominal variable.
   B. a rank-order variable.
   C. an equal-interval variable.
   D. an independent variable.

7. If a student who has a score of 28 on the self-esteem inventory is reporting twice as much self-esteem as a student who has a score of 14, and seven times as much self-esteem as a student who has a score of 6, self-esteem is
   A. a nominal variable.
   B. a rank-order variable.
   C. an equal-interval variable.
   D. an independent variable.

8. When the behavioral scientists talk about the level of measurement at which self-esteem is measured, they are discussing
   A. whether floor or ceiling effects are present.
   B. differences between unimodal and multimodal distributions.
   C. differences between rank-order and equal-interval variables.
   D. whether their distributions will be normal or skewed.

9. Since the scores on the self-esteem inventory can have any value between 0 and 40, the behavioral scientists may want to summarize the data using a grouped frequency table instead of an ordinary frequency table because an ordinary frequency table would
   A. include too many values.
   B. not be able to include all cases.
   C. not depict a skewed distribution.
   D. have to start at 0 (or 0%).

10. In general, the largest number of intervals in a grouped frequency table should be
    A. 5.
    B. 10.
    C. 15.
    D. 20.

11. If the graph the behavioral scientists use to display the data in a frequency table consists of adjacent bars, the graph is a
    A. pie chart.
    B. normal curve approximation.
    C. histogram.
    D. frequency polygon.

12. In a histogram, the vertical (up and down) dimension represents the
    A. frequency of values.
    B. possible values a variable can take.
    C. intensity of the variable.
    D. percentage of scores at each value.

13. If 60 students complete the self-esteem inventory just before the first statistics test and another 60 students complete it close to the end of the semester, the distribution will probably be
    A. unimodal.
    B. bimodal.
    C. normal.
    D. skewed.

14. If the behavioral scientists examine the distributions of student self-esteem scores and find that most of the scores are low with just a few high scores, the distribution is
    A. unimodal.
    B. bimodal.
    C. positively skewed.
    D. negatively skewed.

15. If the behavioral scientists examine the distributions of student self-esteem scores and find that most of the scores are high with just a few low scores, the distribution is
    A. unimodal.
    B. bimodal.
    C. positively skewed.
    D. negatively skewed.

16. If the behavioral scientists examine the distributions of student self-esteem scores and find many scores in both ends of the distribution, the distribution is
    A. light-tailed.
    B. heavy-tailed.
    C. normal.
    D. rectangular.

17. If the behavioral scientists examine the distributions of student self-esteem scores and find very few scores in either end of the distribution, the distribution is
   A. light-tailed.
   B. heavy-tailed.
   C. normal.
   D. rectangular.

18. The behavioral scientists may suspect that a floor effect exists if
   A. most of the scores in the distribution are located at the high end.
   B. the curve is skewed to the right.
   C. the distribution is symmetrical, but heavy-tailed.
   D. the distribution describes the spread of a rank-order variable.

19. The behavioral scientists may suspect that a ceiling effect exists if
   A. most of the scores in the distribution are located at the high end.
   B. the curve is skewed to the right.
   C. the distribution is symmetrical, but heavy-tailed.
   D. the distribution describes the spread of a rank-order variable.

20. When the behavioral scientists create distributions of self-esteem scores, the standard of comparison when describing the shape of these distributions is a
   A. rectangular distribution.
   B. flat distribution.
   C. normal curve.
   D. square curve.

Problems

1. The behavioral scientists administered the self-esteem inventory to 22 students in a statistics class and obtained the following scores:

15 29 26 23 24 21 16 23 20 23 24 18 20 22 23 17 28 19 21 20 28 25

Make a frequency table.
Use the frequency table to make a histogram.
Describe the shape of the distribution.

2. The behavioral scientists then administered the self-esteem inventory to 38 more students in statistics classes and obtained the following scores:

35 24 27 30 26 30 32 20 32 33 24 19 25 18 17 33 31 19 30 28 20 35 16 29 27 21 27 24 31 36 22 26 20 25 28 24 22 29

Add the 38 new scores to the 22 scores obtained earlier and make a frequency table. Explain why a grouped frequency table might be preferred in this instance.

3. Using the self-esteem inventory data, explain what a ceiling effect is, and contrast it to a floor effect.

Additional Practice: Complete any Practice Problems in Set I that your instructor has not assigned and compare your responses to those provided by the authors. Pay particular attention to the problems that require you to explain your results to someone who has never taken a course in statistics.

SPSS Applications

Note: At the time of this writing, SPSS software is called IBM SPSS Statistics. Recent versions of SPSS were also called SPSS Statistics and PASW Statistics. The problem solutions and examples in this Study Guide were obtained using PASW Statistics Version 17.0.2. Your institution may have a different version of the software, but the versions available in most academic computing centers should be adequate to follow the problems in this Study Guide. In general, any differences in the procedural steps and output across different versions of the software will be very minor. Versions available in most academic computing centers should be adequate to follow the problems in this Study Guide. If you are using SPSS for the first time, you will want to read Appendix I before attempting the applications that follow. Remember that ⌐Ѳ indicates a single left mouse click.

Application 1

Open SPSS.
Enter the self-esteem inventory scores used in Problem 1in one column of a data window. Follow the instructions in the Appendix to name the variable and remove the zeros following the decimal. Again, the scores are

15 29 26 23 24 21 16 23 20 23 24 18 20 22 23 17 28 19 21 20 28 25

To create a frequency table:
⌐Ѳ Analyze.
⌐Ѳ Descriptive statistics.
⌐Ѳ Frequencies.
⌐Ѳ the name of the variable and ⌐Ѳ the arrow to move the variable to Variable(s) window.
The screen should look like the one in Figure 1.

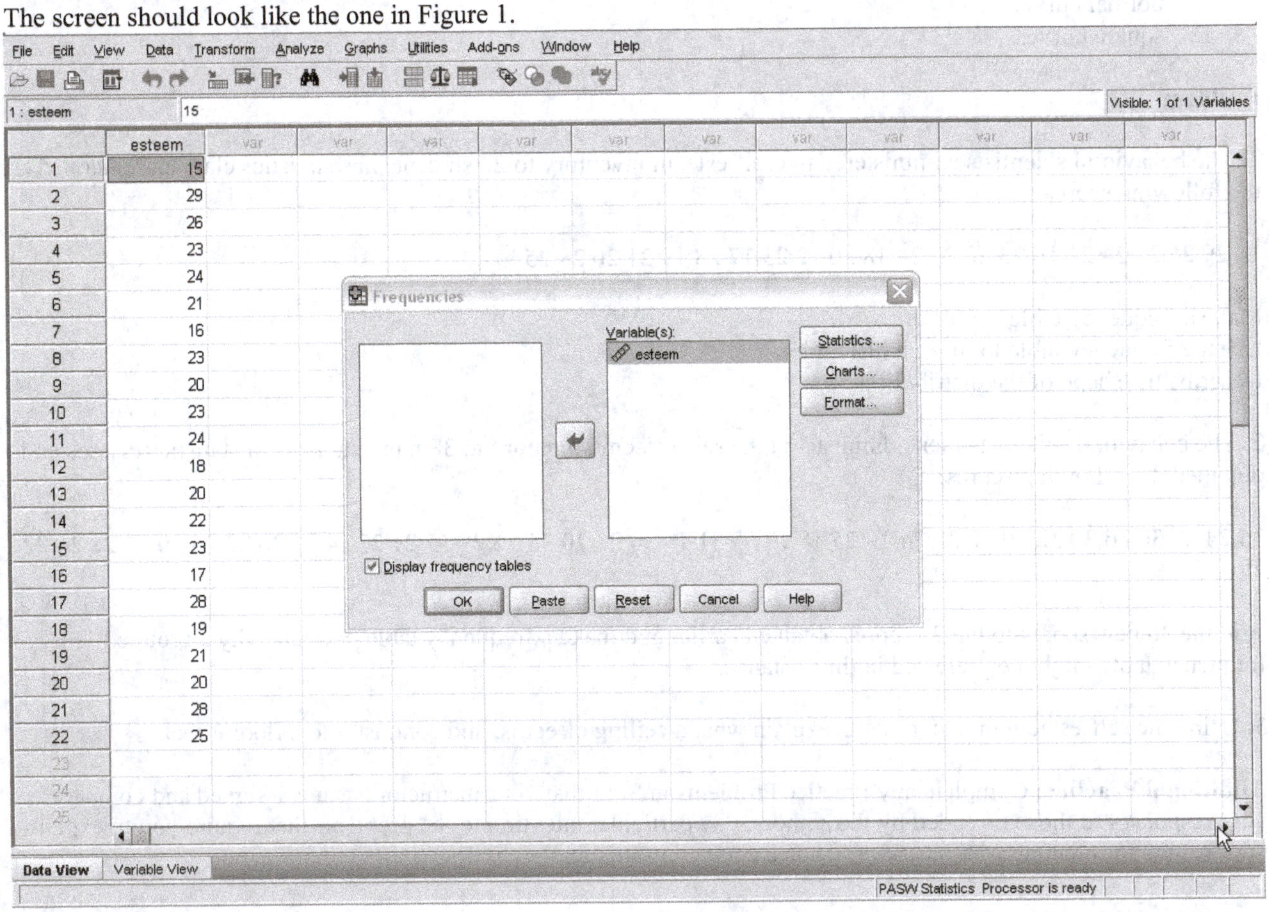

Figure 1

⤶ OK.
The output should look like the output in Figure 2.

esteem

		Frequency	Percent	Valid Percent	Cumulative Percent
Valid	15	1	4.5	4.5	4.5
	16	1	4.5	4.5	9.1
	17	1	4.5	4.5	13.6
	18	1	4.5	4.5	18.2
	19	1	4.5	4.5	22.7
	20	3	13.6	13.6	36.4
	21	2	9.1	9.1	45.5
	22	1	4.5	4.5	50.0
	23	4	18.2	18.2	68.2
	24	2	9.1	9.1	77.3
	25	1	4.5	4.5	81.8
	26	1	4.5	4.5	86.4
	28	2	9.1	9.1	95.5
	29	1	4.5	4.5	100.0
	Total	22	100.0	100.0	

Figure 2

To create a histogram:
⤶ Analyze.
⤶ Descriptive statistics.
⤶ Frequencies.
⤶ the name of the variable and ⤶ the arrow to move the variable to Variable(s) window.
⤶ Charts, ⤶ Histograms, ⤶ Continue.
⤶ OK.
The output should look like the output in Figure 3.

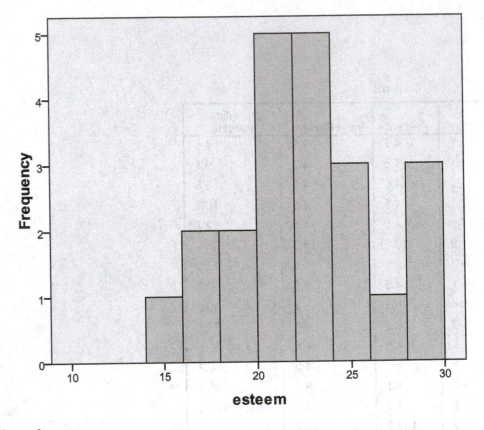

Histogram

Mean =22.05
Std. Dev. =3.823
N =22

Figure 3

As indicated in the Appendix, you can save this data if you wish. As is also indicated in the Appendix, you do not necessarily need to reenter data if you are using the same computer. Simply open SPSS, but instead of choosing "Type in data," choose "Open an existing data source." Then choose one of the SPSS datasets listed, for example, Appendix Data.sav as shown in Figure 10 in the Appendix.

Application 2
Open SPSS.
Enter the following motivation scores in one column of a data window. Follow the instructions in the Appendix to name the variable and to set the number of decimals at 1. The scores are:

1, 4.5, 9, 7.5, 4.5, 8.5, 5.5, 2.5, 4.5, 9, 4.5, 5, 6.5, 7.5, 8, 8.5, 6, 2.5, 7, 3.5, 8, 1.5, 2.5, 6.5, 3.5, 5.5, 9.5, 6.5, 1.5, 7.5

To create a frequency table:
🖱 Analyze.
🖱 Descriptive statistics.
🖱 Frequencies.
🖱 the name of the variable and 🖱 the arrow to move the variable to Variable(s) window.
The screen should look like the one in Figure 4.

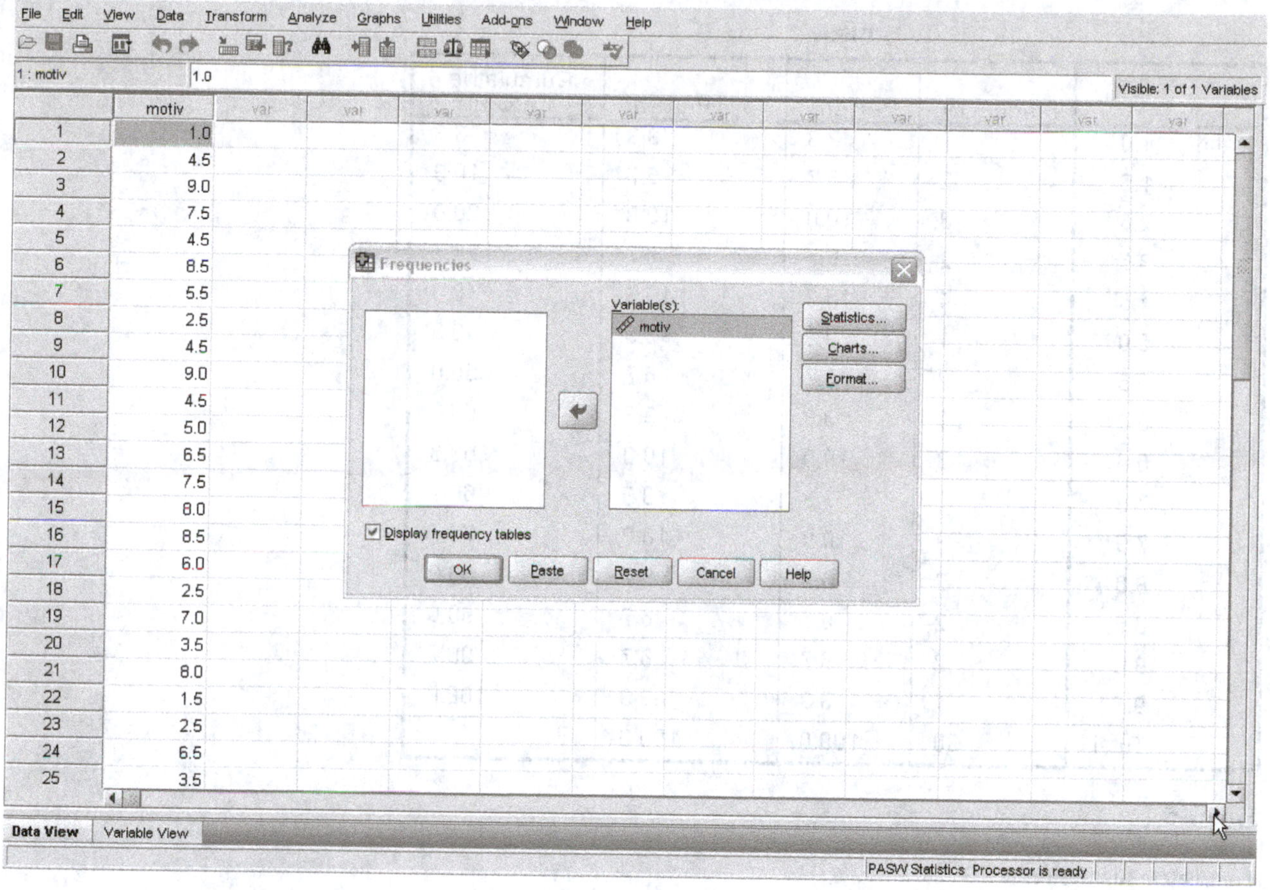

Figure 4

🖱 OK.

The output should look like the output in Figure 5.

motiv

		Frequency	Percent	Valid Percent	Cumulative Percent
Valid	1.0	1	3.3	3.3	3.3
	1.5	2	6.7	6.7	10.0
	2.5	3	10.0	10.0	20.0
	3.5	2	6.7	6.7	26.7
	4.5	4	13.3	13.3	40.0
	5.0	1	3.3	3.3	43.3
	5.5	2	6.7	6.7	50.0
	6.0	1	3.3	3.3	53.3
	6.5	3	10.0	10.0	63.3
	7.0	1	3.3	3.3	66.7
	7.5	3	10.0	10.0	76.7
	8.0	2	6.7	6.7	83.3
	8.5	2	6.7	6.7	90.0
	9.0	2	6.7	6.7	96.7
	9.5	1	3.3	3.3	100.0
	Total	30	100.0	100.0	

Figure 5

To create a histogram:
- ⌐Ⓗ Analyze.
- ⌐Ⓗ Descriptive statistics.
- ⌐Ⓗ Frequencies.
- ⌐Ⓗ the name of the variable and ⌐Ⓗ the arrow to move the variable to Variable(s) window.
- ⌐Ⓗ Charts, ⌐Ⓗ Histograms, ⌐Ⓗ Continue.
- ⌐Ⓗ OK.

The output should look like the output in Figure 6.

Histogram

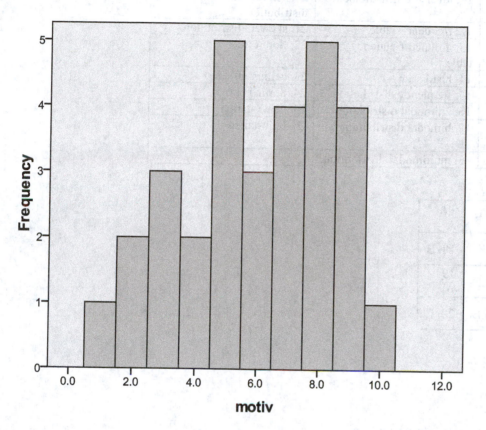

Mean =5.6
Std. Dev. =2.489
N =30

Figure 6

Chapter 1 Key

Completion Items

1. statistics	10. nominal variable	19. rectangular distribution
2. inferential statistics	11. levels of measurement	20. symmetrical distribution
3. descriptive statistics	12. frequency table	21. skewed distribution
4. variable	13. grouped frequency table	22. floor effect
5. values	14. histogram	23. ceiling effect
6. score	15. frequency distribution	24. normal curve
7. numeric variables	16. unimodal distribution	25. heavy-tailed
8. equal-interval variable	17. bimodal distribution	26. light-tailed
9. rank-order variable	18. multimodal distribution	

Multiple-Choice Items

1. B	5. A	9. A	13.B	17. A
2. A	6. C	10. C	14. C	18. B
3. D	7. B	11. C	15.D	19. A
4. D	8. C	12. A	16.B	20. C

Problems

1.
Frequency Distribution

esteem

		Frequency	Percent	Valid Percent	Cumulative Percent
Valid	15	1	4.5	4.5	4.5
	16	1	4.5	4.5	9.1
	17	1	4.5	4.5	13.6
	18	1	4.5	4.5	18.2
	19	1	4.5	4.5	22.7
	20	3	13.6	13.6	36.4
	21	2	9.1	9.1	45.5
	22	1	4.5	4.5	50.0
	23	4	18.2	18.2	68.2
	24	2	9.1	9.1	77.3
	25	1	4.5	4.5	81.8
	26	1	4.5	4.5	86.4
	28	2	9.1	9.1	95.5
	29	1	4.5	4.5	100.0
	Total	22	100.0	100.0	

Histogram

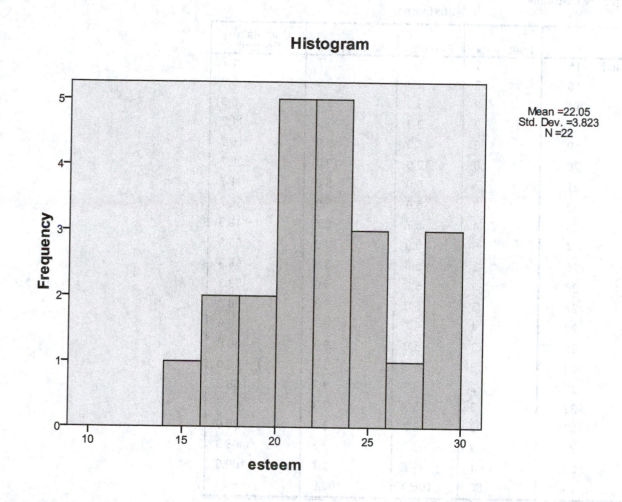

Mean =22.05
Std. Dev. =3.823
N =22

Despite the small number of students, the distribution is beginning to assume the shape of a normal curve.

2.
Frequency Distribution

esteem

		Frequency	Percent	Valid Percent	Cumulative Percent
Valid	15	1	1.7	1.7	1.7
	16	2	3.3	3.3	5.0
	17	2	3.3	3.3	8.3
	18	2	3.3	3.3	11.7
	19	3	5.0	5.0	16.7
	20	6	10.0	10.0	26.7
	21	3	5.0	5.0	31.7
	22	3	5.0	5.0	36.7
	23	4	6.7	6.7	43.3
	24	6	10.0	10.0	53.3
	25	3	5.0	5.0	58.3
	26	3	5.0	5.0	63.3
	27	3	5.0	5.0	68.3
	28	4	6.7	6.7	75.0
	29	3	5.0	5.0	80.0
	30	3	5.0	5.0	85.0
	31	2	3.3	3.3	88.3
	32	2	3.3	3.3	91.7
	33	2	3.3	3.3	95.0
	35	2	3.3	3.3	98.3
	36	1	1.7	1.7	100.0
	Total	60	100.0	100.0	

A grouped frequency table would combine scores and make the distribution easier to visualize. Because there are so many scores obtained by two or three students, this frequency table is not much easier to interpret than the ranked individual scores would be.

Grouped frequency table

Interval	Frequency	Percent
15–19	10	16.7
20–24	22	36.7
25–29	16	26.7
30–34	9	15.0
35–39	3	5.0

Histogram

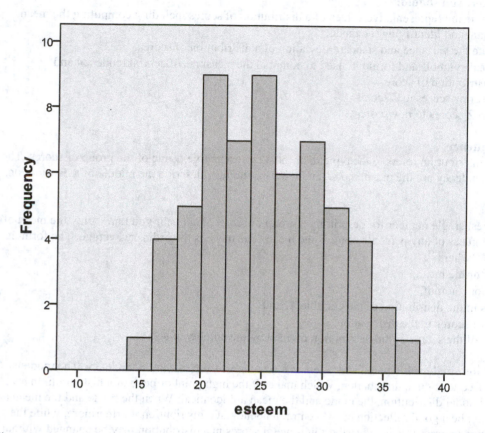

Mean =24.67
Std. Dev. =5.255
N =60

Histogram

3. A ceiling effect would exist if most of the scores on the self-esteem inventory were massed at the high end of the scoring scale, for example, if most of the scores were 30 or higher. In this situation, students with very high self-esteem would not be able to express the full extent of their self-esteem. On the other hand, a floor effect would exist if most of the scores on the self-esteem inventory were massed at the low end of the scoring scale, for example, if most of the scores were less than 10. In this case, students with very low self-esteem would not be able to describe their lack of self-esteem fully.

Chapter 2
The Mean, Variance, Standard Deviation, and Z Scores

Learning Objectives
After studying this chapter, you should:
- Be able to determine the representative values of a distribution of scores including computing the mean, locating the median, and identifying the mode.
- Be able to compute the variance and standard deviation of a distribution of scores.
- Know the statistical symbols and formulas used to compute the measures of central tendency and variability of a distribution of scores.
- Be able to convert raw scores to Z scores.
- Be able to convert Z scores to raw scores.

Measures of Central Tendency
The *central tendency* of a distribution refers to the typical, or most representative, value of the group of scores. The three measures of central tendency are the mean, mode, and median, and they describe the middle of a distribution of scores.

The **mean** is usually the best single number for describing a group of scores. That is, if you know only the mean of a group of scores, the best guess of any person's score is the mean. The mean is the ordinary average. The formula for the mean is $M = \Sigma X / N$, where
- M is the symbol for the mean,
- Σ is the symbol for "sum of,"
- X refers to scores in the distribution of the variable X, and
- N is the number of scores in the distribution.

Thus, the mean is the sum of the scores in the distribution divided by the number of scores.

The **mode**, the most common single value in a distribution, is a second measure of central tendency. The mode is the value with the largest frequency in a distribution, which makes it the high point or peak of a histogram. In a perfectly symmetrical, unimodal distribution, the mode and the mean are identical. When the mode and the mean are not equal, the mode may not be a good reflection of the central tendency of a distribution. Furthermore, while the mean is affected by a change to any score in a distribution, several scores in a distribution may be changed without affecting the mode. Consequently, the mode is rarely used in psychological research.

The **median** is the third measure of central tendency. The value of the median may vary slightly depending on the number of scores in the distribution and on whether two or more scores in the middle of the distribution have the same value.

Steps for Finding the Median
1. Line up all the scores in the distribution from the lowest to the highest.
2. Figure how many scores there are to the middle score by adding 1 to the number of scores and dividing by 2.
3. Count up to the middle score or scores.

If there is one middle score, it is the median. If there are two middle scores, the median is the average of the two middle scores.

Comparing Representative Values
An advantage of the median over the mean is that it is less influenced by extreme (or unrepresentative) cases, called **outliers**.

Variability
Variability refers to the spread of scores in a distribution, and more specifically, to how the scores are spread around the mean.

The Variance

The **variance** of a group of scores is a measure of how the scores in a distribution are spread around the mean. By definition, the variance is the average of each score's squared difference from the mean. The steps in figuring the variance are:

1. Subtract the mean of the distribution from each score in the distribution to obtain the **deviation score**.
2. Square each of these deviation scores (to remove the effect of positive and negative deviations, which would cancel each other when summed).
3. Add all the **squared deviation scores**.
4. Divide this **sum of squared deviations** by the number of scores.

Although the variance plays an important role in many statistical procedures, it is rarely reported as a descriptive statistic because it is based on squared units, which do not give a clear sense of the spread of the distribution in the scores in the units in which they were measured.

The Standard Deviation

The **standard deviation** is the measure most widely used for describing the spread of scores in a distribution. The standard deviation is directly related to the variance in that it is the square root of the variance.

The formula for the variance is $SD^2 = \Sigma(X - M)^2 / N$, where

* SD^2 is the symbol for the variance,
* Σ is the symbol for "sum of,"
* X refers to scores in the distribution of the variable X,
* M is the mean of the distribution, and
* N is the number of scores in the distribution.

The formula for the standard deviation is $SD = \sqrt{SD^2}$.

Computational formulas are equations that are mathematically equivalent to **definitional formulas,** the latter being equations for statistical procedures that directly reflect the meaning of the procedure. The former are useful when statistics are to be calculated by hand using calculators instead of computers. The disadvantage is that the computational formulas do not directly reflect the meaning of the procedure. The variance and standard deviation are sometimes figured using the sum of squared deviations divided by $N - 1$. Appropriate uses of this denominator are described beginning in Chapter 8. Be aware that programmable calculators and computer packages like SPSS may use this formula instead of the formula emphasized in this chapter.

Z Scores

A **Z score** is the number of standard deviations a score lies above or below the mean; that is, a Z score is a score expressed in standard deviation units. Thus, Z scores are units of measure in their own right and will be used in calculations encountered in future chapters. If the actual score is greater than the mean, its Z score will have a positive value. If the actual score is lower than the mean, its Z score will have a negative value. Z scores are useful in determining where scores fall on the normal curve.

The formula used to compute a Z score is $Z = (X - M) / SD$ where X is a **raw score**, an ordinary score, or any other number in a distribution before it has been converted to a Z score or otherwise transformed. Z scores can also be converted to raw scores using the formula $X = (Z) (SD) + M$.

Looking at the formula for Z, if the raw score X is equal to the mean, $X - M = 0$, and 0 divided by any number is 0. Therefore, the mean of a distribution of Z scores is always 0. Similarly, since computation of a Z score involves dividing by the standard deviation, the Z score one standard deviation above the mean is always 1 and the Z score one standard deviation below the mean is always –1. For example, suppose that 10,000 students have taken the inventory designed to measure perceived stress, and that the mean stress score is 36 and the standard deviation is 8. If a student obtains a score of 36, the student's Z score = (36–36) / 8 = (0) / 8 + 0. If another student obtains a score of 44, this student's Z score = (44–36) / 8 = 8 / 8 = 1.00, and if a third obtains a score of 28, this student's Z score = (28–38) / 8 = (–8) / 8 = –1.00.

An advantage of Z scores is that Z scores on completely different variables can be calculated so that a person's standing on each variable can be compared. For example, suppose an inventory designed to measure motivation had a mean of 25 and a standard deviation of 5 and an achievement test had a mean of 60 and a standard deviation of 15. A student with a score on the motivation inventory of 35 would have a Z score = 2.00. If the student had a score of 90 on the achievement test, the student's Z score would also be 2.00. If another student also had a score of 35 on the motivation inventory, but a score of 45 on the achievement test, the student's Z score on the latter would be −1.00, allowing an investigator to say that despite similar motivation, the students performed differently on the achievement test.

Steps to Change a Raw Score to a Z Score
   1. Figure the deviation score: subtract the mean from the raw score.
   2. Figure the Z score: divide the deviation score by the standard deviation.
Formula: $Z = (X - M) / SD$

Example 1:
If the mean score of a large number of people on a self-esteem inventory is 66 and the standard deviation is 8, what is the Z score for a person with a score of 66?
$Z = (X - M) / SD$
$= (66 - 66) / 8$
$= 0 / 8$
$= 0.00$
Because the person's score of 66 is equal to the mean, the Z score is zero.

If the mean score of a large number of people on a self-esteem inventory is 66 and the standard deviation is 8, what is the Z score for a person with a score of 54?
$Z = (X - M) / SD$
$= (54 - 66) / 8$
$= -12 / 8$
$= -1.50$
Because the person's score of 54 is less than the mean, the Z score is negative.

If the mean score of a large number of people on a self-esteem inventory is 66 and the standard deviation is 8, what is the Z score for a person with a score of 78?
$Z = (X - M) / SD$
$= (78 - 66) / 8$
$= 12 / 8$
$= 1.50$
Because the person's score of 78 is greater than the mean, the Z score is positive.

Based on their Z scores, the self-esteem score of the person whose score is 54 is as far below the mean as the self-esteem score of the person whose score is 78 is above the mean in standard deviation units.

Example 2:
If the mean score of a large number of people on a self-esteem inventory is 66 and the standard deviation is 8, what is the Z score for a person with a score of 56?
$Z = (X - M) / SD$
$= (56 - 66) / 8$
$= -10 / 8$
$= -1.25$

If the mean score of a large number of people on a depression inventory is 16 and the standard deviation is 4, what is the Z score for a person with a score of 11?

$Z = (X - M) / SD$

$= (11 - 16) / 4$

$= -5 / 4$

$= -1.25$

Based on their Z scores, the self-esteem score of the person whose score is 58 is as far below the mean self-esteem score as the depression score of the person whose score is 11 is below the mean depression score. Thus, converting scores on different variables to Z scores places the score on the same scale, permitting comparisons of variables measured on different scales.

Steps to Change a Z Score to a Raw Score

1. Figure the deviation score: multiply the Z score by the standard deviation.
2. Figure the raw score: add the mean to the deviation score.

Formula: $X = (Z) (SD) + M$

Example 1:

If the mean score of a large number of people on a self-esteem inventory is 66 and the standard deviation is 8, what is the raw score for a person with a Z of 0.00?

$X = Z (SD) + M$

$= (0.00) (8) + 66$

$= 0 + 66$

$= 66$

Because the Z score for the mean is always zero, the Z score of a person who obtains a score equal to the mean will have a Z score of 0.

If the mean score of a large number of people on a self-esteem inventory is 66 and the standard deviation is 8, what is the raw score for a person with a Z score of -1.50?

$X = Z (SD) + M$

$= (-1.50) (8) + 66$

$= -12 + 66$

$= 54$

Because the person's Z score is negative, the raw score will be less than the mean.

If the mean score of a large number of people on a self-esteem inventory is 66 and the standard deviation is 8, what is the raw score for a person with a Z score of 1.50?

$X = (Z) (SD) + M$

$= (1.50) (8) + 66$

$= 12 + 66$

$= 78$

Because the person's Z score is positive, the raw score will be greater than the mean.

Example 2:

If the mean score of a large number of people on a self-esteem inventory is 66 and the standard deviation is 8, what is the raw score for a person with a Z score of -1.25?

$X = (Z) (SD) + M$

$= (-1.25) (8) + 66$

$= -10 + 66$

$= 56$

If the mean score of a large number of people on a depression inventory is 16 and the standard deviation is 4, what is the raw score for a person with a Z score of 11?

$X = (Z)(SD) + M$
$ = (-1.25)(4) + 66$
$ = -5 + 16$
$ = 11$

A self-esteem score of 58 is as far below the mean self-esteem score as a depression score of 11 is below the mean depression score. Again, Z scores place scores on different measuring instruments on the same scale, permitting comparison of variables measured on different scales.

Characteristics of Z Score Distributions

1. As demonstrated above, the Z score for the mean is always 0.
2. The standard deviation is always 1.0 because converting a raw score to a Z score involves dividing the difference between the raw score and the mean by the standard deviation. From the previous example, if the mean score of a large number of people on a self-esteem inventory is 66 and the standard deviation is 8, a person who has a raw score of 74 will have a Z score of 1.00 because:

   $Z = (X - M) / SD$
   $ = (74 - 66) / 8$
   $ = 8 / 8$
   $ = 1.00$

   Similarly, a person who has a raw score of 58 will have a Z score of –1.00 because:

   $Z = (X - M) / SD$
   $ = (58 - 66) / 8$
   $ = -8 / 8$
   $ = -1.00$

3. The variance is always 1.00 because it is the square of the standard deviation, and $1.00^2 = 1.00$.

Central Tendency and Variability in Research Articles

The mean and standard deviation are commonly reported in research articles, and in a variety of ways—either in the text or in tables. The variance is sometimes reported. However, Z scores rarely appear in research articles.

Chapter Self-Tests

The practice test items that follow are based on the following scenario. A group of behavioral scientists has administered an inventory designed to measure perceived stress to 100 students. The inventory consists of 18 statements about stressful situations. Students use a 4-point scale to indicate the extent to which each statement describes their behavior. The responses are scored 1–4 so that scores can range from 18–72.

Understanding Key Terms in Chapter 2
Directions: Using the word bank that follows, complete each statement.
Word Bank: central tendency / computational formula / definitional formula / deviation score / mean / median / mode / N / outlier / raw score / $\sum$ / squared deviation score / standard deviation / sum of squared deviations / variance / X / Z score

The behavioral scientists are interested in the scores that describe the most typical or representative values of the distribution of stress scores, so they need to examine the measures of **(1)** _____. If the behavioral scientists find that the arithmetic average of the 100 scores is 29.3, they have calculated the **(2)** _____. If eight students have a score of 26, but no more than five students obtain any other score, 26 is the **(3)** _____. If the behavioral scientists rank the scores of the 100 students and find that 50 of the scores are greater than 27 and 50 are less than 27, then 27 is the **(4)** _____. If most of the student scores range from 15 to 55, a score of 68 would be an **(5)** _____.

Now the behavioral scientists want to obtain an index of how the scores are spread about the mean. They begin their calculations by subtracting the mean from each score, which yields a **(6)** _____. This difference is squared, yielding a **(7)** _____, and then summed, yielding the **(8)** _____. This last sum is divided by 100, yielding the **(9)** _____. Finally, the square root of the result of the last calculation is the **(10)** _____.

The formula $SD^2 = \sum(X - M)^2 / N$ is an example of a **(11)** _____. Mathematically equivalent formulas designed to simplify hand calculations are **(12)** _____. In this formula, the operation of summing the deviations from the mean is indicated by **(13)** _____. The number of students in the analysis is designated by **(14)** _____, and each student's stress score is represented by **(15)** _____. Each student's stress score is also referred to as the student's **(16)** _____ on the stress inventory. The location of each student's score in relation to the mean can be indicated by calculating each student's **(17)** _____.

Multiple-Choice Items

1. If the behavioral scientists want to describe the central tendency of the stress scores, they will report the
   A. variance.
   B. kurtosis.
   C. median.
   D. standard deviation.

2. If the behavioral scientists compute a statistic using the formula $\sum X / N$, they are computing the
   A. variance.
   B. standard deviation.
   C. mean.
   D. median.

3. In the formula $\sum X / N$, $\sum$ instructs the behavioral scientists to
   A. add.
   B. subtract.
   C. multiply.
   D. divide.

4. In the formula $\Sigma X / N$, N refers to the
   A. normal curve.
   B. normative scores.
   C. natural logarithm.
   D. number of students.

5. If the behavioral scientists examine a frequency distribution of the 100 stress scores and find that more students had a score of 35 than any other score, they have determined the
   A. mode.
   B. median.
   C. variance.
   D. standard deviation.

6. If the behavioral scientists examine a frequency distribution of the 100 stress scores and find that a score of 36 divides the distribution in half, they have determined the
   A. mode.
   B. median.
   C. variance.
   D. standard deviation.

7. If the behavioral scientists examine a frequency distribution of the 100 stress scores and find that most of the scores are between 25 and 45, scores of 11 and 55 would be considered
   A. normal.
   B. outliers.
   C. variant.
   D. deviant.

8. If the behavioral scientists compute a statistic using the formula $\Sigma(X - M)^2 / N$, they are computing the
   A. variance.
   B. standard deviation.
   C. skewness.
   D. kurtosis.

9. In the formula $\Sigma(X - M)^2 / N$, $X - M$ is a
   A. sum of squares.
   B. standard deviation.
   C. deviation score.
   D. range.

10. In the formula $\Sigma(X - M)^2 / N$, $(X - M)^2$ is a
    A. sum of squares.
    B. standard deviation.
    C. squared deviation score.
    D. squared range.

11. If the behavioral scientists determine that the variance of the distribution of 100 stress scores is 49, the standard deviation is
    A. $\sqrt{49}$.
    B. 49^2.
    C. $\sqrt{49}$ / 100.
    D. 49^2 / 100.

12. If the behavioral scientists use a calculator to compute the mean and standard deviation "by hand," they may use formulas developed for this purpose called
    A. definitional formulas.
    B. computational formulas.
    C. logarithmic formulas.
    D. notational formulas.

13. If the behavioral scientists use a calculator to compute the mean and standard deviation "by hand" following all the steps required by $\Sigma X / N$ and $\Sigma(X - M)^2 / N$, they are using
    A. definitional formulas.
    B. computational formulas.
    C. logarithmic formulas.
    D. notational formulas.

Items 14–15 are related.
14. If the total of a student's responses on the stress inventory is 22, this number is the student's
    A. expected relative frequency.
    B. raw score.
    C. standard score.
    D. Z score.

15. In the formulas for the measures of central tendency and variability, 22 would be represented by
    A. Z.
    B. N.
    C. X.
    D. Σ.

16. If the total of a student's responses on the stress inventory is converted so that it can be located on a distribution with a mean of 0.00 and a standard deviation of 1.00, the behavioral scientists have calculated a
    A. expected relative frequency.
    B. raw score.
    C. standard score.
    D. Z score.

Problems

1. The behavioral scientists administered the stress inventory to 25 students in a freshman orientation session and obtained the following scores:

49 14 35 47 38 24 46 27 41 32 44 15 36 37 22 38 48 31 42 34 26 17 38 49 12

Using the definitional formulas described in the text:
What is the mode?
What is the median?
Compute the mean, the variance, and the standard deviation.
Explain your calculations as you would to a person who has never taken statistics.

2. Returning to the data described in Chapter 1, remember that the behavioral scientists administered the self-esteem inventory to 22 students in a statistics class and obtained the following scores:

15 29 26 23 24 21 16 23 20 23 24 18 20 22 23 17 28 19 21 20 28 25

Again, using the definitional formulas described in the text:
What is the mode?
What is the median?

Compute the mean, the variance, and the standard deviation.
Explain your calculations as you would to a person who has never taken statistics.

3. If the mean score on the depression scale is 12 and the standard deviation is 3, what is the Z score for a student whose depression score is 9?

4. If the mean score on the depression scale is 12 and the standard deviation is 3, what is the Z score for a student whose depression score is 18?

5. If the mean score on the depression scale is 12 and the standard deviation is 3, what is the Z score for a student whose depression score is 16?

6. If the mean score on the depression scale is 12 and the standard deviation is 3, what is the Z score for a student whose depression score is 11?

Additional Practice: Complete any Practice Problems in Set I that your instructor has not assigned and compare your responses to those provided by the authors. Pay particular attention to the problems that require you to explain your results to someone who has never taken a course in statistics.

SPSS Applications

Application 1
Open SPSS.
Enter the stress inventory scores used in Problem 1 in one column of a data window. Rename the variable "stress" and remove the zeros following the decimal. (You need not adjust the number of decimal places in any application unless you find it easier to work with the data.) Again, the scores are

49 14 35 47 38 24 46 27 41 32 44 15 36 37 22 38 48 31 42 34 26 17 38 49 12

ᵔᵗ Analyze.
ᵔᵗ Descriptive statistics.
ᵔᵗ Frequencies.
ᵔᵗ the name of the variable and ᵔᵗ the arrow to move the variable to Variable(s) window.
ᵔᵗ Statistics.
ᵔᵗ Mean, ᵔᵗ Median, ᵔᵗ Mode, ᵔᵗ Std. deviation, ᵔᵗ Variance, ᵔᵗ Continue.
Unless you want more practice examining frequency tables, ᵔᵗ the box labeled *Display frequency tables*, which will suppress the frequency table that would be constructed for the dataset.
ᵔᵗ OK.

Note: You can ᵔᵗ Analyze from either the Data View window or the Variable View window. All the instructions in this Study Guide are based on returning to the Data View window after you have named your variables and adjusted the decimals.

The output should look like the output in Figure 1.

Statistics

stress

N	Valid	25
	Missing	0
Mean		33.68
Median		36.00
Mode		38
Std. Deviation		11.430
Variance		130.643

Figure 1

Compare the results to those you obtained using your calculator for Problem 1. Remember that the computer calculates the variance and standard deviation using $N-1$ in the denominator so that these statistics should be slightly larger than those you calculated by hand.

Application 2
Open SPSS.
Enter the self-esteem scores presented in Chapter 1 and again in this chapter in one column of a data window. If you saved the scores after you completed the application in Chapter 1, you may ⌐ on the SPSS icon for the file to open both the file and SPSS, or you may open SPSS and use the *existing data source* window. Name the variable if necessary and remove the decimals. If you did not save the file, the scores are

15 29 26 23 24 21 16 23 20 23 24 18 20 22 23 17 28 19 21 20 28 25

⌐ Analyze.
⌐ Descriptive statistics.
⌐ Frequencies.
⌐ the name of the variable and ⌐ the arrow to move the variable to Variable(s) window.
⌐ Statistics.
⌐ Mean, ⌐ Median, ⌐ Mode, ⌐ Std. deviation, ⌐ Variance, ⌐ Continue.
Again, unless you want more practice examining frequency tables, ⌐ the box labeled *Display frequency tables* to suppress the frequency table that would be constructed for the dataset.
⌐ OK.

The output should look like the output in Figure 2.

Statistics

esteem

N	Valid	22
	Missing	0
Mean		22.05
Median		22.50
Mode		23
Std. Deviation		3.823
Variance		14.617

Figure 2

Compare the results to those you obtained using your calculator for Problem 1. Remember that the computer calculates the variance and standard deviation using $N - 1$ in the denominator so that these statistics should be slightly larger than those you calculated by hand.

Since you will use the dataset in the next application, you may want to leave the SPSS dataset open or save it.

Application 3
You can use SPSS to create a new variable with the variance and standard deviation calculated using N instead of $N - 1$ in the denominator as is shown on pages 59–61 in the text. The procedure applied to the esteem data follows.

As you just determined, the mean of the esteem scores is 22.05.
🖱 Transform.
🖱 Compute variable.

The window should look like the one in Figure 3.

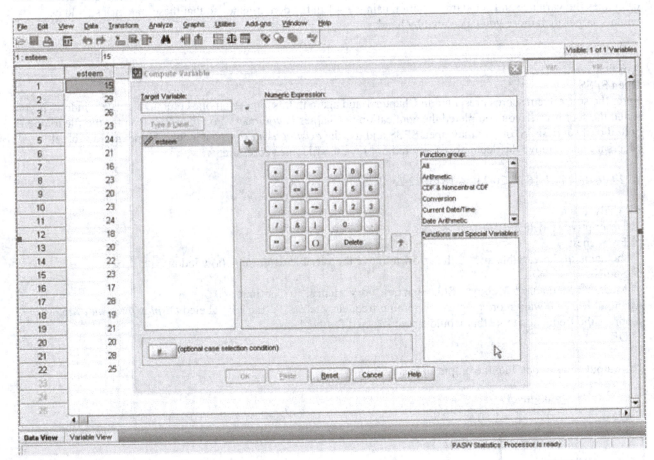

Figure 3

In the Target Variable window, name the new variable "stdev"
🖱 "esteem" in the Type & Label window and 🖱 the arrow to move the variable to the Numeric Expression window.
Modify the Numeric Expression window so that it contains the formula ("esteem" – 22.05) * ("esteem" – 22.05), which will calculate the squared deviation score.
🖱 OK.

The second column in the Data View window now contains the values of the computed variable for each student. (See Figure 4, which follows.)

Since the mean of the squared deviation scores is the variance ($SD^2 = \Sigma(X - M)^2 / N$), you can use the Frequencies procedure just as you have been doing to SPSS to calculate the mean of "stdev," which is 13.95. Since the standard deviation is the square root of the variance, the standard deviation is 3.73. These are the same values you obtained using the definitional formulas when you solved Problem 2.

Statistics

stdev

N	Valid	22
	Missing	0
Mean		13.9525

Since you will use the dataset in the next application, you may want to leave the SPSS dataset open or save it.

Application 4

SPSS can also be used to transform raw scores to Z scores using the mean and standard deviation for the distribution of scores. From your previous calculations, you know that the mean self-esteem score is 22.05 and the standard deviation is 3.73. Again, you will use the SPSS capability to create a new variable to calculate a standard score called "zesteem".

⌐ Transform.
⌐ Compute variable.
In the Target Variable window, name the new variable "zesteem".
Clear the Numeric Expression window.
⌐ "esteem" in the Type & Label window and ⌐ the arrow to move the variable to the Numeric Expression window.
Modify the Numeric Expression window so that it contains the formula ("esteem" – 22.05) / 3.73, which will calculate the Z scores.
⌐ OK.

The third column in the Data View window now contains self-esteem Z scores for each student. Compare your Z scores to those in Figure 4.

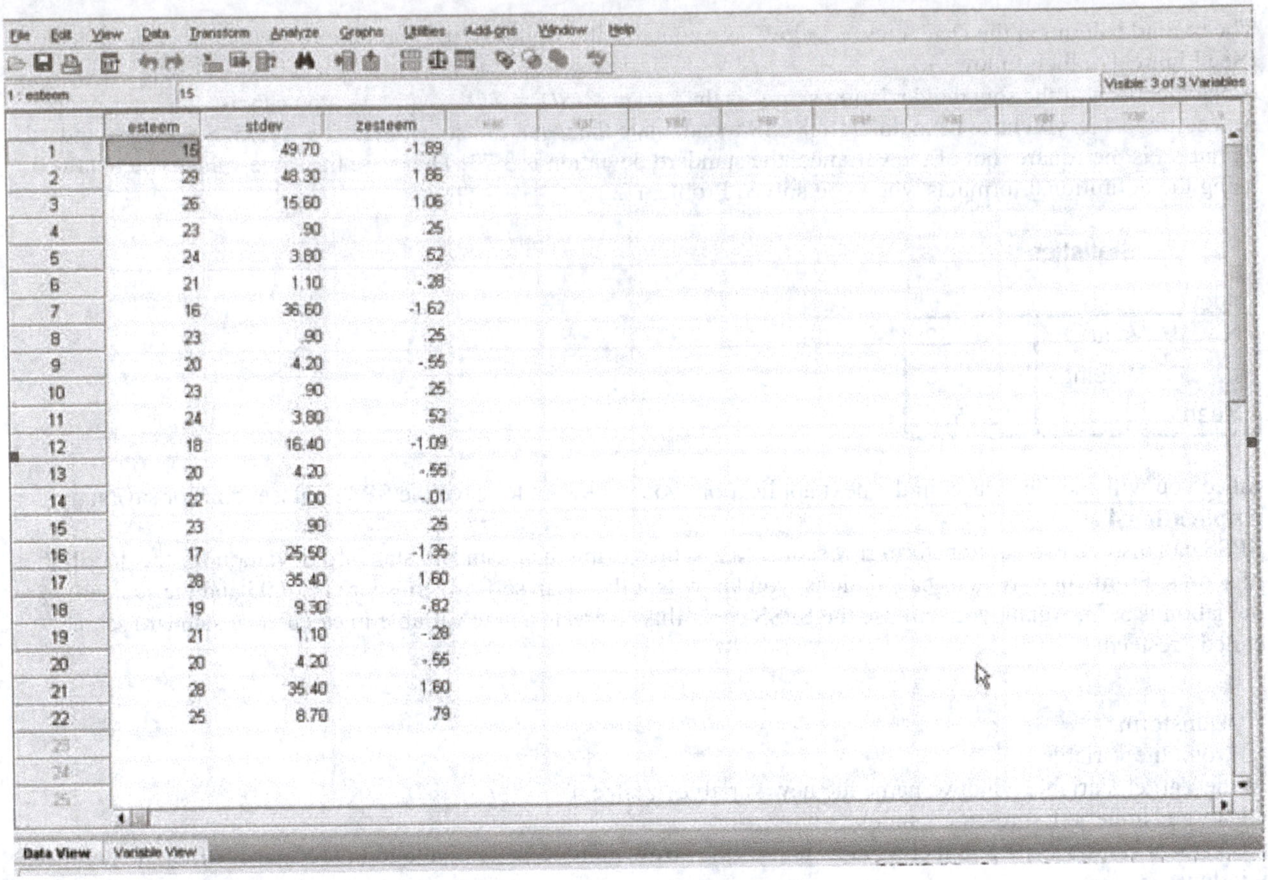

Figure 4

Chapter 2 Key

Completion Items

1. central tendency	7. squared deviation score	13. Σ
2. mean	8. sum of squared deviations	14. N
3. mode	9. variance	15. X
4. median	10. standard deviation	16. raw score
5. outlier	11. definitional formula	17. Z score
6. deviation score	12. computational formula	

Multiple Choice Items

1. C	5. A	9. C	13. A
2. C	6. B	10. C	14. B
3. A	7. B	11. A	15. C
4. D	8. A	12. B	16. D

Problems

1. Stress scores

Mode	38
Median	36
Mean	33.68
Variance	125.42
Standard deviation	11.20

2. Self-esteem scores

Mode	23
Median	22.50
Mean	22.05
Variance	13.95
Standard deviation	3.73

3. $Z = -1.00$
4. $Z = 2.00$
5. $Z = 1.33$
6. $Z = -0.33$

Chapter 3
Correlation and Prediction

Learning Objectives
After studying this chapter, you should:
- Be able to create and interpret scatter diagrams.
- Be able to interpret the patterns of correlation.
- Know how to calculate a correlation coefficient.
- Be able to explain the relationship between correlation and causality.
- Have a general understanding of the meaning of a statistically significant correlation coefficient.
- Know the difference between predictor and criterion variables.
- Know how to predict Z scores and raw scores for a criterion variable using r and the Z score of a predictor variable.
- Be able to explain why prediction is also called regression.
- Know how to calculate and interpret the proportion of variance accounted for.
- Be able to interpret the results of correlation and prediction studies in research articles.
- ADVANCED TOPIC: Understand the difference between multiple regression and multiple correlation.
- ADVANCED TOPIC: Be able to interpret the results of multiple regression and multiple correlation in research articles.
- APPENDIX: Know how to use tables to estimate power and sample size for correlation coefficients.

Correlation is the extent to which two equal-interval numeric variables are related. Conceptually, correlation can be understood by considering whether the pattern of scores is such that high scores on one variable are associated with high scores on the other variable, low scores are associated with low scores, and moderate scores are associated with moderate scores. For example, do people with higher levels of intellectual ability demonstrate higher levels of educational achievement?

Graphing Correlations
One way to examine the relationship between two variables is to create a graph called a **scatter diagram** (also called a *scatterplot*), which displays the degree and pattern of the relationship between the two variables. Creating a scatter diagram involves three steps:

1. **Draw the axes and decide which variable goes on which axis**. In many studies, either variable can be placed on either axis. However, in some studies, one variable is thought of as predicting the other. In these studies, the predictor variable is placed on the horizontal axis, and the predicted variable is placed on the vertical axis.
2. **Determine the range of values to use for each variable and mark them on the axes**. The values should increase on each axis, starting from the point at which the axes meet. Typically, the low value on each axis is zero. However, if zero is not a reasonable value, the values on an axis can begin with a higher number. The values then continue to the highest value the measure can have. If no obvious or reasonable lowest or highest possible value can be identified, the values should extend to the highest score that a participant in a study is likely to achieve. The horizontal and vertical axes should be approximately the same length so that the scatter diagram appears to be square.
3. **Mark a dot for each pair of scores**. This process involves first locating the place on the horizontal axis for a participant's score on the predictor variable. Then, imagine extending a line parallel to the vertical axis upward to the top of the graph. Next, locate the participant's score on the predicted variable and imagine extending a line parallel to the horizontal axis to the right side of the graph. Finally, make a dot where the imaginary lines intersect. If two have identical scores on both variables, put the number "2" in that place, or locate a second dot as close as possible to the first, preferably touching each other. Whichever method is used, the presence of two dots in the same place should be evident.

As an example, consider the 10 pairs of stress and depression scores obtained from emergency health care providers that follow.

Stress: 39 29 43 18 26 45 32 26 22 33
Depression: 26 16 33 22 15 23 18 18 12 15

1. **Draw the axes and determine which variable will be placed on which axis**. Although either variable could be placed on either axis, stress is used as a predictor of depression in many studies. Therefore, stress can logically be placed on the horizontal axis, and depression can be placed on the vertical axis.
2. **Determine the range of values to use for each variable and mark them on the axes.** Instead of zero, the scatter diagram that follows begins with a score of 15 on the horizontal axis and 10 on the vertical axis. The horizontal and vertical axes are the same length so that the scatter diagram appears to be square.
3. **Mark a dot for each pair of scores**, which has been done. Note that all the dots are separate.

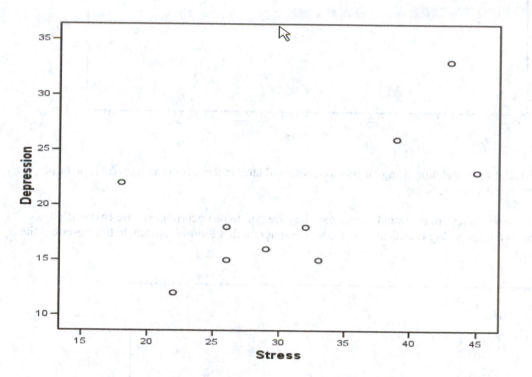

[This scatter diagram was created using SPSS, which will be demonstrated later in this chapter.]

Patterns of Correlation
Patterns of correlation can be identified by the general pattern of dots in a scatter diagram.
1. A **linear correlation** is present when the pattern of dots follows a straight line. In the scatter diagram of stress and depression scores, the pattern of the scores can be described by a straight line extending from the lower left area of the diagram to the upper right area. Therefore, the scatter diagram shows a linear correlation.
2. A **curvilinear correlation** is present when the relationship between two variables does not follow a straight line, but instead follows a curving, or more complex, pattern. Modification of the stress and depression scores in the example resulted in the scatter diagram that follows. This diagram indicates that both low and high levels of stress are associated with low levels of depression, but moderate levels of stress are associated with high levels of depression.

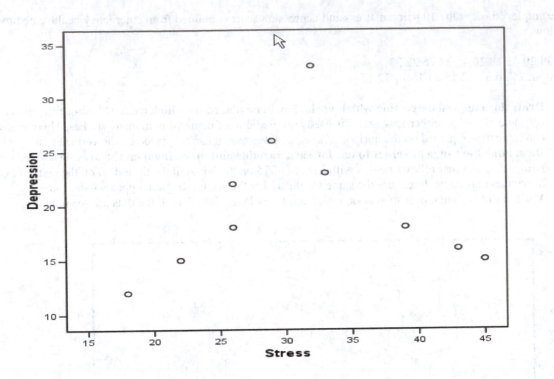

In this case, calculating correlation using the method presented later in the chapter will reveal little or no correlation between the two variables.

3. When the two variables are essentially unrelated, they are said to be uncorrelated—**no correlation** is present. Such a relationship is indicated by the scatter diagram that follows. No single line describes the relationship.

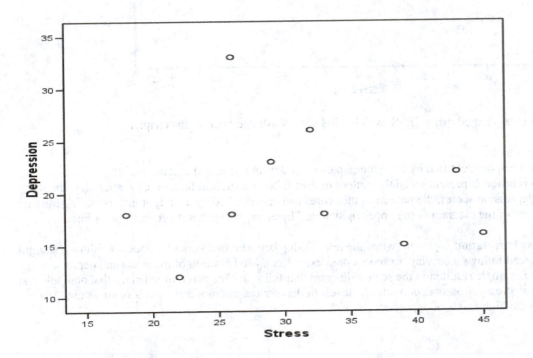

Correlations can also be categorized in another way.

1. A **positive correlation** is present when, as noted previously, low scores on one variable are associated with low scores on the other variable, moderate scores are associated with moderate scores, and high scores are associated with high scores.

2. On the other hand, **negative correlation** is present when low scores on one variable are associated with high scores on the other variable, moderate scores are associated with moderate scores, and high scores are associated with low scores. In a scatter diagram, the dots follow a line that slopes from the upper left area of the graph to the lower right area of the graph. The scatter diagram that follows shows a negative correlation between stress and job satisfaction for a group of emergency health care workers.

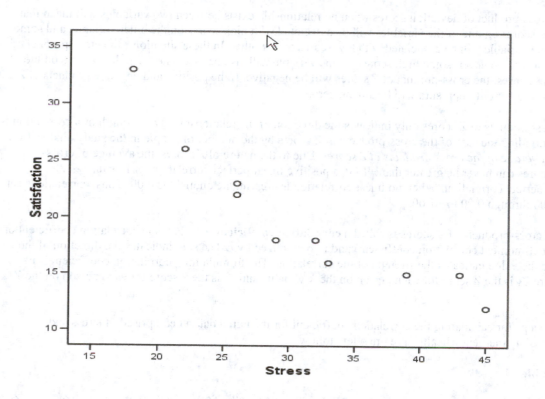

The *strength of a correlation* is often described by the clarity of the relationship between two variables. In other words, how frequently do high scores go with other high scores, moderate scores with other moderate scores, and low scores with other low scores? The closer the dots in a scatter diagram reflect a straight line, the stronger the correlation.

The Correlation Coefficient

Scatter diagrams only provide a general idea of the relationship between two variables. Therefore, a number that provides an exact index of the direction and strength of the relationship is useful. Remember that the logic of correlation is that the scores on each variable are related in a certain way. Specifically, if two variables are positively correlated, high scores on one variable are associated with high scores on the other variable, moderate scores with moderate scores, and low scores with low scores. If two variables are negatively correlated, high scores on one variable are associated with low scores on the other variable, with moderate scores being associated with moderate scores. Thus, the calculation of the number that summarizes the relationship between two variables must consistently identify high and low scores on two different variables.

Z scores can be used for this calculation. As you learned in Chapter 2, *Z* scores permit comparison of variables measured on different scales. In addition, any score that is greater than the mean of the distribution of scores for a variable will have a positive *Z* score, and any score that is below the mean will have a negative *Z* score. Therefore, the **cross-product of *Z* scores** obtained by multiplying a positive *Z* score by another positive *Z* score will be positive, and the cross-product of *Z* scores obtained by multiplying a negative *Z* score by another negative *Z* score also will be positive. Consequently, if the high scores on one variable are associated with high scores on the other variable, and if the low scores on one variable are associated with low scores on the other variable, the cross-product of deviation scores will be positive, and when these cross-products are summed, the result will be a large positive number.

On the other hand, obtaining the cross-product of Z scores obtained by multiplying a positive Z score by a negative Z score will be negative. Therefore, if most of the high scores on one variable are associated with low scores on the other variable, the cross-product of Z scores will be negative, and when these cross-products are summed, the result will be a large negative number.

Obtaining the cross-product of deviation scores when no relationship exists between two variables will mean that while some high scores on one of the variables will be associated with high scores on the other variable, and some low scores on one variable will be associated with low scores on the other. In these situations, the cross-product of the Z will be positive. However, some high scores on one variable will also be associated with low scores on the other, and in these cases, the cross-product of Z scores will be negative. If the positive and negative products of Z scores cancel each other out, their sum will be around zero.

Adding the cross-products of Z scores only indicates the direction of the relationship. The strength of a correlation is determined by dividing the sum of the cross-products of Z scores by the number of people in the study, that is, by calculating the *average of the cross-products of Z scores*. Due to the nature of Z scores, the average of cross-products of Z scores can never be greater than +1.00, a positive linear perfect correlation, or less than −1.00, a negative linear perfect correlation. When no linear correlation is present, the quotient is 0.00. Thus, correlations can range from −1.00 through 0.00 to +1.00.

The average of cross-products of Z scores is called a **correlation coefficient** (or a Pearson correlation coefficient or a Pearson product-moment correlation coefficient) and is symbolized by r. The sign indicates the direction of the correlation, and the value indicates the strength of the correlation. The formula for a correlation coefficient is $r = \Sigma Z_X Z_Y / N$, where Z_X is the Z score for each person on the X variable and Z_Y is the Z score for each person on the Y variable.

Example: The steps for calculating the correlation coefficient for the initial dataset comprised of stress and depression scores of emergency health care providers follow.

Calculation Table

Stress (X)	(X − M)	(X − M)²	Zx	Depression (Y)	(Y − M)	(Y − M)²	Zy	ZxZy
39	7.7	59.29	0.91	26	6.2	38.44	1.04	0.95
29	−2.3	5.29	−0.27	16	−3.8	14.44	−0.64	0.17
43	11.7	136.89	1.39	33	13.2	174.24	2.21	3.07
18	−13.3	176.89	−1.58	22	2.2	4.84	0.37	−0.58
26	−5.3	28.09	−0.63	15	−4.8	23.04	−0.81	0.51
45	13.7	187.69	1.62	23	3.2	10.24	0.54	0.87
32	0.7	0.49	0.08	18	−1.8	3.24	−0.30	−0.03
26	−5.3	28.09	−0.63	18	−1.8	3.24	−0.30	0.19
22	−9.3	86.49	−1.10	12	−7.8	60.84	−1.31	1.44
33	1.7	2.89	0.20	15	−4.8	23.04	−0.81	−0.16
Σ = 313		Σ = 712.1		Σ = 198		Σ = 355.6		Σ = 6.43
M = 31.3		SD² = 71.21		M = 19.8		SD² = 35.56		r = 0.64
		SD = 8.44				SD = 5.96		

Steps for Figuring the Correlation Coefficient
1. Change all scores to Z scores.
2. Figure the cross-product of the Z scores for each person.
3. Add up the cross-products of the Z scores.
4. Divide by the number of people in the study to obtain the correlation of 0.64.

Causality and Correlation

Remember that when constructing scatter diagrams, if justification exists, the convention is to place the predictor variable on the horizontal axis and the variable being predicted on the vertical axis. However, the presence of a statistically significant correlation does not permit a statement about which variable is causing variation in the other variable. That is, the **direction of causality** cannot be identified from a correlation coefficient, even if it is statistically significant. For any particular correlation between variables X and Y, there are three possible directions of causality:
1. X is causing Y,
2. Y is causing X, or
3. Some third factor is causing both X and Y.

In the example,
1. Stress could be causing depression,
2. Depression could be causing stress, or
3. Some other factor like job satisfaction could be causing both stress and depression.

Sometimes a possible direction of causality can be logically eliminated, for example, when one of the variables cannot logically cause the other. For example, think about a study in which age is one of the variables. Age may be correlated with depression, and growing older may lead to depression. However, depression does not cause age (chronologically, at least). A **longitudinal study**, in which people are measured at two or more different times, may be used to rule out at least one direction of causality, as may a **true experiment**, in which participants are randomly assigned to a particular level of a variable and then measured on another variable. The most important fact to remember is that knowing that two variables like stress and depression are correlated does not indicate that one causes the other.

Statistical Significance of a Correlation Coefficient

The correlation coefficient by itself is a descriptive statistic that describes the degree and direction of a linear relationship. However, experimenters are often more interested when the relationship between two variables is representative of a larger group that has not been studied. For example, are stress and depression correlated in the population of all emergency health care workers? A correlation is said to be **statistically significant** if there is a small probability, say .05 or .01, that there is no correlation in the larger population. [The statistical significance of correlation coefficients is discussed more fully in the Appendix to this chapter.]

Prediction

Correlation and regression differ in that in regression, one variable is considered to be the **predictor variable** and the other is the variable being predicted, or **criterion variable**. The predictor variable is usually labeled X, and the criterion variable is labeled Y. In other words, X is said to predict Y.

The **prediction model**, or *prediction rule*, finds a person's Z score on the criterion variable by multiplying the **standardized regression coefficient** by the person's Z score on the predictor variable. The symbol for the standardized regression coefficient is the Greek letter **beta (β)**. The formula for the prediction model is Predicted $Z_Y = (\beta)(Z_X)$.

The correlation coefficient is also the standardized regression coefficient. Remembering from the earlier example that the correlation between stress and depression is .64, the predicted depression score (in Z score units) for an emergency health care provider with a stress score of 45 ($Z = 1.62$) is Predicted $Z_Y = (\beta)(Z_X) = (.64)(1.62) = 1.04$. Similarly, the predicted depression score (in Z score units) for an emergency health care provider with a stress score of 18 ($Z = -1.58$) is Predicted $Z_Y = (\beta)(Z_X) = (.64)(-1.58) = -1.01$.

Prediction is also called regression because of the less than perfect correlation between most variables. The predicted criterion variable Z score is the fraction of the predictor variable Z score indicated by the correlation coefficient. As a result, the predicted criterion Z score regresses back to a Z of 0.

Predictions involving raw scores can also be made using the formula $Z_X = (X M_X) / SD_X$.
1. Change the person's raw score on the predictor variable to a Z score.
2. Multiply the standardized regression coefficient (β) by the person's Z score on the predictor variable.
3. Change the person's predicted Z score on the criterion variable to a raw score.

Remembering from the earlier example that the mean stress score was 31.3 with a standard deviation of 8.44, and the mean depression score was 19.8 with a standard deviation of 5.96, the calculations in the steps above for the emergency health care provider with a stress score of 45 would be:
1. $Z_X = (X - M_X) / SD_X = (45 - 31.3) / 8.44 = 13.7 / 8.44 = 1.62$
2. Predicted $Z_Y = (\beta)(Z_X) = (.64)(1.62) = 1.04$
3. Predicted $Y = (SD_Y)(\text{Predicted } Z_Y) + M_Y = (5.96)(1.04) + 19.8 = 6.20 + 19.8 = 25.99$

In the case of the emergency health care worker with a stress score of 18, the calculations would be:
1. $Z_X = (X - M_X) / SD_X = (18 - 31.3) / 8.44 = -13.3 / 8.44 = -1.58$
2. Predicted $Z_Y = (\beta)(Z_X) = (.64)(-1.58) = -1.01$
3. Predicted $Y = (SD_Y)(\text{Predicted } Z_Y) + M_Y = (5.96)(-1.01) + 19.8 = -6.02 + 19.8 = 13.78$

Review of the Calculation Table for Example 1 shows the relationships between the values used in the calculations and the effect of the correlation on the predicted values.

The Correlation Coefficient and the Proportion of Variance Accounted For
Correlation coefficients indicate the strength of linear relationships, and the larger the value of r, the stronger the relationship. Larger values of r, or values farther from zero, indicate greater degrees of correlation. However, differences between correlation coefficients are not proportional. For example, $r = .60$ is not twice as large as $r = .30$. Most experimenters use r^2 to compare correlations, which is called the **proportion of variance accounted for**. Squaring $.60 = .36$ and squaring $.30 = .09$, which means that $r = .60$ is four times stronger than $r = .30$.

Correlation and Prediction in Research Articles
Scatter diagrams are sometimes included in research articles, and correlation coefficients are often described in the text and in tables. The correlation coefficient obtained in the example could be reported as: $r = .64$, $p < .05$. When several variables are included in a study, a table of all the correlations called a **correlation matrix** is included. Research articles reporting prediction models with only one predictor variable are rare. Research articles describing *multiple regression models* in which two or more predictor variables are used are much more common.

ADVANCED TOPIC: Multiple Regression
Multiple correlation involves determining the association between a criterion variable and two or more predictor variables, while making predictions in this situation is called **multiple regression**. In multiple regression, each predictor variable has its own regression coefficient, and the predicted Z score for the criterion variable is determined by multiplying the Z score for each predictor variable by its standardized regression coefficient and summing the results. Thus, a general multiple regression formula including four variables would be Predicted $Z_Y = (\beta_1)(Z_{X1}) + (\beta_2)(Z_{X2}) + (\beta_3)(Z_{X3}) + (\beta_4)(Z_{X4})$. Suppose that in addition to stress, the behavioral scientists included self-esteem, coping skills, and anxiety as predictors of depression. The multiple regression formula would be Predicted $Z_{Depression} = (\beta_1)(Z_{Stress}) + (\beta_2)(Z_{Self-esteem}) + (\beta_3)(Z_{Coping \ Skills}) + (\beta_4)(Z_{Anxiety})$.

Remember that when using one predictor variable, the standardized regression coefficient is the correlation coefficient, $\beta = r$. However, in multiple regression, any given β will be closer to 0 than r because what makes one variable successful in predicting the criterion variable will overlap with what makes the other variables successful predictors. Thus, in multiple regression, each standardized regression coefficient indicates the unique contribution of that variable to the prediction of the criterion variable. Therefore, in multiple regression, the overall correlation between all the predictor variables and the criterion variable is call the **multiple correlation coefficient**, or R, and the proportion of variance accounted for in multiple regression is R^2.

ADVANCED TOPIC: Multiple Regression and Multiple Correlation in Research Articles
Multiple correlation results are rarely reported in research articles, but multiple regression results are frequently reported. The results usually include the unstandardized regression coefficients, their standard errors (a concept that will be described in Chapter 6), and the standardized regression coefficients.

Chapter Self-Tests

The test items that follow are based on the following scenario. The behavioral scientists studying depression have administered an inventory to assess the level of anxiety experienced by their clients so that they can examine the relationship between these two variables.

Understanding Key Terms in Chapter 3
Directions: Using the word bank that follows, complete each statement.
Word Bank: correlation / correlation coefficient / correlation matrix / criterion variable / cross-product of Z scores / curvilinear correlation / direction of causality / linear correlation / longitudinal study / multiple correlation / multiple correlation coefficient / multiple regression / negative correlation / no correlation / perfect correlation / positive correlation / prediction model / predictor variable / proportion of variance accounted for / scatter diagram / standardized regression coefficient / statistically significant / true experiment / r / R / Z_X / Z_Y

Since the behavioral scientists are interested in the relationship between depression and anxiety, they are interested in a **(1)** _____. As a first step in examining their data, the behavioral scientists will make a graph of each client's depression scores and anxiety scores. This graph is called a **(2)** _____. If the behavioral scientists find that higher depression scores are associated with higher anxiety scores, lower depression scores are associated with lower anxiety scores, and moderate depression scores are associated with moderate anxiety scores, the relationship is called a **(3)** _____. However, if higher depression scores are associated with lower anxiety scores, lower depression scores are associated with higher anxiety scores, and moderate depression scores are associated with moderate anxiety scores, the relationship is called a **(4)** _____. If the pattern of pairs of depression scores and anxiety scores approximates a straight line, the behavioral scientists are observing a **(5)** _____. However, if higher depression scores are associated with higher anxiety scores, lower depression scores are associated with lower anxiety scores, and some moderate depression scores are associated with higher anxiety scores and some with lower anxiety scores, the relationship is called a **(6)** _____. If the dots representing the pairing of depression scores and anxiety scores have no apparent pattern, the data reflect **(7)** _____.

In order to identify high scores and low scores, the behavioral scientists calculate two Z scores labeled **(8)** _____ and **(9)** _____. The product of these Z scores is called the **(10)** _____, and dividing the sum of these products yields a **(11)** _____, which is symbolized by **(12)** _____. If each client's depression Z score is equal to his or her anxiety Z score, a **(13)** _____ will result. Although the behavioral scientists anticipate that higher levels of depression will be associated with higher levels of anxiety, the single number they have calculated to summarize the relationship does not allow them to say whether depression causes anxiety or whether anxiety causes depression because the **(14)** _____ cannot be determined from this analysis. If the research design that the behavioral scientists have used to collect the depression and anxiety data involves measuring the depression and anxiety perceived by their clients every 3 months for 2 years, they are conducting a **(15)** _____. If the behavioral scientists have randomly assigned clients to one of two groups based on whether a client's level of anxiety is categorized as low, moderate, or high, they are conducting a **(16)** _____. If they can conclude that the results of their study would be unlikely if there were no association between depression and anxiety in the larger group of all clients like theirs, the results of the study would be considered **(17)** _____.

Based on their review of previous studies, the psychologists have decided to analyze their data using the following formula, Predicted $Z_Y = (\beta)(Z_X)$, in which X represents anxiety, which means the psychologists are designating anxiety as the **(18)** _____ and depression as the **(19)** _____ variable. This kind of formula is known as the **(20)** _____, and β is also known as the **(21)** _____. The behavioral scientists base a statement about the strength of the relationship between depression and anxiety on r^2, which is called the **(22)** _____. If the behavioral scientists also correlate the number of activities of daily living with both depression and anxiety, they will report the results of all these correlations in a **(23)** _____. If they include age and a rating of general health made on a 10-point scale as additional predictor variables, they would examine the association between the criterion variable and the predictor variables using **(24)** _____. Making predictions in this situation would be called **(25)** _____. The correlation between the criterion variable and the predictor variables taken together is called the **(26)** _____, which is symbolized by **(27)** _____.

Multiple-Choice Items

1. If the dots in a scatter diagram containing depression and anxiety scores lie close to a straight line extending from the lower left side of the graph to the upper right side, the behavioral scientists will report that the correlation is
    A. positive.
    B. negative.
    C. curvilinear.
    D. rectangular.

2. If the dots in a scatter diagram containing depression and anxiety scores resemble an inverted U, the behavioral scientists will report that the correlation is
    A. positive.
    B. negative.
    C. curvilinear.
    D. rectangular.

3. If the dots in a scatter diagram containing depression and anxiety scores spread evenly across all areas of the graph, the behavioral scientists will report that
    A. the two variables are positively correlated.
    B. no correlation is present.
    C. an error has been made during data collection.
    D. the correlation is perfect.

4. If the dots in a scatter diagram containing depression and anxiety scores lie close to a straight line extending from the upper left side of the graph to the lower right side, the behavioral scientists will report that the correlation is
    A. positive.
    B. negative.
    C. curvilinear.
    D. rectangular.

5. If the dots in a scatter diagram containing depression and anxiety scores lie on a straight line extending from the lower left side of the graph to the upper right side, the behavioral scientists will obtain a correlation coefficient of
    A. +1.00.
    B. ±.50.
    C. 0.00.
    D. −1.00.

6. If the dots in a scatter diagram containing depression and anxiety scores lie on a straight line extending from the upper left side of the graph to the lower right side, the behavioral scientists will obtain a correlation coefficient of
    A. +1.00.
    B. +.75.
    C. −.75.
    D. −1.00.

Items 7–11 are based on the following information.
Based on prior studies, the behavioral scientists know that the relationship between depression and anxiety is positive and the relationship between depression and the number of activities of daily living performed is negative.

7. Which of the following correlation coefficients indicates the strongest correlation between depression and anxiety?
    A. +.75
    B. +.60
    C. .00
    D. −.60

8. Which of the following correlation coefficients indicates the strongest correlation between depression and number of activities of daily living performed?
    A. –.45
    B. +.60
    C. .00
    D. –.60

9. If the behavioral scientists obtain a correlation coefficient of +.50 between depression and anxiety, they can state that
    A. depression causes anxiety.
    B. anxiety causes depression 50% of the time.
    C. low levels of depression are associated with low levels of anxiety.
    D. low levels of anxiety are associated with high levels of depression.

10. On the other hand, if the behavioral scientists obtain a correlation coefficient of –.50 between depression and the number of activities of daily living performed, they can state that
    A. the number of activities causes depression.
    B. 50% of depression is related to the number of activities performed.
    C. low levels of depression are associated with performing fewer activities.
    D. performing fewer activities is associated with high levels of depression.

11. If the behavioral scientists obtain a correlation coefficient between depression and number of activities of daily living performed of –0.90, they would interpret this coefficient as evidence of a
    A. strong negative linear correlation.
    B. weak negative linear correlation.
    C. strong positive linear correlation.
    D. weak positive linear correlation.

12. The behavioral scientists have calculated a correlation coefficient of +1.05, which indicates
    A. a strong positive correlation.
    B. a calculation error.
    C. a curvilinear correlation.
    D. no correlation.

Items 13–14 are related.
The behavioral scientists have obtained a correlation coefficient of .60 between depression and anxiety, which means that $r^2 = .36$.

13. This value of r^2 is called
    A. Pearson product-moment correlation.
    B. Spearman's rho.
    C. the proportion of variance accounted for.
    D. the unreliability coefficient.

14. The valid interpretation of this r^2 value is that
    A. depression causes anxiety 36% of the time.
    B. the combined unreliability of the depression and anxiety scores is .36.
    C. restriction of range has reduced the explanatory power of the correlation by 36%.
    D. 36% of the variation in depression and anxiety can be explained by the correlation between them.

15. Since correlation coefficients are measures of effect size, a large effect is defined by a correlation coefficient of
    A. .10.
    B. .20.
    C. .30.
    D. .50.

16. If the behavioral scientists have calculated correlation coefficients between all possible pairings of depression, anxiety, number of activities of daily living performed, health status, and perceived quality of life, they will present these coefficients in a research article
    A. in a correlation matrix.
    B. as products of deviation scores.
    C. as the proportion of variance accounted for.
    D. in a series of scatter diagrams.

Items 17–21 are related.
Remember that the psychologists are examining the relationship between depression and anxiety using the formula Predicted $Z_Y = (\beta)(Z_X)$.

17. In this formula, the criterion variable is represented by
    A. Z_Y.
    B. β.
    C. R.
    D. Z_X.

18. In this formula, the predictor variable is represented by
    A. Z_Y.
    B. β.
    C. R.
    D. Z_X.

19. In this formula, the standardized regression coefficient is represented by
    A. Z_Y.
    B. β.
    C. R.
    D. Z_X.

20. The formula itself is called a
    A. multiple regression.
    B. multiple correlation.
    C. prediction model.
    D. proportion of variance.

21. If the psychologists devise a prediction model using stress and anxiety to predict depression, they are
    A. applying multiple regression.
    B. setting the intercept to zero.
    C. incorporating a standardized regression coefficient.
    D. making a bivariate prediction.

22. If the psychologists are primarily interested in the association between stress, anxiety, and depression, they are interested in
    A. controlling for outliers.
    B. adjusting for restriction in range.
    C. the multiple correlation.
    D. the standardized regression coefficient.

23. The symbol for a multiple correlation coefficient is
    A. R.
    B. β.
    C. R^2.
    D. $\hat{Y}$.

Problems

1. The behavioral scientists conducted their study of depression and anxiety using a sample of 12 depressed clients and obtained the following scores.

Depression: 44 47 39 43 45 57 56 48 52 48 44 48
Anxiety: 39 50 44 49 51 65 47 49 60 59 40 58

Construct a scatter diagram and describe the general pattern of the relationship. Calculate the correlation coefficient. Explain the procedure to someone who is unfamiliar with correlation, but who does understand the mean, deviation scores, and Z scores. Describe the three possible directions of causality.

2. The behavioral scientists also examined the relationship between depression and the number of activities of daily living performed by the sample of 12 depressed clients and obtained the following scores.

Depression: 44 47 39 43 45 57 56 48 52 48 44 48
Activities: 17 14 16 14 15 12 16 15 10 12 15 14

Construct a scatter diagram and describe the general pattern of the relationship. Calculate the correlation coefficient. Describe the three possible directions of causality.

3. In the stress and depression example presented earlier, the correlation coefficient is .64. What are the predicted Z scores on the depression inventory for emergency health care workers whose stress scores are (a) 15, (b) 20, (c) 25, (d) 30, (e) 35, and (f) 40?

4. If the Z scores on the stress inventory for five emergency health care workers are (a) .50, (b) –.75, (c) 1.25, (d) –1.50, and (e) 2.00, what are their predicted raw scores on the depression inventory?

5. ADVANCED TOPIC: The behavioral scientists also had scores on a self-esteem inventory and an anxiety inventory. If the standardized regression coefficient for stress was .54, for self-esteem –.62, and for anxiety .77, what would be the predicted Z score for depression for an emergency health care worker who had scores of 32 on the stress inventory, 22 on the self-esteem inventory, and 42 on the anxiety inventory?

Additional Practice: Complete any Practice Problems in Set I that your instructor has not assigned and compare your responses to those provided by the authors. Pay particular attention to the problems that require you to explain your results to someone who has never taken a course in statistics.

SPSS Applications

Application 1: Scatter Diagram and Correlation Coefficient for Problem 1
Open SPSS.
Analyze the data for Problem 1. Remember that SPSS assumes that all the scores in a row are from the same participant. In this study, there are 12 participants, each having both a depression score and an anxiety score. When you have entered the data for all 12 clients, move to the Variable View window, change the first variable name to "depress" and the second to "anx." You can enter "Depression" and "Anxiety" in the Label column so the axes of your scatter diagram will be labeled clearly. Set the number of decimals for both variables to zero. Your screen should look like Figure 1.

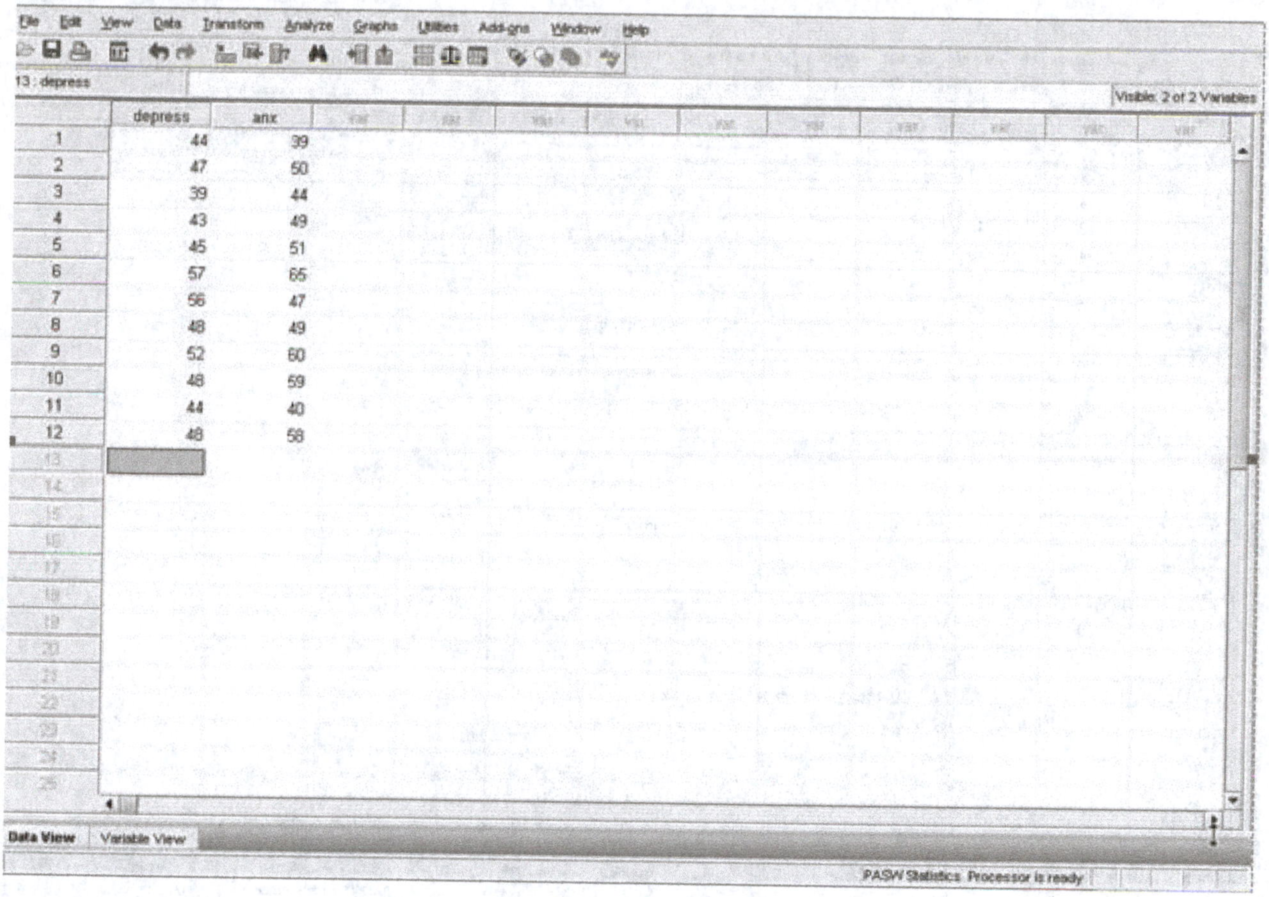

Figure 1

To construct the scatter diagram,

🖰 Graphs.

🖰 Legacy Dialogs.

🖰 Scatter/Dot. The graph labeled Simple Scatter is the default, so

🖰 Define.

🖰 the variable "depress" and 🖰 the arrow next to the box labeled "Y axis" to indicate that the scores for the depression variable should be placed on the Y (vertical) axis.

🖰 the variable "anx" and 🖰 the arrow next to the box labeled "X axis" to indicate that the anxiety variable should be placed on the X (horizontal) axis.

The window should look like Figure 2.

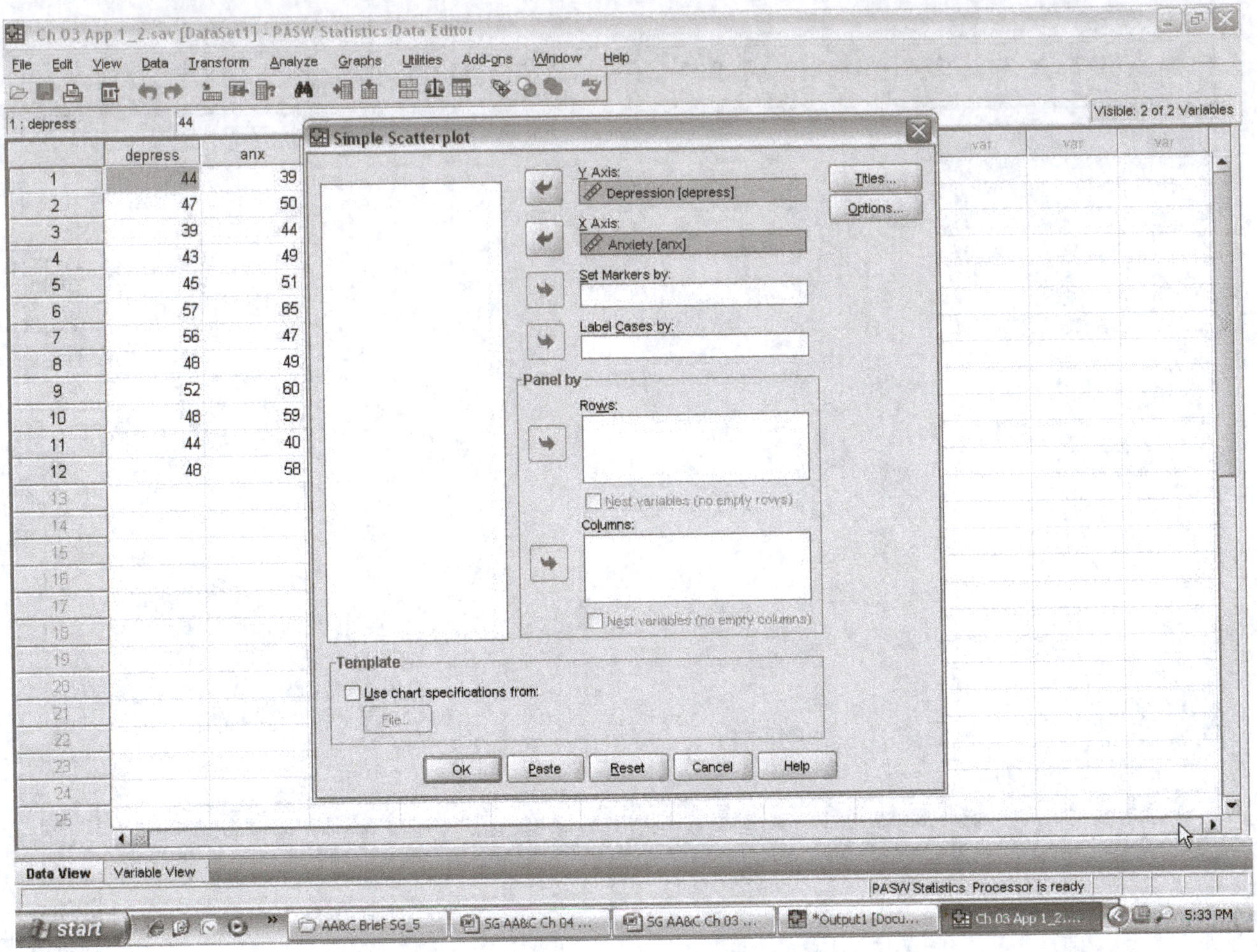

Figure 2

🖱 OK.

The scatter diagram should look like Figure 3.

Graph

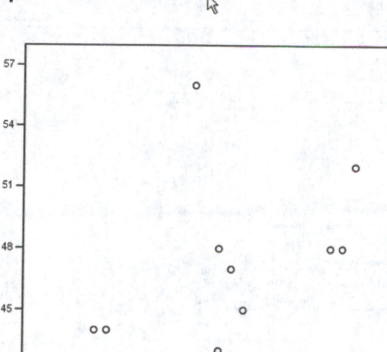

Figure 3

To calculate the correlation coefficient,
 Analyze.
 Correlate.
 Bivariate.
 the variable "depress" and the arrow next to the box labeled "Variables." Then the variable "anx" and the arrow next to the box labeled "Variables," which indicates that the correlation between depression and anxiety is to be calculated.

The window should look like Figure 4.

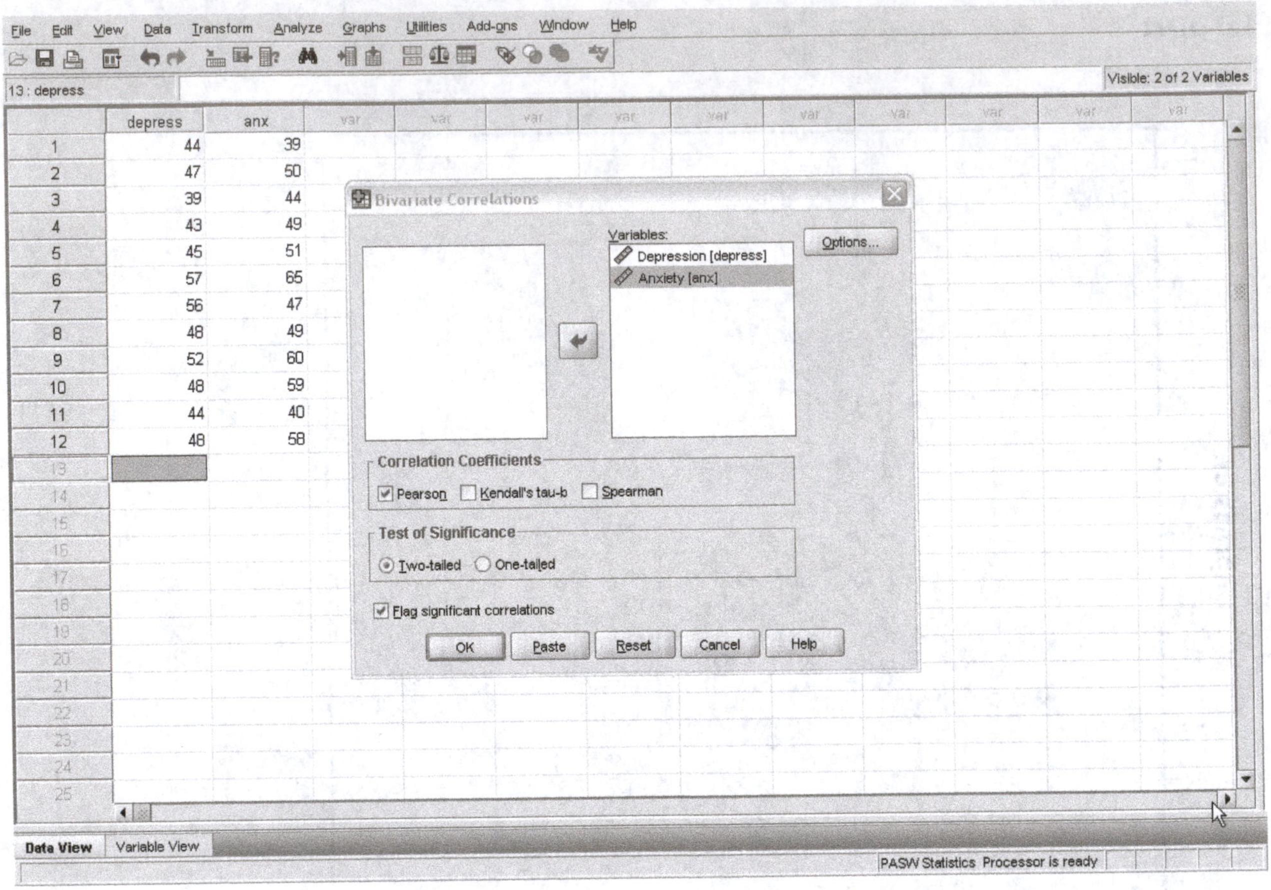

Figure 4

🖰 OK.

The output window should look like Figure 5.

Correlations

		Depression	Anxiety
Depression	Pearson Correlation	1	.625*
	Sig. (2-tailed)		.030
	N	12	12
Anxiety	Pearson Correlation	.625*	1
	Sig. (2-tailed)	.030	
	N	12	12

*. Correlation is significant at the 0.05 level (2-tailed).

Figure 5

The table in Figure 5 shows that the correlation between depression and anxiety is .625, which would be rounded to .63, and that the probability of obtaining a coefficient this large is .030 if the correlation in the population is zero. [The coefficient is close to the one calculated by hand. The difference is most likely due to the fact that SPSS uses $N-1$ in the denominator when calculating the standard deviation. This calculation will be explained in Chapter 8.] The note indicates that the correlation is significant at the .05 level using a two-tailed test. The table also includes the number of people in the analysis. Note that the two cells indicating that the correlation coefficient is 1.00 define the diagonal of the table and indicate the correlation of each variable with itself. Therefore, these cells can be ignored. Also note that the information in the upper right cell and the lower left cell is identical. Since only one coefficient has been obtained, this information would probably be reported in the text of a research article instead of in a table.

Since you will use the dataset in the next application, you may want to leave the SPSS dataset open or save it.

Application 2: Prediction with a Single Predictor for Problem 1
Open SPSS.
If you did not save the dataset you used in Application 1, enter the data for Problem 1. When you have entered the data for all 12 clients, move to the Variable View window, change the first variable name to "depress" and the second to "anx." You can enter "Depression" and "Anxiety" in the Label column so the axes of a scatter diagram (if you choose to create one) will be labeled clearly. Set the number of decimals for both variables to zero.

🖰 Analyze.
🖰 Regression and 🖰 Linear.
🖰 the variable "depress" and 🖰 the arrow next to the box labeled "Dependent" to indicate that depression is the criterion variable, which is also called the dependent variable in prediction studies.
🖰 the variable "anx" and 🖰 the arrow next to the box labeled "Independent" to indicate that anxiety is the predictor variable, which is also called the independent variable in prediction studies.
The Linear Regression window should look like Figure 6.

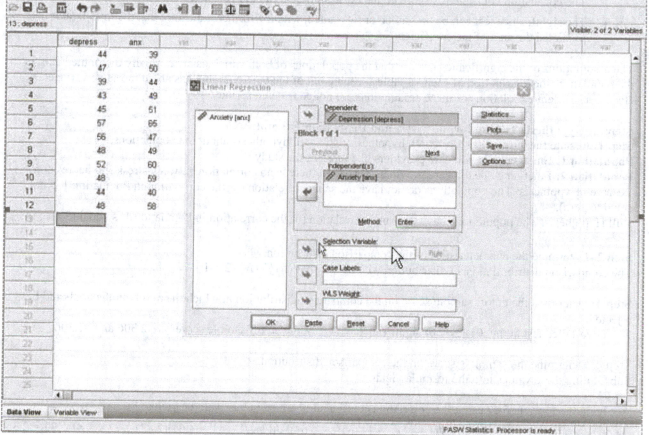

Figure 6
🖰 OK.

At this point, the important part of the output is the table containing the coefficients shown below as Figure 7. (Your instructor may teach you how to interpret the output in the other tables, or you may take a more advanced course.)

Coefficients[a]

Model		Unstandardized Coefficients		Standardized Coefficients	t	Sig.
		B	Std. Error	Beta		
1	(Constant)	26.936	8.252		3.264	.009
	Anxiety	.406	.160	.625	2.531	.030

a. Dependent Variable: Depression

Figure 7

Note that the standardized regression coefficient is .625, or .63, which is the same as the correlation coefficient obtained in earlier analyses.

APPENDIX: Hypothesis Tests and Power for the Correlation Coefficient
Hypothesis testing of correlation coefficients follows the usual steps of hypothesis except that:
1. The null hypothesis is that the correlation in the population is zero.
2. If the assumptions of the test are met, the comparison distribution is a t distribution with $N - 2$ degrees of freedom.
3. The correlation coefficient's score on the t distribution is calculated using $t = (r) \sqrt{(N-2} / \sqrt{1-r^2}$.
4. The significance test can be one-tailed or two-tailed, with the former indicating that the investigator has predicted the sign of the coefficient.

The assumptions of the significance test are that the populations of both variables are normally distributed and, in the population, the distribution of each variable at each point of the other variable has about the same variance. However, moderate violations of these assumptions are not considered serious.

Steps of Hypothesis Testing for the Stress and Depression Example
Step 1: Restate the question as a research hypothesis and a null hypothesis about the populations.
Population 1: Emergency health care providers like those in the study.
Population 2: Emergency health care providers for whom there is no correlation between stress and depression.
Research Hypothesis: The populations do not have the same correlation (or the correlation in Population 1 is not equal to zero).
Null Hypothesis: The populations have the same correlation (or the correlation in Population 1 is equal to zero).

Step 2: Determine the characteristics of the comparison distribution.
The comparison distribution is a t distribution with $df = 8$, that is, $df = N - 2 = 10 - 2 = 8$.

Step 3: Determine the cutoff sample score on the comparison distribution at which the null hypothesis should be rejected.
For a two-tailed test at the .05 level of significance with 8 df, the cutoff sample scores are 2.306 and −2.306.

Step 4: Determine the sample's score on the comparison distribution.
Substituting these values into the formula yields
$r = .64$
Applying the formula for t using the correlation coefficient obtained in the example yields
$t = (r) \sqrt{N-2} / \sqrt{1-r^2} = (.64) \sqrt{(10-2)} / \sqrt{1-.64^2} = (.64) \sqrt{8} / \sqrt{1-.41} = (.64)(2.83) / .77 = 1.81 / .77 = 2.35.$
Step 5: Decide whether to reject the null hypothesis.
Since the t value of 3.07 is more extreme than the cutoff sample t value of 2.306, the null hypothesis can be rejected and the research hypothesis can be accepted.

Effect Size and Power

A correlation coefficient is a measure of effect size. Cohen's conventions for the effect size of a correlation coefficient are

- .10 = small effect
- .30 = medium effect
- .50 = large effect

[Cohen, J. (1988). *Statistical power analysis for the behavioral sciences.* Hillsdale, NJ: Lawrence Erlbaum Associates.]

The effect size for the example is large.

Sample size can be planned using tables like Table 3-14 on page 118.

Appendix Problems

1. What is the power of the following studies in which the statistical significance of a correlation coefficient is tested at the .05 level of significance using both two-tailed and one-tailed tests?

Study	Effect Size	N
(a)	Small	40
(b)	Small	100
(c)	Medium	40
(d)	Medium	100
(e)	Large	40
(f)	Large	100

2. How many participants are needed to have 80% power in the following studies in which the statistical significance of a correlation coefficient will be tested at the .05 level of significance using both two-tailed and one-tailed tests?

Study	Effect Size
(a)	Medium
(b)	Large

Chapter 3 Key

Completion Items

1. correlation	10. cross-product of Z scores	19. criterion variable
2. scatter diagram	11. correlation coefficient	20. prediction model
3. positive	12. r	21. standardized regression coefficient
4. negative	13. perfect correlation	22. proportion of variance accounted for
5. linear	14. direction of causality	23. correlation matrix
6. curvilinear	15. longitudinal study	24. multiple correlation
7. no	16. true experiment	25. multiple regression
8. Z_X	17. statistically significant	26. multiple correlation coefficient
9. Z_X	18. predictor variable	27. R

Multiple-Choice Items

1. A	6. D	11. A	16. A	21. A
2. C	7. A	12. C	17. A	22. C
3. B	8. D	13. C	18. D	23. A
4. B	9. C	14. D	19. B	
5. A	10. D	15. D	20. C	

Problems

1.
Scatter diagram

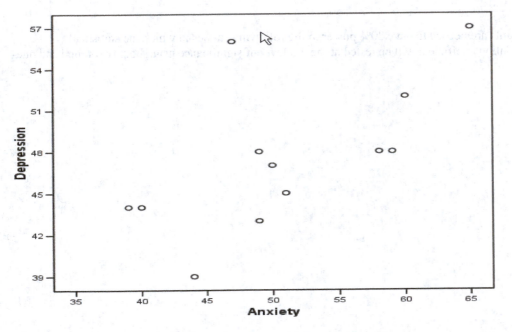

The general pattern of the scatter diagram indicates a positive correlation.

The table that follows shows the calculation of the correlation with Depression = X and Anxiety = Y.

Depression	X – M	$(X-M)^2$	Z_X	Anxiety	Y – M	$(Y-M)^2$	Z_Y	$Z_X Z_Y$
44	–3.58	12.82	–0.71	39	–11.92	142.09	–1.53	1.08
47	–0.58	0.34	–0.11	50	–0.92	0.85	–0.12	0.01
39	–8.58	73.62	–1.70	44	–6.92	47.89	–0.89	1.51
43	–4.58	20.98	–0.91	49	–1.92	3.69	–0.25	0.22
45	–2.58	6.66	–0.51	51	0.08	0.01	0.01	–0.01
57	9.42	88.74	1.86	65	14.08	198.25	1.81	3.36
56	8.42	70.90	1.66	47	–3.92	15.37	–0.50	–0.84
48	0.42	0.18	0.08	49	–1.92	3.69	–0.25	–0.02
52	4.42	19.54	0.87	60	9.08	82.45	1.17	1.02
48	0.42	0.18	0.08	59	8.08	65.29	1.04	0.09
44	–3.58	12.82	–0.71	40	–10.92	119.25	–1.40	0.99
48	0.42	0.18	0.08	58	7.08	50.13	0.91	0.08
$\Sigma = 571$		$\Sigma = 306.92$		$\Sigma = 611$		$\Sigma = 728.92$		$\Sigma = 7.50$
$M_X = 47.58$		$SD^2_X = 25.58$		$M_Y = 50.92$		$SD^2_Y = 60.74$		$r = 0.62$
		$SD_X = 5.06$				$SD_Y = 7.79$		

Compare your explanation of the procedure you followed to the sample response to Practice Problem 6 or Practice Problem 7 in Set 1 in the text.

The three possible directions of causality are
1. depression causes anxiety,
2. anxiety causes depression, or
3. some third variable is causing both depression and anxiety.

2.
Scatter diagram

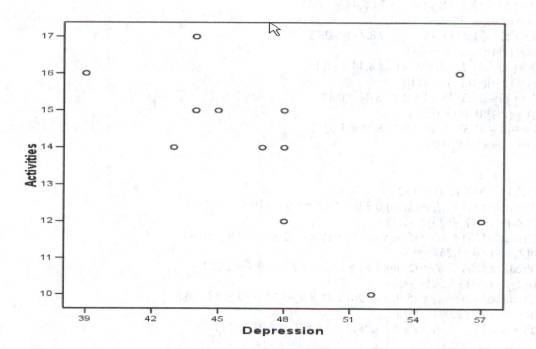

The general pattern of the scatter diagram indicates a negative correlation.

The table that follows shows the calculation of the correlation with Depression = X and Activities of Daily Living = Y.

Depression	$X - M$	$(X - M)^2$	Z_X	Activities	$Y - M$	$(Y - M)^2$	Z_Y	$Z_X Z_Y$
44	−3.58	12.82	−0.71	17	2.83	8.01	1.48	−1.05
47	−0.58	0.34	−0.11	14	−0.17	0.03	−0.09	0.01
39	−8.58	73.62	−1.70	16	1.83	3.35	0.96	−1.62
43	−4.58	20.98	−0.91	14	−0.17	0.03	−0.09	0.08
45	−2.58	6.66	−0.51	15	0.83	0.69	0.43	−0.22
57	9.42	88.74	1.86	12	−2.17	4.71	−1.14	−2.12
56	8.42	70.90	1.66	16	1.83	3.35	0.96	1.59
48	0.42	0.18	0.08	15	0.83	0.69	0.43	0.04
52	4.42	19.54	0.87	10	−4.17	17.39	−2.18	−1.91
48	0.42	0.18	0.08	12	−2.17	4.71	−1.14	−0.09
44	−3.58	12.82	−0.71	15	0.83	0.69	0.43	−0.31
48	0.42	0.18	0.08	14	−0.17	0.03	−0.09	−0.01
$\Sigma = 571$		$\Sigma = 306.92$		$\Sigma = 170$		$\Sigma = 43.67$		$\Sigma = -5.60$
$M_X = 47.58$		$SD^2{}_X = 25.58$		$M_Y = 14.17$		$SD^2{}_Y = 3.64$		$r = -0.47$
		$SD_X = 5.06$				$SD_Y = 1.91$		

The three possible directions of causality are
1. depression causes the number of activities of daily living to be performed,
2. the number of activities of daily living performed causes depression, or
3. some third variable is causing both depression and the number of daily activities performed.

3.
(a) $Z_X = (X - M) / SD = (15 - 31.3) / 8.44 = -16.3 / 8.44 = -1.93$
Predicted $Z_Y = (\beta)(Z_X) = (.64)(-1.93) = -1.24$
(b) $Z_X = (X - M) / SD = (20 - 31.3) / 8.44 = -11.3 / 8.44 = -1.34$
Predicted $Z_Y = (\beta)(Z_X) = (.64)(-1.34) = -0.86$
(c) $Z_X = (X - M) / SD = (25 - 31.3) / 8.44 = -6.3 / 8.44 = -0.75$
Predicted $Z_Y = (\beta)(Z_X) = (.64)(-0.75) = -0.48$
(d) $Z_X = (X - M) / SD = (30 - 31.3) / 8.44 = -1.3 / 8.44 = -0.15$
Predicted $Z_Y = (\beta)(Z_X) = (.64)(-0.15) = -0.10$
(e) $Z_X = (X - M) / SD = (35 - 31.3) / 8.44 = 3.7 / 8.44 = 0.44$
Predicted $Z_Y = (\beta)(Z_X) = (.64)(0.44) = 0.28$
(f) $Z_X = (X - M) / SD = (40 - 31.3) / 8.44 = 8.7 / 8.44 = 1.03$
Predicted $Z_Y = (\beta)(Z_X) = (.64)(1.03) = 0.66$

4.
(a) Predicted $Z_Y = (\beta)(Z_X) = (.64)(0.50) = 0.32$
Predicted $Y = (SD_Y)(\text{Predicted } Z_Y) + M_Y = (5.96)(0.32) + 19.8 = 1.91 + 19.8 = 21.71$
(b) Predicted $Z_Y = (\beta)(Z_X) = (.64)(-0.75) = -0.48$
Predicted $Y = (SD_Y)(\text{Predicted } Z_Y) + M_Y = (5.96)(-0.48) + 19.8 = -2.86 + 19.8 = 16.94$
(c) Predicted $Z_Y = (\beta)(Z_X) = (.64)(1.25) = 0.8$
Predicted $Y = (SD_Y)(\text{Predicted } Z_Y) + M_Y = (5.96)(0.8) + 19.8 = 4.77 + 19.8 = 24.57$
(d) Predicted $Z_Y = (\beta)(Z_X) = (.64)(-1.50) = -0.96$
Predicted $Y = (SD_Y)(\text{Predicted } Z_Y) + M_Y = (5.96)(-0.96) + 19.8 = -5.72 + 19.8 = 14.08$
(e) Predicted $Z_Y = (\beta)(Z_X) = (.64)(2.00) = 1.28$
Predicted $Y = (SD_Y)(\text{Predicted } Z_Y) + M_Y = (5.96)(1.28) + 19.8 = 7.63 + 19.8 = 27.43$

5. ADVANCED TOPIC

Predicted $Z_{Depression} = (\beta_1)(Z_{Stress}) + (\beta_2)(Z_{Self-esteem}) + (\beta_3)(Z_{Coping\ Skills}) + (\beta_4)(Z_{Anxiety}) = (.54)(32) + (-.62)(22) + (.77)(42) = 17.28 + (-13.64) + 32.34 = 35.98$

APPENDIX PROBLEMS

1.

Study	Effect Size	N	Two-Tailed Power	One-Tailed Power
(a)	Small	40	.09	.15
(b)	Small	100	.17	.26
(c)	Medium	40	.48	.60
(d)	Medium	100	.86	.92
(e)	Large	40	.92	.96
(f)	Large	100	*	*

2.

Study	Effect Size	Two-Tailed N	One-Tailed N
(a)	Medium	85	68
(b)	Large	28	22

Chapter 4
Some Key Ingredients for Inferential Statistics: The Normal Curve, Sample versus Population, and Probability

Learning Objectives
After studying this chapter, you should:
- Be able to describe the normal curve.
- Be able to use the normal curve table.
- Be able to figure the percentage of scores above or below a particular raw score or Z score using the normal curve table.
- Be able to figure Z scores and raw scores from percentages using the normal curve table.
- Know the difference between a sample and a population and the associated statistical terminology.
- Be able to define probability and explain the long-run relative-frequency interpretation of probability.
- Be able to differentiate random and nonrandom methods of sampling.

The Normal Distribution
The distributions of many variables, such as the intelligence or reaction times of a large number of people, and many other variables measured by behavioral scientists are unimodal, roughly symmetrical, and bell-shaped. These bell-shaped histograms or frequency polygons approximate a precise and important mathematical distribution called the **normal distribution**, or more simply, the **normal curve**. The normal curve is common in nature because a person's score on any particular variable can be influenced by a large number of essentially random factors that cause most of the scores to cluster around a middle value, with equal but smaller numbers of scores falling above and below the middle value. Mathematics, specifically the *central limit theorem*, will show that in the long run, if the influences are truly random, a precise normal curve will result. However, some distributions in the social sciences do not follow the normal curve. Methods for working with variables that do not follow a normal curve will be presented in Chapter 11.

The shape of the normal curve is standard, so the percentage of scores above or below any particular point in the curve can be determined. Because normal curves are symmetrical, exactly 50% of the cases lie above the mean and exactly 50% lie below the mean. In addition, approximately 34% of the cases fall between the mean and one standard deviation above the mean, and approximately 34% fall between the mean and one standard deviation below the mean. Furthermore, approximately 14% of the cases fall between one and two standard deviations above the mean and between one and two standard deviations below the mean.

Returning to the example of stress scores first mentioned in Chapter 2, remember that the mean was 36 and the standard deviation was 8. Therefore, 50% of the scores will be higher than 36 and 50% will be lower than 36. Considering scores above the mean, approximately 34% of the population will have scores between 36 and 44 (between the mean and one standard deviation above the mean), and approximately 14% of the population will have scores between 44 and 52 (between one standard deviation above the mean and two standard deviations above the mean). Since the normal curve is symmetrical, approximately 34% of the population will have scores between 28 and 36 (between the mean and one standard deviation below the mean), and approximately 14% of the population will have scores between 20 and 28 (between one standard deviation below the mean and two standard deviations below the mean). Since these percentages are constant for any variable that is normally distributed, the percentage of cases that lie above or below any Z score can be determined, as can the percentage of cases that lie between any two Z scores.

The Normal Curve Table and Z Scores
Because the normal curve is exactly defined, it is also possible to determine the exact percentage of cases between any two Z scores. **Normal curve tables** like Table A-1 in the text provide the percentage of cases between the mean (a Z score of 0) and any other Z score. This table also can be used to determine the percentage of cases between any two Z scores, and if raw scores are converted to Z scores, between any two raw scores.

Figuring the Percentage of Scores above or below a Particular Raw Score or Z Score Using the Normal Curve Table

1. If you are beginning with a raw score, first change it to a Z score. $[Z = (X - M) / SD]$
2. Draw a picture of the normal curve, where the Z score falls on it, and shade in the area for which you are finding the percentage.
3. Make a rough estimate of the shaded area's percentage based on the 50%–34%–14% percentages.
4. Find the exact percentage using the normal curve table (Table A-1), adding 50% if necessary.
5. Check that your exact percentage is within the range of your rough estimate from Step 3.

The examples that follow are based on scores on a self-esteem inventory taken by a large number of students that has a mean of 66 and a standard deviation of 8. These examples are designed to reinforce the concepts underlying the process of determining areas under the normal curve. Therefore, you should do the calculations, and then check your answer using the "% in Tail" column in Table A-1.

Example 1:
What percentage of scores is higher than 72?
$Z = (X - M) / SD$
$= (72 - 66) / 8$
$= 6 / 8$
$= 0.75$
From the table of areas under the normal curve, the percentage from the mean to a Z score of 0.75 is 27.34%. Therefore, the number of scores greater than 72 is 50.00% – 27.34% = 22.66% of the scores.

Example 2:
What percentage of scores is higher than 60?
$Z = (X - M) / SD$
$= (60 - 66) / 8$
$= -6 / 8$
$= -0.75$
From the table of areas under the normal curve, the percentage from the mean to a Z score of –0.75 is 27.34%. Therefore, the number of scores greater than 60 is 50.00% + 27.34% = 77.34% of the scores.

Example 3:
What percentage of scores is lower than 72?
$Z = (X - M) / SD$
$= (72 - 66) / 8$
$= 6 / 8$
$= 0.75$
From the table of areas under the normal curve, the percentage from the mean to a Z score of 0.75 is 27.34%. Therefore, the number of scores lower than 72 is 50.00% + 27.34% = 77.34% of the scores.

Example 4:
What percentage of scores is lower than 60?
$Z = (X - M) / SD$
$= (60 - 66) / 8$
$= -6 / 8$
$= -0.75$
From the table of areas under the normal curve, the percentage from the mean to a Z score of –0.75 is 27.34%. Therefore, the number of scores greater than 60 is 50.00% – 27.34% = 22.66% of the scores.

Figuring Z Scores and Raw Scores from Percentages Using the Normal Curve Table

1. Draw a picture of the normal curve and shade in the approximate area for your percentage of area under the curve using the 50%–34%–14% percentages.
2. Make a rough estimate of the Z score where the shaded area stops.
3. Find the exact Z score using the normal curve table (subtracting 50% from your percentage if necessary before looking up the Z score).
4. Check that your exact Z score is within the range of your rough estimate from Step 2.
5. If you want to find a raw score, change it from the Z score. [$X = (Z)(SD) + M$]

Again, the examples that follow use scores on a self-esteem inventory that has a mean of 66 and a standard deviation of 8.

Example 1:
What self-esteem score would place a student in the top 10% of all students?
Referring to Table A-1, the area from the mean to a Z score of 1.28 is 39.97%, leaving 10.03% of the curve in the tail. Solving the formula $X = (Z)(SD) + M$ yields $(1.28)(8) + 66 = 10.24 + 66 = 76.24$. Therefore, a self-esteem score of 76 could be used to identify students in the top 10% of all self-esteem scores.

Example 2:
What self-esteem score would place a student in the top 75% of all students?
Referring to Table A-1, the area from the mean to a Z score of $-.67$ is 24.86%, leaving 25.14% in the tail. Solving the formula $X = (Z)(SD) + M$ yields $(-.67)(8) + 66 = -5.36 + 66 = 60.64$. Therefore, a self-esteem score of 60 could be used to identify students in the top 75% of all self-esteem scores.

Example 3:
What range of self-esteem scores would include students in the middle 60% of all self-esteem scores?
Referring to Table A-1, the area from the mean to a Z score of $-.84$ is 29.95%, leaving 20.05% of the area in the lower tail of the curve. Similarly, the area from the mean to a Z score of .84 is 29.95%, leaving 20.05% of the area in the upper tail of the curve. Solving the formula $X = (Z)(SD) + M$ for the lower tail of the curve yields $(-.84)(8) + 66 = -6.72 + 66 = 59.28$. Solving the formula $X = (Z)(SD) + M$ for the upper tail of the curve yields $(.84)(8) + 66 = 6.72 + 66 = 72.72$. Therefore, the range of self-esteem scores from 59 to 73 would include approximately 60% of all self-esteem scores.

Sample and Population
A **population** is the entire set of things of interest. In this text, the populations are comprised of people with certain characteristics. A **sample** is the subset of the population about which researchers actually have information.

Behavioral scientists study samples instead of populations because studying populations is usually impractical. The general strategy of psychological research is to study a sample of individuals believed to be representative of the general population, or of some particular population of interest. Realistically, researchers try to study people who at least do not differ from the general population in a systematic way that could influence the results of a research study. For example, if researchers are interested in the self-esteem of students who entered college following military service, they would not include students who had no military service in the sample.

Methods of Sampling
Random selection, in which researchers obtain a complete list of members of the population of interest and randomly select some of them for inclusion in the study, is the ideal method for selecting a sample.
Haphazard selection, which may involve selecting anyone who is available or who happens to be first in a list, may result in a sample that is different from the population.

Statistical Terminology for Samples and Populations
Population parameters include the mean, variance, and standard deviation of populations. Population parameters are usually an unknown and can only be estimated from data collected from a sample drawn from the population.
Sample statistics include the mean, variance, and standard deviation calculated from scores collected from a sample. Thus, sample statistics are computed from known information.

Probability
Probability is important in scientific research in general and psychological research in particular because of the role of probability in inferential statistics, which permit researchers to draw conclusions about whether theories or experimental procedures can be applied in other settings. While probability is a broad, controversial topic, only a few key ideas are needed to understand basic inferential statistics.

Probability is the expected relative frequency of a particular outcome.
An **outcome** is the result of an experiment, or virtually any event for which the result is not known in advance.
Frequency is how many times something happens, and r*elative frequency* is the number of times something happens relative to the number of times it could have happened.
The **expected relative frequency** is the frequency obtained when an experiment is repeated many times, and interpretation of research results in terms of this frequency is known as the **long-run relative-frequency interpretation of probability**.

A probability is equal to the number of possible successful outcomes divided by the number of all possible outcomes. As a formula: Probability = Possible successful outcomes / All possible outcomes.
Probabilities can range from 0, when something has no chance of happening, to 1, when something is certain to happen.
Probability is usually symbolized by the letter p and is expressed as being equal to, greater than, or less than some fraction or percentage.
The normal distribution can also be thought of as a probability distribution because the percentage of scores between any two Z scores is the same as the probability of selecting a case between those two Z scores.

Normal Curves, Probabilities, Samples, and Populations as Described in Research Articles
Although important to understanding the statistical procedures that follow, the topics in this chapter are rarely discussed explicitly in research articles. The normal curve is sometimes mentioned when describing the distribution of scores on a particular variable, and the method of selecting the sample from the population may be described, particularly if the study reports the results of a survey. Probability also is rarely discussed directly, except in the context of statistical significance, which will be discussed in later chapters.

Chapter Self-Tests

The practice test items that follow are based on the following scenario. A group of behavioral scientists plans to administer an inventory designed to measure depression in the general population to a sample of college students. The inventory asks students to indicate whether they have experienced any of 20 thoughts or feelings during the past week. Students use a 4-point scale in which responses are scored 0–3, so that scores can range from 0 to 60.

Understanding Key Terms in Chapter 4
Directions: Using the word bank that follows, complete each statement.
Word Bank: expected / haphazard selection / long-run relative frequency / normal curve / normal curve table / normal distribution / outcome / *p* / population / population parameters / probability / random selection / sample / sample statistics

The behavioral scientists are now preparing to perform inferential statistical analyses. Although they have enrolled only 40 students in their **(1)** _____, they are interested in applying what they learn to the **(2)** _____ of all students. If a graph of the distribution of depression scores is unimodal, approximately symmetrical, and shaped like a bell, the graph reflects the **(3)** _____, or more simply, the **(4)** _____. Because this curve is a precise mathematical curve, the percentage of scores between two points on the curve can be found using the **(5)** _____. If the behavioral scientists created the sample by administering the depression inventory to the 40 students enrolled in one of their classes, they have used **(6)** _____. The ideal method for selecting a sample for a study is **(7)** _____.

The behavioral scientists find that the mean on the depression scale for the 40 students is 12.4 with a standard deviation of 4.6, which are **(8)** _____. If the behavioral scientists could determine the mean depression score and its standard deviation for the population of all students, they would know the **(9)** _____.

If the behavioral scientists state that the expected relative frequency of depressed students in their sample will be four students out of 40, they have defined a **(10)** _____. The symbol for this value is **(11)** _____. The identification of 6 of the 40 students as depressed is an **(12)** _____. If the behavioral scientists were able to repeat their study a large number of times and found that the mean number of depressed students over all the studies was 4, the behavioral scientists would have determined the **(13)** _____ relative frequency. This series of studies would provide data for a **(14)** _____ relative frequency interpretation of probability.

Multiple-Choice Items

1. A description of the normal distribution would include a statement that it is
   A. slightly skewed to the left.
   B. slightly skewed to the right.
   C. unimodal.
   D. bimodal.

2. If the behavioral scientists wanted to determine the precise percentage of students whose depression scores were greater than 2 standard deviations above the mean, they would use a
   A. normal curve table.
   B. population parameter.
   C. sample statistic.
   D. long-run relative-frequency interpretation.

3. If depression is normally distributed among students, the behavioral scientists can expect approximately two-thirds of the students to have depression scores that transform to Z scores between
   A. 0.00 and 1.00.
   B. 0.00 and −1.00.
   C. −1.00 and 1.00.
   D. −2.00 and 2.00.

4. If depression is normally distributed among students, the behavioral scientists can expect approximately one-third of the students to have depression scores that transform to Z scores between
   A.   0.00 and 1.00.
   B.   0.00 and −2.00.
   C.   −1.00 and 1.00.
   D.   −2.00 and 2.00.

5. If the behavioral scientists state that 5% of all students are clinically depressed, they are making a statement about
   A.   the normal distribution.
   B.   a population.
   C.   a sample.
   D.   skewness.

6. If the behavioral scientists choose 40 students from the 400 students taking statistics during a semester to participate in their survey to assess the number of students experiencing clinical depression, the behavioral scientists have selected a
   A.   normal distribution.
   B.   population.
   C.   sample.
   D.   focus group.

7. If the behavioral scientists obtain a numbered list of all 1,000 full-time students enrolled at a school during a semester and a computer identifies students numbered 3, 501, 256, 782, and 650 as the first five participantsto be selected for a sample, the behavioral scientists will be using
   A.   relative selection.
   B.   haphazard selection.
   C.   random selection.
   D.   subjective selection.

8. If the behavioral scientists select participants by posting notices asking for volunteers in all the dormitories on campus, they will have a
   A.   relative selection.
   B.   haphazard selection.
   C.   random selection.
   D.   subjective selection.

9. If the behavioral scientists know that 4 of every 100 students are clinically depressed, the probability of selecting a depressed student at random from a sample of 100 students can be expressed as
   A.   4.0.
   B.   .04.
   C.   40.0.
   D.   .004.

10. If the behavioral scientists repeat the study of depression among students and find that 5% of the students in this second study are clinically depressed, the result is the
   A.   outcome.
   B.   relative frequency.
   C.   probability.
   D.   expected relative frequency.

11. If the behavioral scientists repeat the study of depression among students several more times and find that approximately 5% of the students in all these studies are clinically depressed, the behavioral scientists can expect that many more replications will yield the same result. In this case, the behavioral scientists can say that a 5% rate of clinical depression is the
   A. probability.
   B. relative frequency.
   C. outcome.
   D. expected relative frequency.

12. If the behavioral scientists state that any investigation of depression among students is likely to yield a 5% rate of clinical depression, the behavioral scientists are
   A. interpreting population parameters.
   B. using normal curve tables.
   C. transforming raw scores to standard scores.
   D. applying the long-run relative-frequency interpretation of probability.

Problems

Using the 50%–34%–14% approximations of areas under the normal curve, what percentage of normally distributed scores lie:
1. Between 1 standard deviation below the mean and 1 standard deviation above the mean?

2. Between 2 standard deviations below the mean and 2 standard deviations above the mean?

3. Between 2 standard deviations below the mean and the mean?

4. Between 2 standard deviations above the mean and the mean?

5. Above 1.5 standard deviations above the mean?

6. Below 0.5 standard deviations below the mean?

Calculate the areas under the normal curve between the following pairs of Z scores.

7. $Z = -0.36$ and $Z = 0.88$

8. $Z = 1.74$ and $Z = 2.05$

9. $Z = -1.51$ and $Z = 1.32$

10. $Z = -0.49$ and $Z = -1.89$

11. $Z = 1.31$ and $Z = -1.61$

12. $Z = 0.68$ and $Z = -1.48$

13. $Z = -2.74$ and $Z = -1.55$

14. $Z = 1.33$ and $Z = 2.33$

Additional Practice: Complete any Practice Problems in Set I that your instructor has not assigned and compare your responses to those provided by the authors. Pay particular attention to the problems that require you to explain your results to someone who has never taken a course in statistics.

SPSS Applications
There are no SPSS applications for this chapter.

Chapter 4 Key

Completion Items

1. sample	8. sample statistics
2. population	9. population parameters
3. normal distribution	10. probability
4. normal curve	11. p
5. normal curve table	12. outcome
6. haphazard selection	13. expected
7. random selection	14. long-run

Multiple-Choice Items

1. C	5. B	9. B
2. A	6. C	10. A
3. C	7. C	11. D
4. A	8. B	12. D

Problems

1. 68%	8. 2.07%
2. 96%	9. 84.11%
3. 48%	10. 28.27%
4. 48%	11. 85.12%
5. 9%	12. 68.23%
6. 33%	13. 5.75%
7. 45.12%	14. 8.19%

Chapter 5
Introduction to Hypothesis Testing

Learning Objectives
After studying this chapter, you should:
- Be able to apply the core logic of hypothesis testing.
- Be able to define the populations involved in hypothesis testing.
- Write research hypotheses.
- Write null hypotheses.
- Define the comparison distribution.
- Determine the cutoff score on the comparison distribution.
- Define significance and know the conventional levels of significance.
- Know when to reject the null hypothesis and the implications of this decision.
- Know when not to reject the null hypothesis and the implications of this decision.
- Be able to follow the steps of hypothesis testing.
- Know the difference between directional and nondirectional hypotheses.
- Know the difference between one-tailed and two-tailed tests.
- Know how results of studies using hypothesis-testing procedures are reported in research articles.

Research in behavioral or social sciences often begins with a **hypothesis**, which is a prediction about the results of a research study. This hypothesis is often derived from a **theory**, or a set of principles that explain one or more facts, relationships, or events. **Hypothesis testing** is a procedure for deciding whether the outcome of a study conducted with a sample of participants supports a theory or innovation that can, in turn, be applied to a population.

The Core Logic of Hypothesis Testing
The principle underlying hypothesis testing is that researchers test the idea that an experimental treatment makes no difference—that it has no effect. If the idea that the experimental treatment makes no difference can be rejected, then researchers can accept the idea that the treatment does make a difference. In other words, the researchers can conclude that the treatment has an effect. In other words, researchers draw conclusions by evaluating the probability of getting the observed research results if the opposite of what they are predicting is true. This double-negative, roundabout logic is awkward, but necessary, because researchers use comparison distributions (which will be described in later chapters) to determine the probability of obtaining the observed results if the opposite of what they are predicting is true.

The Steps of Hypothesis Testing
Suppose that a group of behavioral scientists has measured the stress perceived by students and wants to see if a 1-hour counseling session each week for 6 weeks will reduce stress. Although such a study would most likely involve more than one student, suppose that the behavioral scientists have selected only one student to undergo the six counseling sessions. In order to conduct the study, the behavioral scientists will follow the five steps that follow.

Step 1: Restate the question as a research hypothesis and a null hypothesis about the populations.
Research is conducted using samples to test hypotheses about populations. One population (*Population 1*) includes the people who undergo the experimental treatment. The other population (*Population 2*) includes the people who have not been exposed to the experimental treatment. In this example,
Population 1: Students who undergo 1 hour of counseling per week for 6 weeks.
Population 2: Students who do not undergo 1 hour of counseling per week for 6 weeks.

The **research hypothesis** is a statement about the predicted difference between populations. Typically, the research hypothesis states that the means of the populations will be different, or perhaps more specifically, that one population mean will be higher or lower than the other population mean. The **null hypothesis** is the crucial opposite of the research hypothesis, and states that the means of the populations will be different, or, that if a difference is observed, it will be in the opposite direction from the predicted direction. Thus, the research hypothesis and the null hypothesis are opposites and mutually exclusive. The research hypothesis is also called the *alternative hypothesis* because researchers are interested in rejecting the null hypothesis to make a decision about its alternative. The hypotheses for the hypothetical stress study will be presented later.

Step 2: Determine the characteristics of the comparison distribution.

The question in hypothesis-testing procedures is "Given a particular sample result, what is the probability of obtaining this result if the null hypothesis is true?" In order to answer this question, researchers must know the characteristics of the **comparison distribution**. The comparison distribution is the distribution of the variable being measured if the null hypothesis is true, that is, in the absence of an experimental treatment, or if an experimental treatment has no effect. Thus, the comparison distribution is the distribution for Population 2 in Step 1. Stated another way, if the null hypothesis is true, the distributions for Population 1 and Population 2 in Step 1 are identical; and any score is equally likely to come from either population. In this example, the comparison distribution is a normal distribution that reflects the scores of students who do not undergo 1 hour of counseling per week for 6 weeks.

Step 3: Determine the cutoff sample score on the comparison distribution at which the null hypothesis should be rejected.

Before conducting a study, researchers should determine how extreme a sample score must be to reject the null hypothesis. This score is called the **cutoff sample score** (or the *critical value*). Cutoff sample scores are expressed as Z scores instead of in the units in which the experimental variable is measured, in this case, stress inventory scores. These Z scores are selected based on the percentage of area in one or both tails of the comparison distribution. For example, if the mean stress score for a large number of students is 52 and the standard deviation is 8, a score more extreme than 36 ($Z = -2.00$) would occur fewer than 2% of the time. Therefore, the behavioral scientists might decide to reject the null hypothesis if the student in the study obtains a score on the stress inventory lower than 36 after undergoing 1 hour of counseling per week for 6 weeks. If the student's stress score is greater than (or equal to) 36, the behavioral scientists will not reject the null hypothesis.

Behavioral scientists, however, generally select cutoff sample scores that will be observed less than 5% of the time if the null hypothesis is true, or if they want to be more conservative, less than 1% of the time. These probabilities are written as $p < .05$ and $p < .01$, respectively. These cutoff percentages are known as the **conventional levels of significance**, and are also called the 5% (or .05) and the 1% (or .01) significance levels. When sample values are so extreme that researchers reject the null hypothesis, the results are said to be *statistically significant*. Since the goal of this study is stress reduction, the cutoff sample score on the normal curve might be -2.33 if the behavioral scientists want to reject the null hypothesis if any observed stress reduction would occur less than 1% of the time if students did not receive counseling.

Step 4: Determine the sample's score on the comparison distribution.

After conducting a study, the raw score result is converted to a Z score so that it can be compared to the cutoff sample score. For example, if a student in the sample study obtains a stress inventory score of 32 after undergoing 1 hour of counseling per week for 6 weeks, the student's Z score will be -2.50. If the null hypothesis is true, a score this extreme will occur less than 1% of the time.

Step 5: Decide whether to reject the null hypothesis.

This step involves simply comparing the sample's Z score obtained in Step 4 with the cutoff sample score determined in Step 3. If the sample score is more extreme than the cutoff sample score, the researchers will reject the null hypothesis and accept the research hypothesis. If the sample score is not more extreme than the cutoff sample score, the researchers will fail to reject the null hypothesis. In Step 4 above, the student in the sample study obtained a stress inventory score of 32 after undergoing 1 hour of counseling per week for 6 weeks, yielding a Z score of -2.50. Since the student's Z score is more extreme than the cutoff sample score of -2.33, the behavioral scientists will reject the null hypothesis and accept the research hypothesis.

Implications of Rejecting or Failing to Reject the Null Hypothesis

Since the decision to reject or fail to reject the null hypothesis is based on probabilities, three points should be remembered.

1. Even if the null hypothesis is rejected, the results do not prove the research hypothesis. The research hypothesis cannot be *proved* because the results of research studies are based on probabilities. All that a study can do is demonstrate that the likelihood of obtaining those results due to chance alone is very low *if the null hypothesis is true*.

2. When the results are not sufficiently extreme to reject the null hypothesis, behavioral scientists do not say that the results support the null hypothesis. Demonstrating that the null hypothesis is true would require that there be

absolutely no difference between the two populations. The experimental treatment may cause a difference between or among the groups, but the difference may be too small to attribute conclusively to the treatment. Therefore, when the results are not sufficiently extreme to reject the null hypothesis, they are said to be inconclusive.

3. It should be emphasized that obtaining a statistically significant result does not indicate that the results of a study are important or suggest any practical application of the results.

One-Tailed and Two-Tailed Hypothesis Tests

Studies with Directional Hypotheses

In the example described earlier, the behavioral scientists are planning to measure the stress perceived by students and wanted to see if a weekly 1-hour counseling session for 6 weeks would reduce student stress levels. Therefore, the behavioral scientists were expecting that the counseling sessions would reduce stress levels. In this case, the behavioral scientists would state a **directional hypothesis**. Behavioral scientists state directional hypotheses when they are interested in predicting the direction of the effect of the experimental treatment; that is, whether the value of the variable being measured will increase or decrease.

A directional research hypothesis states that the Population 1 mean is higher (or lower, if that is the prediction) than the Population 2 mean. The directional hypothesis for the sample study would be that the level of stress perceived by a student who attends a 1-hour counseling session each week for 6 weeks will be lower than the level of stress perceived by students who do not attend such counseling sessions. If the behavioral scientists were conducting a study to increase the student's self-esteem, the directional hypothesis would be that attending a 1-hour counseling session each week for 6 weeks would increase self-esteem.

The null hypothesis is that the Population 1 mean is the same as, or is in the opposite direction from, the Population 2 mean. The null hypothesis for the sample study would be that the level of stress perceived by a student who attends a 1-hour counseling session each week for 6 weeks will be the same as, or higher than, the level of stress perceived by students who do not attend such counseling sessions. Again, if the behavioral scientists were interested in increasing the student's self-esteem, the null hypothesis would be that attending a 1-hour counseling session each week for 6 weeks would result in the same level of self-esteem or would lead to a decrease in self-esteem.

Therefore, if the 5% level of significance is being used, the obtained score has to lie in either the upper or lower 5% of the comparison distribution in order to reject the null hypothesis. That is, the score after the experimental treatment must lie in only one tail of the comparison distribution. For this reason, the statistical tests of such hypotheses are called **one-tailed tests**.

Studies with Nondirectional Hypotheses

Human behavior is difficult to predict. Despite the behavioral scientists' expectation that the counseling sessions will reduce stress, suppose that discussion of the student's problems in one area leads to discussion of problems in other areas of the student's life. Awareness of these additional problems may lead to increased perceptions of stress. If the behavioral scientists are unsure about the effect of the proposed experimental treatment, they may state a **nondirectional hypothesis**, in which they state that one population will be different from the other, but they do not specify whether Population 1 scores will be higher or lower than Population 2 scores.

A nondirectional research hypothesis states that the Population 1 mean is different than the Population 2 mean. The nondirectional hypothesis for the example study would be that the level of stress perceived by a student who attends a 1-hour counseling session each week for 6 weeks will be different than the level of stress perceived by students who do not attend such counseling sessions. If the behavioral scientists were interested in the effect of the experimental treatment on the student's self-esteem, the nondirectional hypothesis would be that attending a 1-hour counseling session each week for 6 weeks will result in a different level of self-esteem.

The null hypothesis is that the Population 1 mean will be no different than the Population 2 mean. The null hypothesis for the example study would be that the level of stress perceived by a student who attends a 1-hour counseling session each week for 6 weeks will be *no* different than the level of stress perceived by students who do not attend such counseling sessions. Again, if the behavioral scientists were interested in increasing the student's self-esteem, the null hypothesis would be that attending a 1-hour counseling session each week for 6 weeks will have no effect on self-esteem.

Since the 5% level of significance is being used, the null hypothesis can be rejected if the obtained score lies in either the upper 2.5% or the lower 2.5% of the comparison distribution. Therefore, the 5% probability being used to make the decision about the null hypothesis must be divided to accommodate the possibility of either an increase or decrease in the amount of the variable being measured, and the Population 1 score after the experimental treatment can lie in either tail of the comparison distribution. For this reason, the statistical tests of such hypotheses are called **two-tailed tests**.

Note that the cutoff sample scores for two-tailed tests are more extreme than the cutoff sample scores for one-tailed tests. The cutoff sample scores for a two-tailed test at the .05 level are +1.96 and −1.96, while for a one-tailed test, the scores are +1.64 and −1.64. At the .01 level, the scores are +2.58 and −2.58 and +2.33 and −2.33, respectively.

When to Use One-Tailed versus Two-Tailed Tests
In principle, one-tailed tests are used when the hypothesis is clearly directional, and two-tailed tests are used when the hypothesis is clearly nondirectional. In practice, the situation is not so simple. Obtaining a statistically significant result is "easier" using a one-tailed test because the sample value after the experimental treatment does not have to be as extreme as the sample value for a two-tailed test. However, the price is that extreme results in the opposite direction do not permit rejection of the null hypothesis, no matter how extreme or interesting the result. For this reason, using one-tailed tests introduces the risk of having to ignore potentially important results. Consequently, many researchers use two-tailed tests for both types of hypotheses. In most behavioral or social science articles, unless the researcher specifically notes that a one-tailed test was used, a two-tailed test is assumed. In studies, the conclusion is not really affected by the choice of a one-tailed or a two-tailed test. Usually the results of studies are sufficiently extreme to reject or fail to reject the null hypothesis using either test. On the other hand, if the null hypothesis would be rejected by the result of a one-tailed test, but not by the result of a two-tailed test, the results of the study should be interpreted cautiously pending further research.

Decision Errors
In statistics, **decision errors** are NOT due to making mistakes in calculations or using an inappropriate procedure. Instead, decision errors are made when experimenters make the wrong decision about the null hypothesis based on their experimental data.
Remember:
1. The hypothesis-testing process involves studying samples to draw inferences about populations of interest. In the sample study, the question is whether the effect of six weekly 1-hour counseling sessions on the stress perceived by a student can be generalized to all students like the one in the study.
2. This inference is based on the probability that any observed difference in perceived stress would have occurred even if the counseling sessions were ineffective. For example, suppose the student received unanticipated financial aid that removed an important source of stress.
3. The hypothesis-testing procedure is designed to make the probability of errors as small as possible, but the possibility of error is always present.

One error is rejecting the null hypothesis when it is true, that is, concluding that the experimental treatment has an effect when it does not. This error is a **Type I error**, and the probability of making a Type I error is determined by the level of significance chosen, usually either .05 or .01. A second error is failing to reject the null hypothesis when it is false, that is, concluding that the experimental treatment is ineffective when it does have an effect. This error is a **Type II error**.

The problem posed by these errors is that experimenters never know when they are making either of these errors. In the case of Type I errors, ineffective treatments may be presented as effective. For example, a 1-hour counseling session each week for 6 weeks may appear to reduce stress when it actually does not. On the other hand, the effectiveness of a 1-hour counseling session each week for 6 weeks will be missed if a Type II error is made. Type I and Type II errors are related. Since the probability of making a Type I error is determined by the level of significance, using larger significance levels like .20 decreases the chance of making a Type II error (of failing to identify a potentially effective treatment), but it increases the chance of making a Type I error (of deciding that a treatment that is actually ineffective is effective). Using a more conservative significance level like .001 has the opposite effect. In this situation, the probability of making a Type I error is reduced, but the probability of making a Type II error is increased. This difficulty is resolved by using the conventional levels of significance, .05 and .01.

Hypothesis Tests As Reported in Research Articles

Decisions based on hypothesis tests are typically reported in the context of one of the statistical procedures described in later chapters. Articles usually include the symbol describing the statistic used (for example, F for analysis of variance), the value of the statistic, and a statement about statistically significant results accompanied by notation like $p < .05$. Results that are not statistically significant are said to be nonsignificant or are indicated by the letters ns. Since statistical packages like SPSS provide exact probabilities for statistical procedures, many experimenters report exact p values like $p = .033$ or $p = .333$. Experimenters will usually note if statistical tests are one-tailed. The absence of such descriptions indicates that the tests were most likely two-tailed. In tables, statistically significant results often are indicated by one or more asterisks. Be aware that the research and null hypotheses are not stated explicitly in many articles, and decision errors are rarely mentioned.

Summary of the Hypothesis-Testing Procedure

Step 1: Restate the question as a research hypothesis and a null hypothesis about populations.
Identify the two populations.

- Population 1: people like those who are exposed to the experimental treatment.
- Population 2: people like members of Population 1 who have not been exposed to the experimental treatment—the population to which the results of the experiment are to be generalized.

State the hypotheses.

- Research Hypothesis: how is the experimental treatment expected to affect Population 1 (is the hypothesis directional or nondirectional)?
- Null Hypothesis: the hypothesis that Population 1 and Population 2 will be the same with respect to the variable being measured after Population 1 has been exposed to the experimental treatment (the treatment will have no impact).

Step 2: Determine the characteristics of the comparison distribution.

- The comparison distribution is the Population 2 distribution.

Step 3: Determine the cutoff sample score on the comparison distribution at which the null hypothesis should be rejected.

- Select the significance level (.05 or .01).
- Determine the percentage of cases between the mean and Z score that will serve as the cutoff sample score on the normal curve. (For a one-tailed test at the .05 level, the Z score is $+1.64$ or -1.64, depending on the expected effect of the experimental treatment. For a two-tailed test at the .05 level, the Z scores are $+1.96$ and -1.96.)

Step 4: Determine the sample's score on the comparison distribution.

- Observe the raw score of the individual exposed to the experimental treatment.
- Convert the raw score to a Z score and locate the Z score on the comparison distribution.

Step 5: Decide whether to reject the null hypothesis.

- If the Z score of the individual exposed to the experimental treatment (Step 4) is more extreme than the cutoff Z score (Step 3), reject the null hypothesis and accept the research hypothesis.
- If the Z score of the individual exposed to the experimental treatment (Step 4) is not more extreme than the cutoff Z score (Step 3), do not reject the null hypothesis and state that the results of the experiment are inconclusive.

Chapter Self-Tests

The practice test items that follow are based on the following scenario. A group of behavioral scientists have decided to conduct the sample study described in this chapter. A student has been asked to attend a 1-hour counseling session each week for 6 weeks. At the end of the 6 weeks, the student's level of perceived stress will be measured using an 18-statement inventory, each statement describing a possible response to stress. The student will use a 4-point scale on which responses are scored 1–4, so that scores can range from 18 to 72.

Understanding Key Terms in Chapter 5
Directions: Using the word bank that follows, complete each statement. **Some words maybe used more than once.**
Word Bank: comparison / conventional / cutoff sample / decision error / directional / hypothesis / hypothesis testing / nondirectional / null / one-tailed / research / statistically significant / theory / two-tailed / Type I error / Type II error

After reviewing previous research about the effect of counseling on stress, the behavioral scientists develop a set of principles that will guide their study. This set of principles is called a **(1)** _____. Based on these principles, the behavioral scientists make the prediction that counseling will reduce stress among students. This prediction is called a **(2)** _____. The general procedure the behavioral scientists will use to determine whether six weekly counseling sessions are effective in reducing the student's level of perceived stress is **(3)** _____. If the behavioral scientists believe that the counseling sessions will reduce stress, they have stated their **(4)** _____ hypothesis. If they make a formal statement to this effect as they plan their statistical analysis, the behavioral scientists will be stating a **(5)** _____ hypothesis, and they will analyze their data using a **(6)** _____ test. If the behavioral scientists are not sure what effect the counseling sessions will have on the student's stress, they may state a **(7)** _____ hypothesis and analyze their data using a **(8)** _____ test. The statement that the student's level of stress after the six counseling sessions will be no different than the levels of students who have not experienced counseling is a **(9)** _____ hypothesis.

In order to make a decision about the effectiveness of the counseling sessions, the behavioral scientists will locate the student's score after the six sessions on the distribution for Population 2. This distribution is called the **(10)** _____ distribution. If the student's score is more extreme than the **(11)** _____ score, the behavioral scientists will reject the **(12)** _____ hypothesis and accept the **(13)** _____ hypothesis. The behavioral scientists may decide that the student's score must be so extreme that it will occur fewer than either 5% of the time or 1% of the time if the counseling sessions have no effect. These values are known as the **(14)** _____ levels of significance. If the student's score is so extreme that the behavioral scientists conclude that the sessions were effective in reducing stress, the results are said to be **(15)** _____.

Although the behavioral scientists performed a well-planned statistical analysis and double-checked their calculations before concluding that six weekly counseling sessions can be expected to reduce stress, several replications of the study have not demonstrated significant reductions in stress. These replications suggest that the behavioral scientists may have made a **(16)** _____. If the null hypothesis stated that the level of stress would be the same as, or higher than, the level before the counseling sessions, and the behavioral scientists have erroneously concluded that the sessions effectively reduced stress, they have made a **(17)** _____. Had the behavioral scientists concluded that the sessions were ineffective, but replications indicated that they were effective, the behavioral scientists may have made a **(18)** _____.

Multiple-Choice Items

Items 1–3 are based on the hypothesis that a student's level of stress after attending one counseling session per week for 6 weeks will be no different from the student's level of stress before the counseling sessions.

1. This hypothesis is an example of
    A. a comparison hypothesis.
    B. a conventional hypothesis.
    C. a null hypothesis.
    D. a research hypothesis.

2. This hypothesis is also an example of
    A. a directional hypothesis.
    B. a nondirectional hypothesis.
    C. a Type I hypothesis.
    D. a Type II hypothesis.

3. The statistical analysis of this hypothesis will be
    A. Type I.
    B. Type II.
    C. one-tailed.
    D. two-tailed.

Items 4–6 are based on the hypothesis that a student's level of stress after attending one counseling session per week for 6 weeks will be the same as, or higher than, the student's level of stress before the counseling sessions.

4. This hypothesis is an example of
    A. a comparison hypothesis.
    B. a conventional hypothesis.
    C. a null hypothesis.
    D. a research hypothesis.

5. This hypothesis is also an example of
    A. a directional hypothesis.
    B. a nondirectional hypothesis.
    C. a Type I hypothesis.
    D. a Type II hypothesis.

6. The statistical analysis of this hypothesis will be
    A. Type I.
    B. Type II.
    C. one-tailed.
    D. two-tailed.

7. The overall procedure reflected in **Items 1–6** is
    A. alpha testing.
    B. beta testing.
    C. conventional testing.
    D. hypothesis testing.

8. The research hypothesis may also be called the
    A. alternative hypothesis.
    B. cutoff hypothesis.
    C. decision hypothesis.
    D. significant hypothesis.

9. The comparison distribution is the distribution that describes
    A. Population 1.
    B. Population 2.
    C. decision errors.
    D. conventional levels of significance.

10. Comparison distributions may also be called
    A. conventional distributions.
    B. cutoff distributions.
    C. sampling distributions.
    D. Type I distributions.

11. The target score against which researchers will compare their experimental result is called
    A. beta.
    B. the cutoff sample score.
    C. significance.
    D. the type error score.

12. The conventional levels of statistical significance include
    A. .10 and .20.
    B. .05 and .10.
    C. .05 and .20.
    D. .05 and .01.

13. An experimental result is said to be statistically significant when the
    A. research hypothesis is rejected.
    B. Type II errors are identified.
    C. null hypothesis is rejected.
    D. alpha level is set prior to the analysis.

14. If the behavioral scientists are using the .05 level of significance and find that the observed reduction in the student's level of stress would occur fewer than 2 times in 100, they
    A. can accept the research hypothesis.
    B. have proved the null hypothesis.
    C. should report that the results are inconclusive.
    D. must use a more conservative alpha.

15. The behavioral scientists are said to have made a decision error when they
    A. miscalculate the student's Z score after the counseling sessions.
    B. use the normal curve table incorrectly and obtain an incorrect cutoff sample score.
    C. use a significance level of .10 instead of one of the conventional levels of significance.
    D. reject the null hypothesis when the counseling sessions had no effect on the student's stress.

16. The behavioral scientists have committed a Type I error when they
    A. reject the null hypothesis when it is true.
    B. fail to prove the research hypothesis.
    C. incorrectly estimate beta.
    D. use a one-tailed test.

17. The behavioral scientists have committed a Type II error when they
    A. fail to prove the research hypothesis.
    B. incorrectly estimate beta.
    C. use a conventional level of alpha.
    D. fail to reject the null hypothesis when it is false.

18. If the behavioral scientists could know that they were making a Type II error, their concern would be that
    A. the experiment must be repeated to confirm their results.
    B. they had incorrectly rejected the null hypothesis.
    C. a potentially useful practice would not be implemented.
    D. their results would not be statistically significant.

19. If the behavioral scientists report a difference between the student's stress level after counseling and the stress level of students in general and include the notation "$p < .05$" to describe this difference, they are indicating that
    A. the result is not statistically significant at the .05 level.
    B. the sample score falls in either the upper 5% or the lower 5% of the comparison distribution.
    C. there is a 95% chance that the research hypothesis is true.
    D. the chance of obtaining this result is less than 5% if the null hypothesis is true.

Problems

1. What is the difference between the null hypothesis and the research hypothesis of a study? What is the difference between directional and nondirectional research hypotheses and how are the corresponding null hypotheses different?

2. A group of behavioral scientists wants to see if a 10-week self-defense training program will increase the self-esteem of an adolescent student being bullied by classmates. Describe the two populations of interest and write both directional and nondirectional research hypotheses with the corresponding null hypotheses for this study.

3. If the normal curve is the comparison distribution, what are the cutoff sample scores for both conventional levels of significance?

4. Why are behavioral scientists reluctant to use directional hypotheses and the corresponding one-tailed tests?

5. Suppose the behavioral scientists interested in the effect of a 10-week self-defense program on the self-esteem of bullied adolescent students know that the population distribution of self-esteem scores is normally distributed with Population $M = 66$ and Population $SD = 12$. Calculate the Z score for each of the following students, enter the cutoff sample score, and indicate the appropriate decision about the null hypothesis.

Student	Student Score	p	Tails of Test
1	90	.05	2
2	84	.05	1
3	94	.01	2
4	94	.01	1

6. Suppose the behavioral scientists interested in the effect of a 10-week self-defense program on the self-esteem of bullied adolescent students also want to see if the program reduces the students' anxiety. They know that the population distribution of anxiety scores is normally distributed with Population $M = 32$ and Population $SD = 8$. Calculate the Z score for each of the following students, enter the cutoff sample score, and indicate the appropriate decision about the null hypothesis.

Student	Student Score	p	Tails of Test
1	20	.05	2
2	14	.05	1
3	10	.01	2
4	18	.01	1

7. Using the five steps of hypothesis testing, describe how a group of behavioral scientists would determine the effect of the 12-week exercise program on the life satisfaction of a person whose score on a satisfaction with life scale after the program is 75. The population distribution of life satisfaction scores is normal with Population $M = 50$ and Population $SD = 10$. Just for practice, write both directional and nondirectional hypotheses and test each hypothesis at both the .05 and .01 levels. Explain your decisions about the null hypothesis at each level of significance in enough detail that someone who is not familiar with hypothesis testing, but who is familiar with the mean, standard deviation, and Z scores, can understand the process.

8. Now the behavioral scientists want to determine the effect of the 12-week exercise program on the depression of a person whose depression score after the program is 9. The population distribution of depression scores is normal with Population $M = 15$ and Population $SD = 3$. Using the five steps of hypothesis testing, describe how the behavioral scientists would conduct the study. Just for practice, write both directional and nondirectional hypotheses and test each hypothesis at both the .05 and .01 levels. Explain your decisions about the null hypothesis at each level of significance in enough detail that someone who is not familiar with hypothesis testing, but who is familiar with the mean, standard deviation, and Z scores, can understand the process.

Additional Practice: Complete any Practice Problems in Set I that your instructor has not assigned and compare your responses to those provided by the authors. Pay particular attention to the problems that require you to explain your results to someone who has never taken a course in statistics.

SPSS Applications
There are no SPSS applications for this chapter.

Completion Items

1. theory	6. one-tailed	11. cutoff sample	16. decision error
2. hypothesis	7. nondirectional	12. null	17. Type I error
3. hypothesis testing	8. two-tailed	13. research	18. Type II error
4. research	9. null	14. conventional	
5. directional	10. comparison distribution	15. statistically significant	

Multiple-Choice Items

1. C	5. A	9. B	13. C	17. D
2. B	6. C	10. C	14. A	18. C
3. D	7. D	11. B	15. D	19. D
4. C	8. A	12. D	16. A	

Problems

1. The null hypothesis states that there will be no difference between Population 1 and Population 2 after the experimental treatment. In other words, the experimental treatment will have no effect on behavior. The research hypothesis indicates the predicted relationship between Population 1 and Population 2 after the experimental treatment. That is, the research hypothesis expresses the experimenters' expectation that the treatment will have some effect. A directional research hypothesis states that the behavior being measured will increase or decrease. In this case, the null hypothesis is that the behavior being measured will not change, or will change in the opposite direction. A nondirectional research hypothesis states that the behavior being measured will change, but no direction for the change is specified. The corresponding null hypothesis is that the behavior being measured will not change.

2.
Population 1: Bullied adolescents who participate in the 10-week self-defense training program.
Population 2: Bullied adolescents who do not participate in the 10-week self-defense training program.

Directional Research Hypothesis: The self-esteem of bullied adolescents who participate in a 10-week self-defense training program will be higher than the self-esteem of bullied adolescents who do not participate in the program.
Directional Null Hypothesis: The self-esteem of bullied adolescents who participate in a 10-week self-defense training program will be the same as, or lower than, the self-esteem of bullied adolescents who do not participate in the program.

Nondirectional Research Hypothesis: The self-esteem of bullied adolescents who participate in a 10-week self-defense training program will be different than the self-esteem of bullied adolescents who do not participate in the program.
Nondirectional Null Hypothesis: The self-esteem of bullied adolescents who participate in a 10-week self-defense training program will be no different than the self-esteem of bullied adolescents who do not participate in the program.

3.
Two-tailed .05 = ±1.96
Two-tailed .01 = ±2.58
One-tailed .05 = +1.64 or −1.64
One-tailed .01 = +2.33 or −2.33

4. Behavioral and social scientists are reluctant to use directional hypotheses and their associated one-tailed tests because results in the opposite direction of the scientists' prediction, which may be interesting, important, or both, must be treated as simple failures to reject the null hypothesis—as if the treatment had no effect.

5.

Student	Student Score	p	Tails of Test	Z Score	Cutoff Score	Decision
1	90	.05	2	2.00	+1.96	Reject
2	84	.05	1	1.50	+1.64	Fail to Reject
3	94	.01	2	2.33	+2.58	Fail to Reject
4	94	.01	1	2.33	+2.33	Reject

6.

Student	Student Score	p	Tails of Test	Z Score	Cutoff Score	Decision
1	20	.05	2	−1.50	−1.96	Fail to Reject
2	14	.05	1	−2.25	−1.64	Reject
3	10	.01	2	−2.75	−2.58	Reject
4	18	.01	1	−1.75	−2.33	Fail to Reject

7.

Step 1: Restate the question as a research hypothesis and a null hypothesis about the populations.
Population 1: People who participate in the 12-week exercise program.
Population 2: People who do not participate in the 12-week exercise program.

Directional Research Hypothesis: The life satisfaction of people who participate in a 12-week exercise program will be higher than the life satisfaction of people who do not participate in the program.
Directional Null Hypothesis: The life satisfaction of people who participate in a 12-week exercise program will be the same as, or lower than, the life satisfaction of people who do not participate in the program.

Nondirectional Research Hypothesis: The life satisfaction of people who participate in a 12-week exercise program will be different from the life satisfaction of people who do not participate in the program.
Nondirectional Null Hypothesis: The life satisfaction of people who participate in a 12-week exercise program will be no different from the life satisfaction of people who do not participate in the program.

Step 2: Determine the characteristics of the comparison distribution.
The comparison is a normal distribution with Population $M = 50$ and Population $SD = 10$.

Step 3: Determine the cutoff sample score on the comparison distribution at which the null hypothesis should be rejected.
The cutoff sample score for the one-tailed tests that would be used for the directional research hypothesis would be +1.64 at the .05 level of significance and +2.33 at the .01 level of significance.
The cutoff sample score for the two-tailed tests that would be used for the nondirectional research hypothesis would be +1.96 at the .05 level of significance and +2.58 at the .01 level of significance.
[Remember that if this study was to be conducted, either a directional or a nondirectional hypothesis would be stated, and only one level of significance would be selected as the criterion for statistical significance.]

Step 4: Determine the sample's score on the comparison distribution.
The participant's Z score = $(75 − 50) / 10 = +2.50$.

Step 5: Decide whether to reject the null hypothesis.
Since +2.50 is more extreme than both +1.64 and +2.33, the null hypotheses for the directional research hypotheses at both .05 and .01 levels of significance will be rejected and the conclusion will be that the exercise program did increase life satisfaction—the results are statistically significant. Also, +2.50 is more extreme than +1.96, so the null hypothesis for the nondirectional research hypothesis will be rejected at the .05 level of significance and the same conclusion about the effects of exercise on life satisfaction will be drawn. However, +2.50 is not more extreme than +2.58. Therefore, the decision will be to fail to reject the null hypothesis for the nondirectional research hypothesis at the .01 level, and the results will be described as inconclusive.

8.
Step 1: Restate the question as a research hypothesis and a null hypothesis about the populations.
Population 1: People who participate in the 12-week exercise program.
Population 2: People who do not participate in the 12-week exercise program.

Directional Research Hypothesis: The depression of people who participate in a 12-week exercise program will be lower than the depression of people who do not participate in the program.
Directional Null Hypothesis: The depression of people who participate in a 12-week exercise program will be the same as, or higher than, the depression of people who do not participate in the program.

Nondirectional Research Hypothesis: The depression of people who participate in a 12-week exercise program will be different than the depression of people who do not participate in the program.
Nondirectional Null Hypothesis: The depression of people who participate in a 12-week exercise program will be no different than the depression of people who do not participate in the program.

Step 2: Determine the characteristics of the comparison distribution.
The comparison is a normal curve with Population $M = 15$ and Population $SD = 3$.

Step 3: Determine the cutoff sample score on the comparison distribution at which the null hypothesis should be rejected.
The cutoff sample score for the one-tailed tests that would be used for the directional research hypothesis would be -1.64 at the .05 level of significance and -2.33 at the .01 level of significance.
The cutoff sample score for the two-tailed tests that would be used for the nondirectional research hypothesis would be -1.96 at the .05 level of significance and -2.58 at the .01 level of significance.
[Again, remember that if this study was to be conducted, either a directional or a nondirectional hypothesis would be stated, and only one level of significance would be selected as the criterion for statistical significance.]

Step 4: Determine the sample's score on the comparison distribution.
The participant's Z score $= (9 - 15) / 3 = -2.00$.

Step 5: Decide whether to reject the null hypothesis.
Since -2.00 is more extreme than -1.64, the null hypotheses for the directional research hypothesis at the .05 level of significance will be rejected, and the conclusion that the exercise program did reduce depression will be drawn—the results are statistically significant. However, -2.00 is not more extreme than -2.58. Therefore, the decision will be to fail to reject the null hypothesis for the directional research hypothesis at the .01 level, and the results will be described as inconclusive. Similarly, -2.50 is more extreme than -1.96, so the null hypothesis for the nondirectional research hypothesis at the .05 level of significance will be rejected, and the conclusion that the exercise program reduced depression will be drawn. Again, -2.00 is not more extreme than -2.58. Therefore, the decision will be to fail to reject the null hypothesis for the nondirectional research hypothesis at the .01 level, and the results will be described as inconclusive.

Chapter 6
Hypothesis Tests with Means of Samples

Learning Objectives
After studying this chapter, you should:

- Be able to explain the use of a distribution of means as a comparison distribution for experimental samples that include more than one individual.
- Be able to describe the hypothetical method for constructing a distribution of means.
- Know how to calculate the mean of a distribution of means and explain its relationship to the mean of the population of individual cases.
- Know how to calculate the variance of a distribution of means and explain why it is smaller than the variance of the population of individual cases.
- Know how to calculate the standard deviation of a distribution of means.
- Be able to explain why a distribution of means tends to be unimodal and symmetrical.
- Be able to describe the conditions under which a distribution of means is, or closely approximates, the normal curve.
- Know how to apply the five steps of hypothesis testing using samples that include more than one person and a known population distribution.
- Know how the results of studies using the Z test are reported in research articles.
- ADVANCED TOPIC: Know how to calculate and interpret confidence intervals.
- ADVANCED TOPIC: Know how confidence intervals are used in reporting research results.

The Distribution of Means as a Comparison Distribution

When testing hypotheses with a sample of more than one individual, the comparison distribution defined in Step 2 of the hypothesis-testing procedure changes. Specifically, the comparison distribution is no longer the distribution of Population 2, the general population of individuals who are not exposed to the experimental treatment. Instead, when a sample of two or more individuals experiences the treatment, the score of interest is the mean of the group of scores. Therefore, the appropriate comparison distribution becomes a **distribution of means** (or *sampling distribution of the mean*), which is a distribution of all possible means of samples of the same size as the sample in an experiment.

Suppose that a group of behavioral scientists is interested in reducing the stress perceived by college freshmen and has enrolled a group of 40 freshmen in a self-help discussion group. Since this group of freshmen comprises Population 1, the behavioral scientists need to describe the distribution for Population 2, the comparison distribution. The intuitive approach to the problem of describing the comparison distribution is to select a random sample of 40 freshmen who are not receiving the experimental treatment from the population of all freshmen, measure their perceived stress, calculate the sample mean, and plot it as the first value in a frequency distribution. Then repeat the process for a second sample of 40 untreated freshmen and plot the mean for this sample. After repeating this process many times, the mean and standard deviation of this frequency distribution of means can be calculated and the distribution can be used as a comparison distribution just like a normal distribution of scores of individuals. [Note that the characteristics of a distribution of means can be determined without this process of repeated sampling, as will be shown in the next section.]

Characteristics of a Distribution of Means

The three characteristics of a comparison distribution that must be determined are its mean, variation (variance and then standard deviation), and shape. Due to the relationships between distributions of means and the populations of individual cases from which samples are drawn, the characteristics of the distribution of means can be determined directly from knowledge of the characteristics of the population and the size of the samples involved by applying three rules.

Rule 1: The **mean of the distribution of means** (Population M_M) is the same as the mean of the population of individuals.

Expressed as a formula, this rule states that Population M_M = Population M, where Population M_M represents the mean of the distribution of means and Population M represents the mean of the population of individual scores.

The rationale for this rule is that as random samples of a given size are drawn, the effect of extremely low scores in a sample on the mean of the sample are canceled by the effects of extremely high scores and *vice versa*. For this reason, sample means will tend to cluster about the mean of the population of individual scores, and if an infinite number of samples are drawn, the mean of all the sample means will be equal to the population mean.

Rule 2a: The **variance of a distribution of means (Population SD^2_M)** is the variance of the distribution of the population of individuals divided by the number of individuals in each sample. The distribution of means will have less variation than the population of individual cases from which the samples are drawn because the probability that all the scores in a sample will be extremely high or extremely low is low. That is, in any sample, extreme scores tend to be balanced out by scores in the middle of the distribution, or by extreme scores in the opposite direction. With fewer extreme values for the means, the variance of the means is smaller. Expressed as a formula, this rule states that Population SD^2_M = Population SD^2 / N, where Population SD^2_M is the variance of the distribution of means, Population SD^2 is the variance of the distribution of individual scores, and N is the number of cases in each sample.

Rule 2b: The **standard deviation of a distribution of means (Population SD_M)** is the square root of the variance of the distribution of means.

Expressed as a formula, this rule states that Population $SD = \sqrt{\text{Population } SD^2_M} = \sqrt{\text{Population } SD^2 / N}$, where Population SD^2_M is the variance of the distribution of means, Population SD^2 is the variance of the distribution of individual scores, and N is the number of cases in each sample.
The standard deviation of the distribution of means is also called the **standard error (SE)**, or *standard error of the mean*.

Rule 3: The **shape of a distribution of means** is approximately normal if either (a) each sample includes 30 or more individuals or (b) the distribution of the population of individuals is normal.

Distributions of means tend to be unimodal due to the process of extreme scores balancing each other described in the discussion of the variance of distributions of means. Distributions of means tend to be symmetrical for the same reason—since skew is caused by extreme scores, the presence of fewer extreme scores results in distributions that are more symmetrical. As the number of participants in a sample increases, the distribution of means for samples of that size becomes an increasingly closer approximation to the normal curve. When samples include 30 or more individuals, even if the population of individual cases is quite skewed, the distribution of means will closely resemble a normal curve, and the percentages of area under the normal curve table will be extremely accurate. If the population distribution of individual cases is normal, any distribution of means obtained from samples drawn from the population will be normal, regardless of sample size.

Determining the Characteristics of a Distribution of Means

Example 1: The distribution of scores of large numbers of individuals on certain widely used intelligence tests is approximately normal with a mean of 100 and a standard deviation of 15. What would be the characteristics of the distribution of means for a sample of 25 individuals?

Rule 1: The mean of the distribution of means is the same as the mean of the population of individuals. Since the mean of the population is 100, the mean of the distribution of means will also be 100.

Rule 2a: The variance of a distribution of means is the variance of the distribution of the population of individuals divided by the number of individuals in each sample. The standard deviation of the population is 15, so the variance of the population is 15^2, or 225. The variance of the distribution of means is 225 / 25 = 9 [Population SD^2_M = Population SD^2 / N].

Rule 2b: The standard deviation of a distribution of means is the square root of the variance of the distribution of means. The standard deviation of the distribution of means is the square root of 9, or 3.

[Population $SD_M = \sqrt{\text{Population } SD^2_M} = \sqrt{\text{Population } SD^2 / N}$.]

Rule 3: The shape of a distribution of means is approximately normal if either (a) each sample includes 30 or more individuals or (b) the distribution of the population of individuals is normal. Although the sample only includes 25 individuals, the distribution of individual scores is described as normal.

Example 2: A widely used achievement test also has a mean of 100 and a standard deviation of 15, but the population distribution is slightly skewed. What would be the characteristics of the distribution of means for a sample of 60 individuals?

Rule 1: The mean of the distribution of means is the same as the mean of the population of individuals. Since the mean of the population is 100, the mean of the distribution of means will also be 100.

Rule 2a: The variance of a distribution of means is the variance of the distribution of the population of individuals divided by the number of individuals in each sample. The standard deviation of the population is 15, so the variance of the population is 15^2, or 225. The variance of the distribution of means is $225 / 60 = 3.75$ [Population SD^2_M = Population SD^2 / N].

Rule 2b: The standard deviation of a distribution of means is the square root of the variance of the distribution of means. The standard deviation of the distribution of means is the square root of 3.75, or 1.94.

$$[\text{Population } SD_M = \sqrt{\text{Population } SD^2_M} = \sqrt{\text{Population } SD^2 / N} .]$$

Rule 3: The shape of a distribution of means is approximately normal if either (a) each sample includes 30 or more individuals or (b) the distribution of the population of individuals is normal. Although the distribution of individual scores is slightly skewed, the sample includes 60 individuals. Therefore, the distribution of means will be normally distributed.

Hypothesis Testing with a Distribution of Means: The *Z* Test

The *Z test* is the hypothesis-testing procedure used to compare a single sample mean with a population mean when the population variance is known. Again, the distribution of means is the comparison distribution described in Step 2 of the hypothesis-testing procedure, and it is used to determine the likelihood that a sample mean the size of the one obtained could have been selected if the null hypothesis is true. Remember that sample means are now being treated like the scores of individuals, so the formula for Z changes from $Z = (X - M) / SD$ to
$Z = (M - \text{Population } M) / \text{Population } SD_M$. In addition, the sample mean will be located on the distribution of means in Step 4. Otherwise, the hypothesis-testing process is identical to the process described in Chapter 4 when the sample consisted of a single individual.

Example 1: Suppose that the behavioral scientists interested in reducing the stress perceived by college freshmen have enrolled 40 freshmen in a semester-long self-help discussion group based on the idea that discussions will let participants know that others are dealing with the same stressful issues, and may suggest solutions to problems leading to reduced stress. The mean score on a widely used stress inventory is 56 and the standard deviation is 8. The mean stress score of the 40 freshmen at the end of the semester is 52. Conduct a Z test following the five steps of hypothesis testing to determine whether the freshmen report a different level of stress after participating in the discussion group. Use the .05 level of significance.

Step 1: Restate the question as a research hypothesis and a null hypothesis about the populations.
Population 1: Freshmen who participate in a self-help discussion group.
Population 2: Freshmen who do not participate in a self-help discussion group.
Research Hypothesis: The perceived stress of freshmen who participate in a self-help discussion group will be different from the perceived stress of freshmen who do not participate in a self-help discussion group.
Null Hypothesis: The perceived stress of freshmen who participate in a self-help discussion group will be no different from the perceived stress of freshmen who do not participate in a self-help discussion group.

Step 2: Determine the characteristics of the comparison distribution.
Distribution of means with
Mean = 56 [Population mean = 56 by Rule 1]
Variance = $8^2 / 40 = 64 / 40 = 1.60$ [Population SD^2_M = Population SD^2 / N by Rule 2a]

Standard deviation = 1.26 [Population $SD_M = \sqrt{\text{Population } SD^2_M} = \sqrt{\text{Population } SD^2 / N}$ by Rule 2b]
Shape = normal [$N > 30$ by Rule 3]

Step 3: Determine the cutoff sample score on the comparison distribution at which the null hypothesis should be rejected.
Using the .05 level of significance for a two-tailed test, the cutoff sample score is ±1.96.

Step 4: Determine the sample's score on the comparison distribution.
$Z = (M - \text{Population } M) / \text{Population } SD_M = (52 - 56) / 1.26 = -3.17$

Step 5: Decide whether to reject the null hypothesis.
The behavioral scientists would reject the null hypothesis because a Z score of -3.17 is more extreme than the cutoff sample score of -1.96, and they would conclude that the self-help discussion group did reduce the perceived stress of the participants.

Example 2: Suppose that the behavioral scientists interested in reducing the stress perceived by college freshmen decide to replicate their study during the following semester and have enrolled 25 freshmen in the semester-long self-help discussion group. They use the same stress inventory that has normally distributed scores with a mean of 56 and a standard deviation of 8. The mean stress score of the 25 freshmen at the end of the semester is 54. Conduct a Z test following the five steps of hypothesis testing to determine whether the freshmen report a lower level of stress after participating in the discussion group. Use the .01 level of significance.

Step 1: Restate the question as a research hypothesis and a null hypothesis about the populations.
Population 1: Freshmen who participate in a self-help discussion group.
Population 2: Freshmen who do not participate in a self-help discussion group.
Research Hypothesis: The perceived stress of freshmen who participate in a self-help discussion group will be lower than the perceived stress of freshmen who do not participate in a self-help discussion group.
Null Hypothesis: The perceived stress of freshmen who participate in a self-help discussion group will be the same as, or higher than, the perceived stress of freshmen who do not participate in a self-help discussion group.

Step 2: Determine the characteristics of the comparison distribution.
Distribution of means with
Mean = 56 [Population mean = 56 by Rule 1]
Variance = $8^2 / 25 = 64 / 25 = 2.56$ [Population SD^2_M = Population SD^2 / N by Rule 2a]

Standard deviation = 1.60 [Population $SD_M = \sqrt{\text{Population } SD^2_M} = \sqrt{\text{Population } SD^2 / N}$ by Rule 2b]

Shape = normal [Population of individual scores is normally distributed by Rule 3]

Step 3: Determine the cutoff sample score on the comparison distribution at which the null hypothesis should be rejected.
Using the .01 level of significance for a one-tailed test, the cutoff sample score is -2.33.

Step 4: Determine the sample's score on the comparison distribution.
$Z = (M - \text{Population } M) / \text{Population } SD_M = (54 - 56) / 1.60 = -1.25$

Step 5: Decide whether to reject the null hypothesis.
The behavioral scientists would fail to reject the null hypothesis because a Z score of -1.25 is not as extreme as the cutoff sample score of -2.33. The behavioral scientists would report that their results are inconclusive.

Hypothesis Tests about Means of Samples (Z Tests) and Standard Errors in Research Articles

Research measuring variables with known population means and standard deviations is rare in the behavioral and social sciences. Consequently, Z tests are seldom encountered. However, the standard deviation of the distribution of means, which provides an indication of the amount of variation that might be expected among means of samples of a given size from a particular population, may be reported as the *standard error* (*SE*), or *standard error of the mean* (*SEM*). Standard errors are often used in graphs to indicate the extent to which scores on a variable vary around the mean. When used in this manner, the lines reflecting the standard errors are called *error bars*. However, the error bars in graphs may represent standard deviations, so the legends should be read carefully.

ADVANCED TOPIC: Estimation and Confidence Intervals

If researchers want to estimate an unknown population mean from scores in a sample, the best estimate of the population mean is the sample mean. On the other hand, the range of possible means that is likely to include the population mean can be estimated by determining how much the means vary in a distribution of means. This estimate can be made by calculating the standard deviation of a distribution of means. Remember that the standard deviation of a distribution is also called the standard error of the mean.

Assuming that the distribution of means is normally distributed, areas under the normal curve can be used to define intervals with a known probability of including the population mean. For example, 34% of a normally distributed population lies between the mean and one standard deviation above the mean, and the same percentage lies between the mean and one standard deviation below the mean. Therefore, the area under the curve between one standard deviation below the mean and one standard deviation above the mean includes 68% of the area under the curve. Since there is a 68% chance that this area includes the population mean, the area extending from one standard deviation below the mean to one standard deviation above defines a **confidence interval**, specifically the *68% confidence interval*. The values of the variable being measured that lie one standard deviation above the mean and one standard deviation below the mean are the **confidence limits**. Thus, a confidence interval is the range of values calculated from sample data (sample statistics) that has a specified probability of containing a population parameter, and the confidence limits are the upper and lower values of the confidence interval.

Most experimenters want to be more than 68% confident about their estimates, so the 95% confidence interval and the 99% confidence interval are usually calculated. A **95% confidence interval** includes the middle 95% of a normal distribution, leaving 2.5% in each tail. Since the normal curve is symmetrical, 47.5% of the confidence interval is above the mean and 47.5% is below the mean. Using the normal curve table, the Z scores that define this area above and below the mean are $+1.96$ and -1.96, respectively. To calculate the **99% confidence interval**, the Z scores are $+2.57$ and -2.57, respectively. These Z scores include the middle 99% of a normal curve, leaving .5% in each tail.

Steps for Figuring the 95% and 99% Confidence Intervals

1. Estimate the population mean and figure the standard deviation of the distribution of means.
2. Find the Z scores that go with the confidence interval you want.
3. To find the confidence interval, change these Z scores to raw scores.

Example: Using the results of the study in which 40 freshmen participated in a self-help discussion group to help them cope with stress, the sample mean was 52 and the standard deviation of the distribution of means was 1.26.

$M_{Sample} = 52$

$SD^2{}_M = SD^2 / N = 64 / 40 = 1.60$

$SD_M = \sqrt{1.60} = 1.26$ [This value is also the standard error of the mean.]

Formula: 95% confidence interval $= M_{Sample} + (\pm 1.96)\ (SEM)$

Applying the formula for calculating the 95% confidence interval,
the lower limit $= 52 + (-1.96)\ (1.26) = 49.53$,
the upper limit $= 52 + (1.96)\ (1.26) = 54.47$, so that
the 95% confidence interval $= 49.53–54.47$

Applying the formula for calculating the 99% confidence interval,
the lower limit $= 52 + (-2.57)\ (1.26) = 48.76$,
the upper limit $= 52 + (2.57)\ (1.26) = 55.24$, so that
the 99% confidence interval $= 48.76–55.24$

Confidence Intervals and Hypothesis Testing

Confidence intervals can be used to test hypotheses. Specifically, if the confidence interval does not include the mean of the comparison distribution, then the result is statistically significant. Considering the 95% confidence interval in Example 1, the population mean of 56 is not included in the interval, so the results are statistically significant at the .05 level, which confirms the result of the Z test. In addition, the population mean of 56 is not included in the 99% confidence interval, which means that the result is statistically significant at the .01 level, as well.

ADVANCED TOPIC: Confidence Intervals in Research Articles

Confidence intervals are reported in research articles. Remembering that the 95% and 99% confidence intervals extend approximately 2 standard errors and approximately 2.5 standard errors to either side of the mean, respectively, will help in the interpretation of such results.

Chapter Self-Tests

The practice test items that follow are based on the following scenario. In the last chapter, a group of behavioral scientists conducted a study in which a student attended a 1-hour counseling session each week for 6 weeks that was designed to help the student reduce stress. Based on the results of this study, the behavioral scientists have conducted a larger study in which 30 freshmen attended the counseling sessions. At the end of the 6 weeks, the mean score on a stress inventory was 28. Examination of the responses to the inventory by a large number of freshmen collected over several years reveals that the scores of freshmen are normally distributed with a mean of 36 and a standard deviation of 8.

Understanding Key Terms in Chapter 6
Directions: Using the word bank that follows, complete each statement.
Word Bank: confidence interval / confidence limits / distribution of means / mean of the distribution of means / shape of the distribution of means / standard deviation of the distribution of means / standard error / variance of the distribution of means / Z test / 95% confidence interval / 99% confidence interval

When the study involved only a single student, the comparison distribution was the distribution of scores of freshmen who did not participate in counseling sessions. Now that the behavioral scientists have expanded the study to involve a group of freshmen, the appropriate comparison distribution is a **(1)** _____. Knowing that the mean stress score for a large number of freshmen who had taken the inventory previously was 36 informed the behavioral scientists that 36 would be the **(2)** _____. Dividing the square of the standard deviation of the distribution of scores of previous respondents by 30 yields the **(3)** _____, and the square root of this quotient is the **(4)** _____. The normal curve defines the **(5)** _____. At the conclusion of the 6 weeks, the behavioral scientists can use a **(6)** _____ to compare the sample mean and the population mean.

The behavioral scientists are also interested in estimating the range of possible values the mean of groups of 30 freshmen might take. These estimates are based on the standard deviation of the distribution of means, which is also called the **(7)** _____. When such ranges are calculated, they are called **(8)** _____, and the upper and lower values are called **(9)** _____. If the range extends approximately 2 standard errors from the mean of the distribution of means, the **(10)** _____ has been calculated. If the range extends approximately 2.5 standard errors from the mean of the distribution of means, the **(11)** _____ has been calculated.

Multiple-Choice Items

1. Since the behavioral scientists are now comparing the mean of an experimental group with a known population mean, the appropriate comparison distribution is the distribution of
   A. all possible means of 30 freshmen.
   B. freshmen from which the sample was drawn.
   C. freshmen on whom the counseling sessions had no effect.
   D. the distribution of means with a standard error of 2.13.

2. Since the mean for the population of freshmen who have taken the stress inventory is 36 and the standard deviation is 8, the mean of the distribution of means is
   A. 8.
   B. 26.
   C. 36.
   D. 64.

3. The behavioral scientists will calculate the variance of their distribution of means by
   A. multiplying the variance of the population of individual cases by the number of students in the sample.
   B. subtracting the sample's variance from the population variance.
   C. taking the square root of the variance of the distribution of means.
   D. dividing the variance of the population of individual cases by the number of students in the sample.

4. The behavioral scientists will calculate the standard deviation of their distribution of means by
    A. multiplying the variance of the population of individual cases by the number of students in the sample.
    B. subtracting the sample's variance from the population variance.
    C. taking the square root of the variance of the distribution of means.
    D. dividing the variance of the population of individual cases by the number of students in the sample.

5. The standard deviation of the distribution of means calculated by the behavioral scientists is also known as
    A. the standard error.
    B. the confidence limit.
    C. a distribution error.
    D. a variation estimate.

6. In comparison to the distribution of scores for all freshmen who have taken the inventory previously, the shape of the distribution of means will
    A. have more spread.
    B. have less spread.
    C. be skewed.
    D. be rectangular.

7. By using a sample of 30 freshmen, the behavioral scientists can assume that the distribution of means will be
    A. bimodal.
    B. generally rectangular.
    C. seriously skewed.
    D. approximately normal.

8. To determine whether the difference between the sample mean and the population mean is statistically significant, the behavioral scientists will calculate
    A. Σ.
    B. N.
    C. Z.
    D. M.

Items 9–10 are related.
9. If the behavioral scientists state that they are 90% confident that the population mean lies between 25.61 and 30.39, the values 25.61 and 30.39 define
    A. a confidence interval.
    B. a statistically significant Z.
    C. the standard error of the mean.
    D. the population mean.

10. The values 25.61 and 30.39 are called
    A. confidence intervals.
    B. confidence limits.
    C. point estimates.
    D. standard errors.

11. Which of the following formulas would be used in calculating the 90% confidence interval?
    A. $M_{Sample} + (\pm 1.64)\,(SEM)$
    B. $M_{Sample} + (\pm 2.33)\,(SEM)$
    C. $M_{Sample} + (\pm 1.96)\,(SEM)$
    D. $M_{Sample} + (\pm 2.57)\,(SEM)$

12. Which of the following formulas would be used in calculating the 95% confidence interval?
   A. $M_{Sample} + (\pm 1.64)\,(SEM)$
   B. $M_{Sample} + (\pm 2.33)\,(SEM)$
   C. $M_{Sample} + (\pm 1.96)\,(SEM)$
   D. $M_{Sample} + (\pm 2.57)\,(SEM)$

13. Which of the following formulas would be used in calculating the 99% confidence interval?
   A. $M_{Sample} + (\pm 1.64)\,(SEM)$
   B. $M_{Sample} + (\pm 2.33)\,(SEM)$
   C. $M_{Sample} + (\pm 1.96)\,(SEM)$
   D. $M_{Sample} + (\pm 2.57)\,(SEM)$

Problems

1. The standard deviation for the population of freshmen who have taken the stress inventory is 8. Calculate the standard deviation of the distribution of means for samples comprised of (a) 4, (b) 8, (c) 12, and (d) 20 freshmen.

2. ADVANCED TOPIC: If the mean stress score of the 30 freshmen in the behavioral scientists' sample is 28, calculate the 95% confidence interval for the four samples in Problem 1.

3. ADVANCED TOPIC: If the mean stress score of the 30 freshmen in the behavioral scientists' sample is 28, calculate the 99% confidence interval for the four samples in Problem 1.

4. If the behavioral scientists replicate the study with a sample of 25 freshmen and obtain a mean of 53 on the stress inventory, is the sample mean significantly different from the population mean of 56? Remember that the scores of freshmen who have previously taken the inventory are normally distributed. Use the five steps of hypothesis testing to describe how the behavioral scientists would conduct the study. State a nondirectional research hypothesis and use the .05 level of significance to determine the cutoff sample score. ADVANCED TOPIC: Calculate the 95% confidence interval.

5. Based on the results of the studies they have conducted, the behavioral scientists are confident that the counseling sessions are an effective means of reducing stress. In a final replication, they again use a sample of 25 freshmen and obtain a mean of 50 on the stress inventory. Is the sample mean significantly different from the population mean of 56? Use the five steps of hypothesis testing to describe how the behavioral scientists would conduct the study. State a directional research hypothesis and use the .01 level of significance to determine the cutoff sample score. ADVANCED TOPIC: Calculate the 99% confidence interval.

Problems 6 and 7 are based on the following scenario. Having observed the effect of the counseling sessions on student stress, the behavioral scientists have decided to see if the sessions have an effect on other variables. Therefore, in their final replication, they have also measured self-esteem and coping skills. The self-esteem inventory has been used in a number of studies, and the resulting scores are normally distributed with a mean of 65 and a standard deviation of 11. Scores on the measure of coping skills have also been shown to be normally distributed and have a mean of 72 and a standard deviation of 14.

6. After participating in the counseling sessions, the mean self-esteem score of the 25 freshmen was 70. Use the five steps of hypothesis testing to describe this portion of the final replication. State a nondirectional research hypothesis and use the .05 level of significance to determine the cutoff sample score. ADVANCED TOPIC: Calculate the 95% confidence interval. Explain your results to someone who is familiar with the logic of hypothesis testing, the normal curve, Z scores, probability, and the idea of a distribution of means, but not with confidence intervals.

7. After participating in the counseling sessions, the mean coping skills score of the 25 freshmen was 76. Use the five steps of hypothesis testing to describe this portion of the final replication. State a directional research hypothesis and use the .05 level of significance to determine the cutoff sample score. ADVANCED TOPIC: Calculate the 95% confidence interval.

Additional Practice: Complete any Practice Problems in Set I that your instructor has not assigned and compare your responses to those provided by the authors. Pay particular attention to the problems that require you to explain your results to someone who has never taken a course in statistics.

SPSS Applications
There are no SPSS applications for this chapter.

Chapter 6 Key

Completion Items

1. distribution of means	7. standard error
2. mean of the distribution of means	8. confidence intervals
3. variance of the distribution of means	9. confidence limits
4. standard deviation of the distribution of means	10. 95% confidence interval
5. shape of the distribution of means	11. 99% confidence interval
6. Z test	

Multiple-Choice Items

1. A	5. A	9. A	13. D
2. C	6. B	10. B	
3. D	7. D	11. A	
4. C	8. C	12. C	

Problems

1. Population $SD^2_M = 8^2 = 64$ [Population SD^2_M = Population SD^2 / N by Rule 2a]
   Population $SD^2_M = 64 / N$

   Population $SD_M = \sqrt{\text{Population } SD^2_M} = \sqrt{\text{Population } SD^2 / N}$ by Rule 2b

(a) $64 / 4 = 16 = 4$	(b) $64 / 8 = 8 = 2.83$	(c) $64 / 12 = 5.33 = 2.31$	(d) $64 / 20 = 3.20 = 1.79$

2. Formula: 95% confidence interval = $M_{Sample} + (\pm 1.96)$ (*SEM*)
   (a) 20.16–35.84
   (b) 22.4 –33.55
   (c) 23.4 –32.53
   (d) 24.49–31.51

3. Formula: 99% confidence interval = $M_{Sample} + (\pm 2.57)$ (*SEM*)
   (a) 17.72–38.28
   (b) 20.73–35.27
   (c) 22.06–33.94
   (d) 23.4 –32.60

4.
Step 1: Restate the question as a research hypothesis and a null hypothesis about the populations.
Population 1: Freshmen who participate in a self-help discussion group.
Population 2: Freshmen who do not participate in a self-help discussion group.
Research Hypothesis: The perceived stress of freshmen who participate in a self-help discussion group will be different than the perceived stress of freshmen who do not participate in a self-help discussion group.
Null Hypothesis: The perceived stress of freshmen who participate in a self-help discussion group will be no different than the perceived stress of freshmen who do not participate in a self-help discussion group.

Step 2: Determine the characteristics of the comparison distribution.
Distribution of means with
Mean = 56 [Population $M = 56$ by Rule 1]
Variance = $8^2 / 25 = 64 / 25 = 2.56$ [Population SD^2_M = Population SD^2 / N by Rule 2a]

Standard deviation = 1.60 [Population $SD_M = \sqrt{\text{Population } SD^2_M} = \sqrt{\text{Population } SD^2 / N}$ by Rule 2b]

Shape = normal [Population normally distributed by Rule 3]
Step 3: Determine the cutoff sample score on the comparison distribution at which the null hypothesis should be rejected.
At the .05 level of significance, the cutoff sample score is ± 1.96 for a two-tailed test.

Step 4: Determine the sample's score on the comparison distribution.
$Z = Z = (M - \text{Population } M) / \text{Population } SD_M = (53 - 56) / 1.60 = -1.88$

Step 5: Decide whether to reject the null hypothesis.
The behavioral scientists would fail to reject the null hypothesis because a Z score of -1.88 is not as extreme as the cutoff sample score of -1.96 and state that their results are inconclusive.

Formula: 95% confidence interval $= M_{\text{Sample}} + (\pm 1.96) (SEM) = 49.86 - 56.14.$

5.
Step 1: Restate the question as a research hypothesis and a null hypothesis about the populations.
Population 1: Freshmen who participate in a self-help discussion group.
Population 2: Freshmen who do not participate in a self-help discussion group.
Research Hypothesis: The perceived stress of freshmen who participate in a self-help discussion group will be lower than the perceived stress of freshmen who do not participate in a self-help discussion group.
Null Hypothesis: The perceived stress of freshmen who participate in a self-help discussion group will be the same as, or higher than, the perceived stress of freshmen who do not participate in a self-help discussion group.

Step 2: Determine the characteristics of the comparison distribution.
Distribution of means with
Mean = 56 [Population $M = 56$ by Rule 1]
Variance = $8^2 / 25 = 64 / 25 = 2.56$ [Population $SD^2_M = $ Population SD^2 / N by Rule 2a]

Standard deviation = 1.60 [Population $SD_M = \sqrt{\text{Population } SD^2_M} = \sqrt{\text{Population } SD^2 / N}$ by Rule 2b]

Shape = normal [Population normally distributed by Rule 3]

Step 3: Determine the cutoff sample score on the comparison distribution at which the null hypothesis should be rejected.
At the .01 level of significance, the cutoff sample score is -2.33 for a one-tailed test.

Step 4: Determine the sample's score on the comparison distribution.
$Z = (M - \text{Population } M) / \text{Population } SD_M = (50 - 56) / 1.60 = -3.75$

Step 5: Decide whether to reject the null hypothesis.
The behavioral scientists would reject the null hypothesis because a Z score of -3.75 is more extreme than the cutoff sample score of -2.33 and conclude that the counseling sessions did reduce stress.

Formula: 99% confidence interval $= \text{Mean}_{\text{Sample}} + (\pm 2.57) (SEM) = 45.89 - 54.12.$

6.
Step 1: Restate the question as a research hypothesis and a null hypothesis about the populations.
Population 1: Freshmen who participate in a self-help discussion group.
Population 2: Freshmen who do not participate in a self-help discussion group.
Research Hypothesis: The self-esteem of freshmen who participate in a self-help discussion group will be different than the self-esteem of freshmen who do not participate in a self-help discussion group.
Null Hypothesis: The self-esteem of freshmen who participate in a self-help discussion group will be no different than the perceived stress of freshmen who do not participate in a self-help discussion group.

Step 2: Determine the characteristics of the comparison distribution.
Distribution of means with
Mean = 65 [Population $M = 56$ by Rule 1]
Variance = $11^2 / 25 = 121 / 25 = 4.84$ [Population $SD^2_M = $ Population SD^2 / N by Rule 2a]

Standard deviation = 2.20 [Population $SD_M = \sqrt{\text{Population } SD^2_M} = \sqrt{\text{Population } SD^2 / N}$ by Rule 2b]

Shape = normal [Population normally distributed by Rule 3]

Step 3: Determine the cutoff sample score on the comparison distribution at which the null hypothesis should be rejected.
At the .05 level of significance, the cutoff sample score is ±1.96 for a two-tailed test.

Step 4: Determine the sample's score on the comparison distribution.
$Z = (M - \text{Population } M) / \text{Population } SD_M = (70 - 65) / 2.20 = +2.27$

Step 5: Decide whether to reject the null hypothesis.
The behavioral scientists would reject the null hypothesis because a Z score of +2.27 is more extreme than the cutoff sample score of +1.96 and conclude that the counseling sessions did increase self-esteem.

Formula: 95% confidence interval = $M_{\text{Sample}} + (\pm 1.96)\ (SEM) = 65.69–74.31$.

Compare your explanation to the explanation provided for Problem 8 in Set I of the Practice Problems in the text.

7.
Step 1: Restate the question as a research hypothesis and a null hypothesis about the populations.
Population 1: Freshmen who participate in a self-help discussion group.
Population 2: Freshmen who do not participate in a self-help discussion group.
Research Hypothesis: The coping skills scores of freshmen who participate in a self-help discussion group will be higher than the coping skills scores of freshmen who do not participate in a self-help discussion group.
Null Hypothesis: The coping skills scores of freshmen who participate in a self-help discussion group will be the same as, or lower than, the coping skills scores of freshmen who do not participate in a self-help discussion group.

Step 2: Determine the characteristics of the comparison distribution.
Distribution of means with
Mean = 72 [Population M = 56 by Rule 1]
Variance = $14^2 / 25 = 196 / 25 = 7.84$ [Population SD^2_M = Population SD^2 / N by Rule 2a]
Standard deviation = 2.80 [Population $SD_M = \sqrt{\text{Population } SD^2_M} = \sqrt{\text{Population } SD^2 / N}$ by Rule 2b]
Shape = normal [Population normally distributed by Rule 3]

Step 3: Determine the cutoff sample score on the comparison distribution at which the null hypothesis should be rejected.

At the .05 level of significance, the cutoff sample score is +1.64 for a one-tailed test.

Step 4: Determine the sample's score on the comparison distribution.
$Z = (M - \text{Population } M) / \text{Population } SD_M = (76 - 72) / 2.80 = +1.43$

Step 5: Decide whether to reject the null hypothesis.
The behavioral scientists would fail to reject the null hypothesis because a Z score of +1.43 is not as extreme as the cutoff sample score of +1.64 and state that the results are inconclusive regarding the effects of counseling on coping skills.

Formula: 95% confidence interval = $M_{\text{Sample}} + (\pm 1.96)\ (SEM) = 70.51–81.49$.

Chapter 7
Making Sense of Statistical Significance: Effect Size and Statistical Power

Learning Objectives
After studying this chapter, you should:
- Be able to describe effect size.
- Be able to compute effect size.
- Know conventional effect sizes.
- Describe meta-analysis and list its advantages and disadvantages.
- Be able to define statistical power.
- Know how to determine power using available resources.
- Know how to use power tables.
- Be able to list factors that influence power and describe their influence.
- Be able to determine power from effect size.
- Know how to use sample size tables.
- Be able to list the six influences on statistical power and describe each.
- Be able to explain the distinction between statistical significance and practical significance in interpreting research results.
- Be able to explain the role of power in evaluating significant and nonsignificant research results.
- Know how power and effect size are described in research reports.

Effect Size
Statistical significance indicates that the experimental treatment has an effect, for example, counseling sessions reduce the amount of stress perceived by students. However, statistical significance does not indicate the size of the experimental effect, whether the reduction in perceived stress was large or small. **Effect size**, a measure of the difference between population means, does indicate the amount of change in the variable being measured after an experimental treatment.

One way to conceptualize effect size is to think about the distributions of the two populations used in the hypothesis-testing examples in previous chapters, including their means, being drawn on transparencies. If the experimental treatment has no effect, the overlap of the two distributions will be perfect—the transparencies will appear to depict only one distribution. If the experimental treatment is designed to increase the variable being measured, think about sliding the transparency for Population 1 to the right. The more the transparency moves to the right, the less the distributions overlap and the greater the difference between the means becomes, indicating a greater effect of the experimental treatment. If the experimental treatment is designed to decrease the variable being measured, the transparency for Population 1 is simply moved to the left.

The difference between the Population 1 and Population 2 means is a *raw score effect size*, which is useful in interpreting the effect of the experimental treatment in one study, but does not permit comparison with the results of similar studies. However, in a manner analogous to the computation of Z scores, the difference between means can be divided by its population standard deviation, yielding a *standardized effect size*. The formula is Effect Size = (Population 1 M – Population 2 M) / Population SD. Note that the denominator is the standard deviation of the population of individuals, not the standard deviation of the distribution of means. Also, effect size can be positive or negative depending on whether the experimental treatment is designed to increase or decrease the variable being measured.

Based on psychology research results, Cohen developed **effect size conventions**.

Effect Size	Effect Size Value	Overlap between Distributions
Small	.20	85%
Medium	.50	67%
Large	.80	53%

Meta-Analysis

Calculation of standardized effect sizes provides a statistical method for combining the results of studies in a particular area of research called **meta-analysis**. This technique can be useful in making sense of the results of many studies in applied areas of psychology such as clinical treatment for disorders like depression, which can be measured using any of a number of inventories. Since standardized effect sizes can be averaged, a hypothetical meta-analysis might reveal that self-help discussion groups have a mean effect = −.20 (a small effect) on depression, group therapy has a mean effect = −.50 (a medium effect) on depression, and individual therapy has a mean = −.80 (a large effect) on depression. Thus, all three types of therapy reduce depression, but individual therapy is the most effective, self-help discussion groups are the least effective, and group therapy falls between the other two.

Statistical Power

Statistical power, or simply *power*, is the probability that a study will yield a significant result, if the research hypothesis is true. Two points should be remembered about power:

1. If the research hypothesis is not true, researchers do not want to obtain significant results. Significant results in this situation are Type I errors.
2. Even if the research hypothesis is true, a study may not yield significant results if the sample drawn from the population studied is not sufficiently extreme to reject the null hypothesis. For example, in a study involving a treatment to reduce depression, the researchers may draw a sample of individuals whose depression scores are so low that even if the treatment is successful, the sample scores may not demonstrate the improvement in relation to the comparison population. Depending on the goal of the study, such nonsignificant results could be a Type II error.

Determining Power

Three methods are available for determining power:

1. Computer software
2. Internet power calculators
3. **Power tables**

What Determines Power?

The two main influences on power are:

1. Effect size
2. Sample size

Additional influences include:

1. Level of statistical significance
2. Use of a one-tailed or a two-tailed test
3. Type of hypothesis-testing procedure used

Effect Size Influence

Examination of the formula for calculating the effect size, Effect Size = (Population 1 M − Population 2 M) / Population SD, will make the following statements evident. The greater the difference a researcher expects to observe between two populations, as indicated in the numerator of the formula, the greater the effect size will be. The larger the effect size, the greater the power. However, the population standard deviation affects effect size. The smaller the standard deviation, as reflected in the denominator of the formula, the greater the effect size. Another way to view these concepts is that the greater the difference between means, the less the Population 1 and Population 2 distributions will overlap. Likewise, the smaller the standard deviations of the two distributions, the less they will overlap.

Sample Size Influence

In addition to effect size, the other major influence on power is sample size. Simply stated, the larger the sample size, the greater the power. This influence of sample size on power is due to the fact that the variance of a distribution of means is calculated by dividing the variance of the population of individual scores (the Population 2 variance) by the sample size. Therefore, the larger the sample used in a study, the smaller the variance of the distribution of means, and the smaller the variance, the less the overlap between distributions of means. Remember that sample size and effect size are separate influences on power.

Sample Sizes Required for Given Levels of Power
The main reason researchers consider power when planning an experiment is that the desired power determines the number of participants who must be enrolled in an experiment. Consideration of the number of participants is important because too few participants may result in low power, which may result in a Type II error in which the researchers fail to reject the null hypothesis when the research hypothesis is true.

Other Influences on Power
1. The significance level (alpha) used for an experiment affects power because using a less extreme significance level like .05 instead of .01 means that the cutoff sample score will not be as extreme. For example, the cutoff sample score for a two-tailed test at the .05 level is ±1.96, while the cutoff sample for the same test at the .01 level is ±2.58. Since power is the probability of obtaining a significant result when the research is true, testing a hypothesis at the .05 level will increase power.
2. Using a two-tailed test increases the difficulty of obtaining a significant result in any one tail. Therefore, if all other factors are the same, one-tailed tests have more power (for results in the predicted direction) than two-tailed tests. For example, the cutoff sample score for a one-tailed test at the .05 level is + or −1.64, while the cutoff sample for a two-tailed test at the .0 level is ±1.96.
3. Sometimes the data collected in an experiment can be analyzed appropriately by two or more statistical procedures to apply to a given set of results, each of which has its own power. [This possibility will be discussed in Chapter 11.]

Power in Study Planning
If the power of a planned study is low, the study is unlikely to yield significant results, even if the research hypothesis is true. Since conducting the study as planned would be a waste of time and resources, researchers can look for practical ways to increase the power to an acceptable level. One widely cited rule is that if a power of 80% cannot be obtained, the study may not be worth conducting.

Increasing the Power of a Planned Study
1. Although researchers cannot arbitrarily increase the predicted difference between population means, if there is a logical basis for such an increase, the increase will increase power. In the absence of increasing the effect size, changing the way the experiment is conducted, for example, by increasing the intensity of the experimental manipulation, may permit the researcher to expect a larger difference between means. However, such changes may be difficult or costly to implement, or they may change the experimental treatment so much that the results cannot be generalized to the intended population.
2. The population standard deviation can be decreased by using a population that is less diverse than the one originally planned. However, this approach also limits the scope of the population to which the results can be generalized. A second, and recommended, method for reducing the population standard deviation is to use more standardized conditions (for example, laboratory settings) or more precise measures.
3. Increasing the sample size is the most straightforward way to increase power, but the number of available participants may be a limiting factor. In addition, increasing the number of participants may increase the cost of an experiment in both time and money.
4. Using a less extreme level of significance, for example, .10 instead of .05, will increase power. However, the less extreme level will also increase the risk of a Type I error. The .05 level of significance is conventional in behavioral and social science research, so careful justification for the use of a less extreme level will be expected.
5. Using a one-tailed test will increase power. However, the type of test used depends on the logic of the hypothesis being tested, so researchers usually have little opportunity to influence power in this way.
6. Using a more sensitive hypothesis-testing procedure will increase the probability of detecting the effects of the experimental treatment, but researchers typically start with the most powerful procedure available. Again, researchers usually have little opportunity to influence power in this way.

The Role of Power When Interpreting the Results of a Study
Considerations when a result is statistically significant.
Statistical significance indicates that an experiment has had an effect. However, statistical significance does not indicate that the results of an experiment are either theoretically or practically important. While simply knowing that a statistically significant effect (a *real effect*) is present may be theoretically important, the size of an effect may determine the practical importance of an experimental result. For example, a small effect having little practical

importance may be statistically significant if the study has power due to other factors, particularly large sample size. However, if the sample size for an experiment was small, a statistically significant result is probably practically important, as well. Therefore, when comparing two studies, the effect sizes, not the significance levels, should be compared. In other words, a statistically significant result indicates a real effect—the participants changed as a result of the experimental treatment.

The practical importance of the result must be interpreted, however. For example, the stress inventory described earlier has a mean of 56, a standard deviation of 8, and scores can range from 0 to 72. Suppose 100 students had participated in one counseling session per week for 6 weeks, and their mean stress score at the end of the experiment was 54. The decrease is statistically significant [$Z = (54 - 56) / .64 = -3.13$] at any of the conventional levels of significance for either a one-tailed or a two-tailed test. Is the result practically significant? Was the time spent by the 100 students, as well as the behavioral scientists, worth the two-point reduction in perceived stress? If the answer to these questions is "no," what amount of change in a sample of what size would have produced a practically significant result?

Considerations when a result is not statistically significant.
If the power of an experiment is low, nonsignificant results of an experiment are probably inconclusive. Conversely, nonsignificant results from an experiment with high power suggest that
1. The research hypothesis is false.
2. The effect size is smaller than predicted when the power of the study was calculated.

Effect Size and Power in Research Articles
Discussions of effect size are increasingly common in research articles. Power is most often considered during the planning phase of an experiment. When power is mentioned, the context is often the interpretation of other articles or as a possible explanation for nonsignificant results.

Chapter Self-Tests

The practice test items that follow are based on the following scenario. In the last two chapters, a group of behavioral scientists first conducted a study in which one student attended a 1-hour counseling session each week for 6 weeks that was designed to help the student reduce stress. The behavioral scientists then conducted a larger study in which 30 freshmen attended the counseling sessions. Now the behavioral scientists are planning studies in which they will use sample data to estimate population values.

Understanding Key Terms in Chapter 7
Directions: Using the word bank that follows, complete each statement. **You may need to use some terms more than once.**
Word Bank: decreasing / effect size / effect size conventions / extreme / increasing / liberal /meta-analysis / one-tailed / power tables / practically / statistical power / statistically / two-tailed / .20 / .50 / .80

As an initial step in their planning, the behavioral scientists have referred to a study that combines the results of many other studies of activity levels among depressed people. This study is an example of a **(1)** _____ , and its primary data are obtained by calculating the **(2)** _____ of each study reviewed. As they continue planning, the behavioral scientists discuss their desire to conduct a study that will yield a statistically significant result when the research hypothesis is true. These discussions are about the **(3)** _____. As guidelines for planning this aspect of their studies, the behavioral scientists can use Cohen's **(4)** _____. Different studies may have different effects on their participants, and may include different numbers of participants. Therefore, the behavioral scientists may obtain more precise estimates of this aspect of their studies by using **(5)** _____.

According to Cohen's conventions for assessing the power of a study, a small effect size is **(6)** _____, a medium effect size is **(7)** _____, and a large effect size is **(8)** _____. Cohen has also expressed the opinion that investigators should plan studies to have a power of **(9)** _____. In order to increase the power of their statistical analysis, the behavioral scientists might consider **(10)** _____ the size of their sample, using a less **(11)** _____ level of significance, or using a **(12)** _____ test. However, if the behavioral scientists use a very large sample that results in a small, but **(13)** _____ significant, increase in the average number of activities of daily living performed after a treatment like group therapy, their results may not be **(14)** _____ significant.

Multiple-Choice Items

1. The degree to which the stress scores of students who participate in the counseling sessions differ from the scores of students who do not is an indication of
    A. experimental effectiveness.
    B. power.
    C. the effect size.
    D. the significance level.

2. If the behavioral scientists noted that in one of the experiments they conducted, the distribution of the population expected under the research hypothesis had little overlap with the distribution of the known population, the behavioral scientists had observed
    A. the use of a liberal alpha.
    B. the effect of low power.
    C. a large effect size.
    D. a practically significant result.

3. (Population 1M – Population 2M) / Population SD is a formula for calculating
    A. power.
    B. sample size.
    C. raw effect size.
    D. standardized effect size.

4. According to Cohen's conventions for research that compares means, a small effect size would be
   A. .20.
   B. .50.
   C. .80.
   D. .90.

5. According to Cohen's conventions, for research that compares means, a large effect size would be
   A. .20.
   B. .50.
   C. .80.
   D. .90.

6. If the behavioral scientists calculate the average effect size from a number of the studies they review, they will have
   A. conducted a meta-analysis.
   B. set a less extreme alpha.
   C. specified the desired level of power.
   D. determined the number of participants they will need.

7. Statistical power can be defined as the probability
   A. that the results of a study will result in advances in applied psychology.
   B. of rejecting the null hypothesis if the null hypothesis is true.
   C. of obtaining an effect size that will always be significant.
   D. that the study will yield a significant result if the research hypothesis is true.

8. The majority of previous studies the behavioral scientists have reviewed have shown that counseling has significantly reduced the stress perceived by a variety of groups. If the behavioral scientists fail to demonstrate a statistically significant reduction in one of their studies, they might
   A. have used a liberal alpha.
   B. suspect that the power of the study was low.
   C. need to conduct another meta-analysis.
   D. have made a Type I error.

Items 9–10 are related.
9. As the behavioral scientists review previous studies, they will expect to find that the studies having the highest power are those with
   A. smaller samples.
   B. more extreme alphas.
   C. larger population standard deviations.
   D. larger effect sizes.

10. They will expect to find that the studies having the highest power are also those with
    A. smaller samples.
    B. more extreme alphas.
    C. smaller population standard deviations.
    D. greater overlap between populations.

11. Sample size affects power because the size of the sample determines the
    A. effect size.
    B. standard deviation of the distribution of means.
    C. choice of an alpha level.
    D. size of beta.

Items 12–13 are related.
12. Based on previous studies, the behavioral scientists know that the reduction in stress is likely to be small. However, if they believe that uncovering even a small reduction will be useful, they can increase the power of their studies by
    A. increasing the variance of the known population.
    B. selecting students with very different levels of stress.
    C. using an alpha of .01 instead of .05.
    D. increasing the size of the study samples.

13. Power will be greatest if the behavioral scientists use an alpha level of
    A. .10.
    B. .05.
    C. .01.
    D. .025.

14. The behavioral scientists may also increase power by
    A. stating a directional hypothesis.
    B. basing effect sizes on the smallest difference reported in prior studies.
    C. enrolling a small number of very diverse students in the study.
    D. using an alpha of .001.

15. The effect size conventions proposed by Cohen are useful to researchers for
    A. predicting the value of the dependent variable to use for the experimental condition.
    B. determining the power of a planned experiment.
    C. evaluating research results to determine if they are statistically significant.
    D. predicting the effect their independent variable will have on various populations.

16. According to Cohen, for an experiment to be worth conducting, it should have a level of power of about
    A. 1%.
    B. 5%.
    C. 50%.
    D. 80%.

17. If the behavioral scientists want to decrease the standard deviation of the distribution of means in one of the studies they are planning to increase power, they can
    A. use a more extreme alpha level.
    B. use the sample variance in place of the variance of the population.
    C. use a less diverse population.
    D. decrease the predicted difference between population means.

18. The primary change the behavioral scientists can make in their experiments to increase power is to
    A. increase sample size.
    B. increase beta.
    C. use a two-tailed test.
    D. predict a smaller effect.

19. The behavioral scientists' belief that even a relatively small reduction in stress resulting from attending the counseling sessions will cause other therapists to change their practice refers to the study's
    A. effect size.
    B. statistical significance.
    C. power.
    D. practical significance.

Problems

1. Consider the study of the effect of a teaching method designed to increase the probability of successful completion of a statistics course on the self-esteem of students in the course. Again, for the normally distributed known population, the Population $M = 63$ and the Population $SD = 12$. What is the estimated effect size for samples that have completed the treatment and have means of (a) 54, (b) 57, (c) 60, (d) 71, and (e) 78? For each sample mean, indicate whether the effect is approximately small, medium, or large.

2. What will be the predicted effect size of the following studies of student test anxiety if the means are (a) 35, (b) 42, (c) 50, (d) 56, and (e) 60? The known population of students experiencing test anxiety is normally distributed with Population $M = 44$ and Population $SD = 8$. For each sample mean, indicate whether the effect is approximately small, medium, or large.

3. The behavioral scientists have conducted a study of the effect of a teaching method designed to increase the probability of successful completion of a statistics course on the self-esteem of students in the course. The study revealed a statistically significant difference between the Population 1 and Population 2 means ($p < .5$) with $N = 100$ students. How would you interpret this result to a person who understands hypothesis testing, but who has never learned about effect size and power?

4. The behavioral scientists have replicated the study described in Problem 3 and obtained a statistically significant difference between the Population 1 and Population 2 means ($p < .5$), but with $N = 15$. How would you explain how this result would change your interpretation of the results in Problem 3 to a person who understands hypothesis testing, but who has never learned about effect size and power?
5. Use your responses to Problem 3 and Problem 4 as the basis for summarizing the relationship between statistical significance and effect size as concisely as possible.

Additional Practice: Complete any Practice Problems in Set I that your instructor has not assigned and compare your responses to those provided by the authors. Pay particular attention to the problems that require you to explain your results to someone who has never taken a course in statistics.

SPSS Applications

There are no SPSS applications for this chapter.

Completion Items

1. meta-analysis	6. .20	11. extreme
2. effect size	7. .50	12. one-tailed
3. statistical power	8. .80	13. statistically
4. effect size conventions	9. .80	14. practically
5. power tables	10. increasing	

Multiple-Choice Items

1. C	6. A	11. B	16. D
2. C	7. D	12. D	17. C
3. D	8. B	13. A	18. A
4. A	9. D	14. A	19. D
5. C	10. C	15. B	

Problems

1.

Problem	(Pop$_1$ M – Pop$_2$ M) / Pop SD	Estimated Effect Size	Effect Size
(a)	(54 – 63) / 12	–0.75	large
(b)	(57 – 63) / 12	–0.50	medium
(c)	(60 – 63) / 12	–0.25	small
(d)	(71 – 63) / 12	0.67	medium / large
(e)	(78 – 63) / 12	1.25	large

2.

Problem	(Pop$_1$ M – Pop$_2$ M) / Pop SD	Predicted Effect Size	Effect Size
(a)	(35 – 44) / 8	–0.75	large
(b)	(42 – 44) / 8	–0.25	small
(c)	(50 – 44) / 8	0.50	medium
(d)	(56 – 44) / 8	1.50	large
(e)	(60 – 44) / 8	2.00	large

3. The statistically significant difference between the treatment mean and the known population mean indicates that the behavioral scientists have identified a real effect of the treatment. Due to the large sample size, the study should have high power. The question is whether the effect is large enough to be practically significant, that is, to recommend that the teaching method be adopted in other courses.

4. The small sample makes the statistically significant effect of the treatment more convincing in this replication because, other factors being equal, the replication should have had lower power than the original study. If a study sample is small, the assumption that a statistically significant difference is also practically significant is safer.

5. Statistically significant results indicate a real effect, but not necessarily a practical or important effect. Studies with high power attributable to factors like large sample size may reveal statistically significant differences despite small effect sizes. A nonsignificant difference from a study with low power is truly inconclusive. However, a nonsignificant difference from a study with high power suggests that either: (a) the research hypothesis is false or (b) the effect size is smaller than was predicted when power was calculated.

Chapter 8
Introduction to the *t* Test: Single Sample and Dependent Means

Learning Objectives
After studying this chapter, you should:
- Be able to estimate population variances based on sample scores.
- Know when and how to conduct a *t* test for a single sample.
- Be able to describe the differences between *t* distributions and the normal curve.
- Be able to use the *t* table.
- Know when and how to conduct a *t* test for dependent means.
- Be able to define the normality assumption for the *t* test for dependent means and describe its implications.
- Be able to calculate effect sizes for studies requiring a *t* test for dependent means and interpret these effect sizes using Cohen's conventions.
- Be able to use power tables for the *t* test for dependent means.
- Be able to use sample size tables for the *t* test for dependent means.
- Be able to describe the limitations of pretest–posttest designs.
- Be able to interpret results for *t* tests for dependent means as reported in research articles.

The *t* **test** is a hypothesis-testing procedure used to compare *t* scores obtained from a sample of research participants to a comparison distribution called a *t* distribution that is appropriate when the population variance is unknown.

The *t* Test for a Single Sample (One-Sample *t* Test)
The *t* **test for a single sample** is the hypothesis-testing procedure used to compare a sample mean and a known population mean. This test is like the *Z* test introduced in Chapter 6, with two important exceptions:
1. The population variance required to define the comparison distribution in Step 2 of the hypothesis-testing procedure must be estimated.
2. One of a theoretically infinite number of *t* distributions is used to determine the cutoff sample score in Step 3 of the hypothesis-testing procedure.

Estimating the Population Variance from Sample Scores
Estimating the population variance from the sample data is based on the premise that since a sample represents its population, the sample variance is representative of the population variance. However, the variance of a random sample is, on the average, slightly smaller than the variance of the population from which the sample is drawn. Such estimates of the sample variance are said to give a **biased estimate** of the population's variance. An **unbiased estimate of the population variance**, which means that the estimate is equally likely to be too high or too low, is obtained by modifying the formula for the variance by subtracting 1 from the number of people in the sample. Thus, the formula is $S^2 = \Sigma(X - M)^2 / N - 1$. [Dividing any numerator by a smaller denominator yields a larger quotient, which helps adjust for the fact that estimates of population variances using sample data tend to be too small.] Note that S^2 is the symbol used to represent the estimated population variance.

Degrees of Freedom
The denominator in the formula for estimating the population variance from sample data, $\Sigma(X - M)^2 / (N - 1)$, is also called the **degrees of freedom**. The term refers to the number of scores that are "free to vary" when computing a mean. Thus, the formula for computing the estimated population variance can be written $S^2 = \Sigma(X - M)^2 / df$. In order to understand the concept of degrees of freedom, the sum of the numbers 1–5 is 15 and the mean is 3. If any four numbers are known, the fifth score can have only one value that will yield a sum of 15 and a mean of 3. For example, if four numbers are 1, 2, 3, and 4, the fifth value must be 5. Thus, one degree of freedom *to vary* has been lost and is subtracted from the number of scores accordingly.

The Standard Deviation of the Distribution of Means
Once S^2 has been calculated, calculate the variance of the comparison distribution as before, that is, by dividing the variance by *N*, NOT by $N - 1$. The new symbol is S_M^2. Also as before, the standard deviation of the comparison distribution is the square root of the variance, $\sqrt{S_M^2}$ or S_M.

The Shape of the Comparison Distribution When Using an Estimated Population Variance: The *t* Distribution

Hypothesis testing using estimated population variances means researchers have less true information, leaving more room for error. Specifically, drawing samples means that extreme means are more likely than they would be in a normal curve, and the smaller the N, the higher the probability that extreme means will be obtained. Therefore, the appropriate comparison distribution in Step 2 of the hypothesis-testing procedure changes from the normal distribution to a *t* **distribution**.

One *t* distribution exists for every possible number of degrees of freedom. The *t* distributions have more scores in the tails than the normal distribution, which means that sample means must be slightly more extreme to be significantly different from population means when researchers are using a *t* distribution as the comparison distribution instead of the normal distribution. For example, the cutoff sample score for a two-tailed test at the .05 significance level using the normal distribution is ±1.96, regardless of the size of the sample. With a sample N of 11 ($df = 10$), the cutoff sample score for the same test at the same level of significance is ±2.228, and for a sample N of 31($df = 30$), the cutoff sample score is ±2.043. Note that as the sample size increases, the cutoff sample score from a *t* distribution is closer to the cutoff sample score from the normal curve. In fact, when sample size is infinite, the *t* distribution and normal distribution coincide. The two types of distribution yield very similar cutoff sample scores when N is ≥ 30.

The Cutoff Sample Score for Rejecting the Null Hypothesis: Using the *t* Table

Determining the cutoff sample score in Step 3 of the hypothesis-testing process now requires a *t* **table** that lists the cutoff sample *t* scores for any number of degrees of freedom. Appendix Table A-2 in the text is a table of *t* distributions that includes crucial cutoff scores.

Using the *t* table requires specification of the number of degrees of freedom, the chosen significance level, and a decision about whether a one- or two-tailed test will be conducted. As is the case with the table of areas under the normal curve, the values in *t* tables are positive numbers. However, *t* distributions are symmetrical, so the same cutoff sample score can be used for either a positive or a negative experimental effect. For example, if the experimental treatment is designed to increase the self-esteem of a sample of 26 students ($df = 25$), the cutoff sample score for a one-tailed test at the .05 level of significance will be +1.708. If the experimental treatment is designed to reduce the perceived stress of a sample of 26 students (again, $df = 25$), the cutoff sample score for a one-tailed test at the .05 level of significance will be −1.708.

When the exact number of degrees of freedom required by a study is not given in the *t* table, the nearest number that is lower than the required number should be used to minimize the risk of a Type I error. For example, if a two-tailed test at the .05 level of significance is planned, and the actual number $df = 37$, the cutoff sample score for 35 df should be used instead of the cutoff sample score for 40 df. The cutoff sample scores for these two df are 2.030 and 2.021, respectively, making the former more conservative, that is, making the criterion for statistical significance more extreme.

Determining the Score Sample's Mean on the Comparison Distribution: The *t* Score

Step 4 of the hypothesis-testing process, locating the sample mean on the comparison distribution, is identical to the procedure for a Z test. However, due to the estimation of the population variance, the resulting score is called a *t* **score**. The formula is $t = (M - \text{Population } M) / S_M$.

Deciding Whether to Reject the Null Hypothesis

Step 5 of the hypothesis-testing procedure involves the decision about the null hypothesis and is conducted exactly as it was for the Z test.

Example of a *t* Test for a Single Sample

A consulting psychologist is consulting with a national chain of bookstores to monitor customer complaints. The national average for all bookstores is 6.5 complaints per month. Seven stores in the chain have been selected to determine whether the chain has a different average number of complaints than bookstores in general. The numbers of complaints are 4, 8, 9, 0, 3, 5, and 6. Using the .05 level of significance, what should the psychologist conclude?

Step 1: Restate the Question as a Research Hypothesis and a Null Hypothesis about the Populations
Population 1: Bookstores in the chain
Population 2: Bookstores in general

Research Hypothesis: There will be a difference in the average number of complaints received by bookstores in the chain and the average number received by bookstores in general.
Null Hypothesis: There will be no difference in the average number of complaints received by bookstores in the chain and average number received by bookstores in general.

Step 2: Determine the Characteristics of the Comparison Distribution
$M = 4 + 8 + 9 + 0 + 3 + 5 + 6 / 7 = 35 / 7 = 5$
$\Sigma(X–M)^2 = 56$
$S^2 = \Sigma (X–M)^2 / N–1 = 56 / 6 = 9.33$
$S^2_M = S^2 / N = 9.33 / 7 = 1.33$
$S_M = \sqrt{S_M^2} = \sqrt{1.33} = 1.15$
The comparison distribution will be a t distribution with 6 df.

Step 3: Determine the Cutoff Sample Score on the Comparison Distribution at which the Null Hypothesis Will Be Rejected
The cutoff sample score for a t distribution with 6 df using a two-tailed test at the .05 level of significance $= \pm2.447$

Step 4: Determine the Sample's Score on the Comparison Distribution
$t = (M–\text{Population } M) / S_M$
$= (5–6.5) / 1.15$
$= –1.30$

Step 5: Decide Whether to Reject the Null Hypothesis
Since –1.30 is not as extreme as –2.447, the psychologist would fail to reject the null hypothesis and state that the results of the study are inconclusive; the mean number of complaints received by bookstores in the chain is not significantly different than the mean number of complaints received by bookstores in general.

The _t_ Test for Dependent Means
In most research situations, researchers do not have a population mean against which to compare the mean of the sample exposed to the experimental treatment. Instead, researchers have two sets of scores. One such situation occurs when researchers use **repeated-measures designs** (or _within-subjects designs_). In these designs, each participant has two scores on the variable being measured, one collected before, and the second collected after, the experimental treatment. The hypothesis-testing procedure when this design is used is called the **_t_ test for dependent means**. The means are said to be dependent because they both are provided by the same participants. These _t_ tests are also called _paired-sample t tests_, _t tests for correlated means_, _t tests for matched samples_, or _t tests for matched pairs_.

The differences between the _t_ test for a single sample and the _t_ test for dependent means are
1. The use of difference scores and
2. The assumption that the population mean of the difference scores is zero.

Difference Scores
Difference scores (also called _change scores_) are computed by subtracting one of each participant's scores from the other. Researchers often subtract the score obtained at the conclusion of the treatment from the score obtained before the treatment to reflect the direction of the change resulting from the treatment. For example, if the experimental treatment is designed to enhance student self-esteem, a positive difference score in which the post-treatment score is greater than the pre-treatment score would indicate that the treatment had the expected effect. On the other hand, if the treatment is intended to reduce anxiety, a negative difference score would indicate that the treatment had the expected effect. Although the _t_ score will be the same numerically no matter which mean is subtracted from which,

interpretation of the results may be simplified if the sign of the *t* score indicates the direction of the experimental effect. Computing difference scores combines the two sets of scores for each participant into a single score. Once difference scores have been computed, the hypothesis-testing procedure is conducted using difference scores.

Population of Difference Scores with a Mean of Zero

The population of difference scores (Population 2) to which the population represented by the sample (Population 1) will be compared is ordinarily assumed to have a mean of zero. This assumption makes sense because the researchers are comparing their sample's population to a population in which there is, on the average, no difference or change.

Example of a *t* Test for Dependent Means

A psychologist is interested in the effect of a volunteer tutoring program on the reading achievement of a group of students. The reading achievement scores of eight students before and after the tutoring program are listed in the table that follows. Using the .05 level of significance, did the tutoring program increase reading achievement?

Student	Before Score	After Score	Difference Score	Deviation Score	Squared Deviation Score
A	24	31	7	3.37	11.36
B	20	29	9	5.37	28.84
C	22	25	3	−0.63	0.40
D	26	25	−1	−4.63	21.44
E	30	29	−1	−4.63	21.44
F	31	35	4	0.37	0.14
G	27	32	5	1.37	1.88
H	25	28	3	−0.63	0.40
Σ	205	234	29		85.88

Step 1: Restate the Question as a Research Hypothesis and a Null Hypothesis about the Populations
Population 1: Students in the volunteer tutoring program
Population 2: Students whose reading achievement scores do not change

Research Hypothesis: The reading achievement scores of students in the volunteer tutoring program will be higher after the program than before the program.
Null Hypothesis: The reading achievement scores of students in the volunteer tutoring program will be the same as, or lower than, their scores before the program.

Step 2: Determine the Characteristics of the Comparison Distribution
For the difference scores:
$M = 29 / 8 = 3.63$
Population $M = 0$ (The basis of comparison is no change.)
$S^2 = \Sigma(X-M)^2 = / df = 85.88 / 7 = 12.27$
$S^2_M = S^2 / N = 12.27 / 8 = 1.53$

$S_M = \sqrt{S_M^2} = \sqrt{1.53} = 1.24$
The comparison distribution will be a *t* distribution with 7 *df*.

Step 3: Determine the Cutoff Sample Score on the Comparison Distribution at which the Null Hypothesis Will Be Rejected
The cutoff sample score for a *t* distribution with 7 *df* using a one-tailed test at the .05 level of significance = +1.895 because the researchers are interested in an increase in reading achievement scores.

Step 4: Determine the Sample's Score on the Comparison Distribution
$t = (M-\text{Population } M) / S_M$
$= (3.63-0) / 1.24$
$= 2.931$

Step 5: Decide Whether to Reject the Null Hypothesis
Since 2.931 is more extreme than +1.895, the psychologist would reject the null hypothesis and conclude that the volunteer tutoring program did increase reading achievement.

Assumptions of the *t* Test for a Single Sample and the *t* Test for Dependent Means

When sample data are used to estimate the population variance, the comparison distribution will be a *t* distribution only if the distribution of the population of individuals from which the sample is drawn is normally distributed. Otherwise, the shape of the appropriate comparison distribution will have a different shape that is usually unknown. Thus, a normal population distribution is an **assumption**, a logical and mathematical requirement, of the *t* test. Determination of the actual shape of the population of individual scores is rarely possible based on information provided by sample data. However, the results of *t* tests are reasonably accurate even when population distributions are skewed. The only frequent situation in which a *t* test for dependent means may give a seriously inaccurate result is when a one-tailed test is used with a highly skewed population.

Effect Size and Power for the *t* Test for Dependent Means

The effect size for the *t* test for dependent means is Effect Size = M / S, where M is the mean of the difference scores and S is the estimated standard deviation of the population of individual difference scores. In the reading achievement example above, the mean for the difference scores of the eight students is 3.63, and the variance of their difference scores is 12.27. The square root of the variance is 3.50. Solving the equation, Effect Size = M / S, results in Effect Size = (3.63–0) / 3.50 = 1.04. Cohen's conventions for effect sizes for the *t* test for dependent means: a small effect size is .20, a medium effect size is .50, and a large effect size is .80. Thus, the effect size for the reading achievement study is large.

A table is provided in the text that indicates the approximate power for small, medium, and large effect sizes and one- and two-tailed tests at the .05 significance level. This power table is useful for interpreting the practical importance of nonsignificant results presented in research articles. A second table that indicates the approximate number of participants needed to achieve 80% power for estimated small, medium, and large effect sizes using one- and two-tailed tests at the .05 significance level is provided, as well. Remember that Cohen suggested that studies should be designed to have 80% power in order to be worth conducting. Note that repeated-measures designs are powerful because the standard deviation of difference scores is typically small, which is due to the fact that participants are being compared to themselves, so the variation in their scores on each testing may not be as large as when the scores of different individuals is compared.

t Tests for a Single Sample *t* for Dependent Means in Research Articles

The results of *t* tests for single samples are seen rarely, but the results of *t* tests for dependent means are seen more frequently. The format for reporting the results of *t* tests in research articles is fairly standard. For example, the results of the reading achievement study could be reported as $t(7) = 2.931$, $p < .05$ with $t(7)$, indicating that the comparison distribution was a *t* distribution with 7*df*, the *t* value was 2.931, and the result was statistically significant at the .05 level. Since the results are from a one-tailed test, the researchers should note this fact. Otherwise, two-tailed tests are usually assumed. The effect size might also be reported.

Chapter Self-Tests

The test items that follow are based on the following scenario. A group of behavioral scientists has conducted a study to determine the effects of group therapy on the number of activities of daily living performed by depressed people. During this investigation, they measured the number of activities of daily living performed by a sample of 30 depressed clients before and after 6 weeks of group therapy.

Understanding Key Terms in Chapter 8
Directions: Complete each statement using the word bank that follows. **You may use terms more than once.**
Word Bank: assumption / biased estimate / change scores / degrees of freedom / difference scores / repeated-measures design / robustness / t distribution / t score / t table / t test for dependent means / t test for a single sample / t tests / unbiased estimate

The plan for the study is known as a **(1)** _____. Since the behavioral scientists do not know the population variance for the distribution of activities of daily living, they will estimate the variance of the distribution of activities for the population of depressed people, which means they will use $N - 1$ as the denominator in the formula for computing the variance. Using this denominator will provide an **(2)** _____ estimate of the population variance, and it indicates the number of **(3)** _____. This adjustment is necessary because using sample data to compute the population variance yields a value that is too small, which is a **(4)** _____. This adjustment means that the behavioral scientists will analyze their data using one of several **(5)** _____.

If the behavioral scientists knew that the mean number of activities of daily living performed by the population of depressed people was 14 activities per day, but they did not know the variance for the population, the appropriate statistical test would be a **(6)** _____. However, to analyze the data from the design they are using, the behavioral scientists will use a **(7)** _____.

As an initial step in performing the analysis, the behavioral scientists subtract the number of activities each client performs before therapy from the number performed after therapy. This arithmetic yields **(8)** _____, which are also known as **(9)** _____, for each client. The result of the analysis is a **(10)** _____. In order to interpret this result, the behavioral scientists will consult a **(11)** _____ and use the number of **(12)** _____ to select one of an infinite number of **(13)** _____. In order to interpret the results of their analysis correctly, the behavioral scientists need to recognize that activities of daily living should be normally distributed in the population of depressed people. This logical and mathematical requirement of a statistical test is an **(14)** _____.

Multiple Choice Items

1. The *t* tests were developed for situations in which
    A. the population variance is unknown.
    B. the population mean is unknown.
    C. the sample distribution is seriously skewed.
    D. the normal curve is too narrow.

2. The behavioral scientists have conducted the study and found that following therapy, the 30 depressed clients performed an average of 18 activities each day. From their review of earlier studies, the behavioral scientists know that most depressed people perform an average of 14 activities. The appropriate statistical test in this situation is a
    A. *t* test for dependent means.
    B. *t* test for a single sample.
    C. *Z* test.
    D. repeated-measures test.

3. If the behavioral scientists used the same formula to calculate the variance for the sample of depressed clients that they would use to calculate the variance from a population, the result would be
   A. skewed.
   B. kurtotic.
   C. too large.
   D. too small.

4. An unbiased estimate of the population variance based on sample data is
   A. more like the normal curve variance.
   B. equal to the population variance.
   C. equally likely to be too high or too low.
   D. a powerful estimate of the population variance.

5. The degrees of freedom for the statistical test performed by the behavioral scientists on the data collected from the sample of clients would be
   A. $30 + 1$.
   B. 30^2.
   C. $30 - 1$.
   D. $30 / S$.

6. The symbol for the variance estimated from sample data is
   A. S^2.
   B. S.
   C. SD^2.
   D. SD.

7. The denominator for the formula for estimating the population variance from sample data is also called
   A. an unbiased estimator.
   B. the sum of squares.
   C. a t distribution.
   D. degrees of freedom.

8. In the formula for estimating the population variance from sample data, the substitution of N-1 in the denominator alters the interpretation of the test statistic
   A. by making a t distribution the appropriate comparison distribution.
   B. because the normal curve becomes skewed.
   C. due to the use of a repeated-measures design.
   D. by making the test statistic too robust to use the normal curve as the comparison distribution.

9. After calculating a t score, the behavioral scientists will determine whether it is statistically significant by comparing it to
   A. the t distribution.
   B. the appropriate t distribution.
   C. any of an infinite number of t distributions.
   D. the more appropriate of an infinite number of t distributions or the normal distribution.

10. Which of the following statements is true about the comparison of a normal distribution and a t distribution?
    A. A t distribution may be bimodal.
    B. The distributions will be identical when $df = 1$.
    C. The distributions are approximately identical when $N \geq 30$.
    D. A t distribution is more light-tailed when $N \leq 30$.

11. The appropriate cutoff sample score in a *t* table is located by
    A. squaring the variance used to calculate the test statistic.
    B. converting a *Z* score to a *t* score.
    C. transforming *t* scores to *Z* scores.
    D. using the degrees of freedom used to determine the test statistic.

12. If the behavioral scientists use a two-tailed *t* test to test the hypothesis that therapy will increase the number of activities performed at the .05 level, which *t* score will permit them to reject the null hypothesis? (No table should be necessary to respond to this item.)
    A. +1.699.
    B. +1.960.
    C. ±1.960.
    D. +2.045.

Items 13–17 are related.
13. The behavioral scientists plan to determine the effectiveness of the experimental treatment by comparing the number of activities performed before therapy with the number performed after therapy. This research design is a
    A. zero effect design.
    B. repeated-measures design.
    C. robust design.
    D. two-sample design.

14. The appropriate analysis for this design will be a
    A. *t* test for dependent means.
    B. *t* test for a single sample.
    C. *Z* test.
    D. normal deviate test.

15. The behavioral scientists will create a single score for each client by computing
    A. standard scores.
    B. *t* scores.
    C. difference scores.
    D. robust scores.

16. The scores described in Item 15 are also called
    A. dependent scores.
    B. independent scores.
    C. unbiased scores.
    D. change scores.

17. The population mean in the analysis will be
    A. 0.
    B. 1.
    C. 29.
    D. 30.

18. If the behavioral scientists justify calculating a *t* score on their belief that activities are normally distributed in the population of depressed people, they are concerned about
    A. meeting an assumption.
    B. making a biased estimate.
    C. making an unbiased estimate.
    D. using difference scores.

Problems

1. The behavioral scientists are interested in whether depressed people undergoing group therapy will perform a different number of activities of daily living after group therapy. Therefore, the behavioral scientists have randomly selected 12 depressed clients to undergo a 6-week group therapy program. Use the five steps of hypothesis testing to determine whether the average number of activities of daily living (shown below) obtained after therapy is significantly different from a mean number of activities of 14 that is typical for similar depressed people. Test the difference at the .05 level of significance and, for practice, at the .01 level. In Step 2, show all calculations. As part of Step 5, indicate whether the behavioral scientists should recommend group therapy for all depressed people based on evaluation of the null hypothesis at both levels of significance and calculate the effect size.

Client	After Therapy
A	17
B	15
C	12
D	21
E	16
F	18
G	17
H	14
I	13
J	15
K	12
L	19

2. The behavioral scientists are interested in whether depressed people undergoing group therapy will perform a different number of activities of daily living before and after group therapy. Therefore, the behavioral scientists have randomly selected 8 depressed clients in a 6-week group therapy program. Use the five steps of hypothesis testing to determine whether the observed differences in numbers of activities of daily living (shown below) obtained before and after therapy are statistically significant at the .05 level of significance and, for practice, at the .01 level. In Step 2, show all calculations. As part of Step 5, indicate whether the behavioral scientists should recommend group therapy for all depressed people based on evaluation of the null hypothesis at both levels of significance and calculate the effect size.

Client	Before Therapy	After Therapy
A	12	17
B	7	15
C	10	12
D	13	21
E	9	16
F	8	18
G	14	17
H	11	8

3. A psychologist is interested in whether a standard anxiety-reduction program will be effective for reducing test anxiety. The average test anxiety level for a university population is 40, but the variance is unknown. Nine students experiencing test anxiety have enrolled in a 4-week program designed to reduce test anxiety. The students' scores on an anxiety inventory administered the day before a test are listed in the table that follows. Use the five steps of hypothesis testing to determine whether the observed differences in anxiety obtained after therapy are statistically significant at the .05 level of significance and, for practice, at the .01 level. In Step 2, show all calculations. As part of Step 5, indicate whether the behavioral scientists should recommend the therapy for students experiencing test anxiety based on evaluation of the null hypothesis at both levels of significance. Explain the procedure to a person who is familiar with the Z test, but not with the t test.

Student	After Therapy
A	37
B	35
C	42
D	31
E	46
F	48
G	37
H	44
I	43

4. Based on the results obtained with the nine students enrolled in the 4-week anxiety-reduction program, the psychologist expanded the program to 6 weeks and enrolled 10 students. The psychologist also measured anxiety before and after the program. The students' scores on the two administrations of the anxiety inventory are presented in the table that follows. Use the five steps of hypothesis testing to determine whether the observed differences in anxiety obtained after therapy are statistically significant at the .05 level of significance and, for practice, at the .01 level. In Step 2, show all calculations. As part of Step 5, indicate whether the behavioral scientists should recommend the therapy for students experiencing test anxiety based on evaluation of the null hypothesis at both levels of significance and calculate the effect size. Explain the procedure to a person who is familiar with the Z test, but not with the t test.

Student	Before Therapy	After Therapy
A	48	40
B	46	38
C	44	42
D	48	41
E	43	46
F	47	43
G	47	37
H	41	44
I	44	43
J	45	40

5. Determine the power of each of the following studies that will be analyzed using a t test for dependent means at the .05 level of significance.

Study	Effect Size	N	Tails
(a)	Small	50	One
(b)	Medium	40	One
(c)	Small	40	Two
(d)	Small	100	Two
(e)	Medium	40	Two
(f)	Large	20	Two

6. Determine the approximate number of participants that will be needed for the following studies if a t test for dependent means will be used to analyze data at the .05 level of significance.

Study	Predicted Effect Size	Tails
(a)	Medium	One
(b)	Small	Two
(c)	Large	Two

Additional Practice: Complete any Practice Problems in Set I that your instructor has not assigned and compare your responses to those provided by the authors. Pay particular attention to the problems that require you to explain your results to someone who has never taken a course in statistics.

SPSS Applications

Application 1: *t* Test for a Single Sample

Open SPSS.

Enter the number of activities of daily living performed by the depressed clients studied in Problem 1 in the Data View window.

In the Variable View window, change the variable name to "adl" and set the decimals to zero.

🖰 Analyze.

🖰 Compare means.

🖰 One-Sample T Test.

🖰 the arrow to move "adl" to the Variable(s) window.

Enter the population mean (14) in the "Test Value" box.

The screen should look like Figure 1.

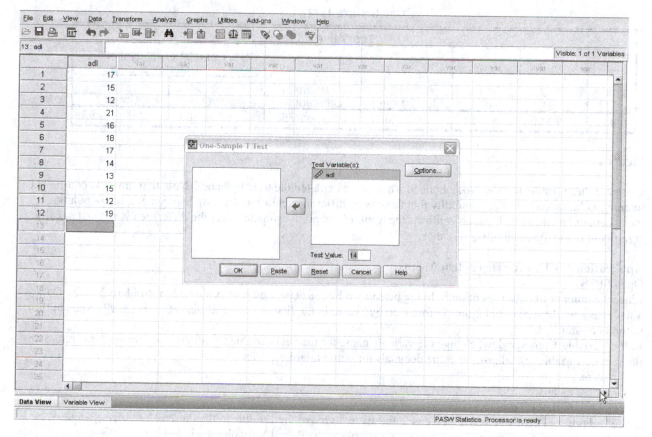

Figure 1

🖰 OK.

The output should look like the output in Figure 2.

T-Test

`[DataSet0]`

One-Sample Statistics

	N	Mean	Std. Deviation	Std. Error Mean
adl	12	15.75	2.800	.808

One-Sample Test

	Test Value = 14					
					95% Confidence Interval of the Difference	
	t	df	Sig. (2-tailed)	Mean Difference	Lower	Upper
adl	2.165	11	.053	1.750	-.03	3.53

Figure 2

Compare these results to those you obtained when you calculated the test "by hand." Note that the 95% confidence interval includes zero, so the possibility that there is no difference between the sample mean and the population mean cannot be eliminated, which confirms the result of the point estimate—that the difference is not statistically significant at the .05 level of significance.

Application 2: *t* Test for Dependent Means

Open SPSS.

Enter the number of activities of daily living performed by the depressed clients studied in Problem 2 in the Data View window. Be sure to enter the "before therapy" score in the first column and the "after therapy" scores in the second column.

In the Variable View window, change the variable name for the first variable to "adlpre" and the variable name for the second variable to "adlpost." Set the decimals for both variables to zero.

⌐ Analyze.

⌐ Compare means.

⌐ Paired-Samples T Test.

Since "adlpre" is already selected, you can ⌐ the arrow to move the variable to the Paired Variable(s) window.

⌐ "adlpost" and then ⌐ the arrow to move the variable to the Paired Variable(s) window.

The screen should look like Figure 3.

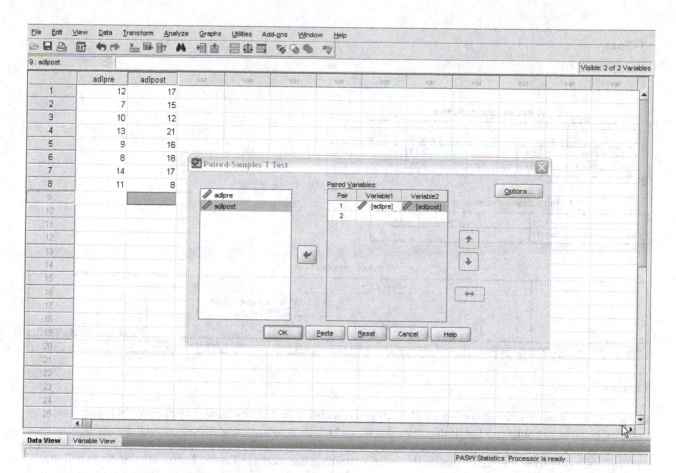

Figure 3

🖰 OK.

The output should look like the output in Figure 4.

T-Test

[DataSet0]

Paired Samples Statistics

		Mean	N	Std. Deviation	Std. Error Mean
Pair 1	adlpre	10.50	8	2.449	.866
	adlpost	15.50	8	3.964	1.402

Paired Samples Correlations

		N	Correlation	Sig.
Pair 1	adlpre & adlpost	8	.206	.625

Paired Samples Test

		Paired Differences					t	df	Sig. (2-tailed)
					95% Confidence Interval of the Difference				
		Mean	Std. Deviation	Std. Error Mean	Lower	Upper			
Pair 1	adlpre - adlpost	-5.000	4.209	1.488	-8.519	-1.481	-3.360	7	.012

Figure 4

Compare these results to those you obtained when you calculated the test "by hand." The *t* score in Figure 4 is negative because the number of activities after therapy, which increased, was subtracted from the number of activities before therapy. Your *t* score would have been positive if you followed the general practice of subtracting the "before" score from the "after" score. However, examining the means in Figure 4 shows that therapy had the desired effect of increasing the number of activities performed by the clients. Note that the 95% confidence interval does not include zero, which confirms that the difference is statistically significant at the .05 level of significance. Examination of the actual probability (.012) in Figure 4 indicates that the change in the number of activities was almost large enough to be statistically significant at the .01 level.

If you would like additional practice, use SPSS to analyze the data for Problem 3 and Problem 4 and compare the results to your calculations and those in the Answer Key.

Completion Items

1. repeated-measures design	6. *t* test for a single sample	11. *t* table
2. unbiased estimate	7. *t* test for dependent means	12. degrees of freedom
3. degrees of freedom	8. difference scores	13. *t* distributions
4. biased estimate	9. change scores	14. assumption
5. *t* tests	10. *t* score	

Multiple-Choice Items

1. A	7. D	13. B
2. B	8. A	14. A
3. D	9. B	15. C
4. C	10. C	16. D
5. C	11. D	17. A
6. A	12. D	18. A

Problems

1.
Step 1: Restate the Question as a Research Hypothesis and a Null Hypothesis about the Populations
Population 1: Depressed people who participate in group therapy
Population 2: Depressed people whose number of activities of daily living is 14

Research Hypothesis: The number of activities of daily living reported by depressed people after group therapy will not be equal to 14.
Null Hypothesis: The number of activities of daily living reported by depressed people after group therapy will be equal to 14.

Step 2: Determine the Characteristics of the Comparison Distribution
$\mu = 14$
For **difference scores**
$M = 15.75$
$S^2 = 86.25 / 11 = 7.84$
$S^2{}_M = S^2 / N = 7.84 / 12 = 0.65$
$S_M = \sqrt{S^2{}_M} = \sqrt{0.65} = 0.81$

The comparison distribution will be a *t* distribution with 11 *df*.

Step 3: Determine the Cutoff Sample Score on the Comparison Distribution at which the Null Hypothesis Will Be Rejected
The cutoff sample score for a *t* distribution with 11 *df* using a two-tailed test at the .05 level of significance will be ±2.20.
The cutoff sample score for a *t* distribution with 11 *df* using a two-tailed test at the .01 level of significance will be ±3.106.

Step 4: Determine the Sample's Score on the Comparison Distribution
$t = (M - \text{Population } M) / S_M$
$= (15.75 - 14) / 0.81$
$= 2.16$

Step 5: Decide Whether to Reject the Null Hypothesis
Since 2.16 is not more extreme than +2.201, the behavioral scientists will fail to reject the null hypothesis at the .05 level of significance and state that the results are inconclusive. Similarly, since 2.16 is not more extreme than +3.106, the behavioral scientists will fail to reject the null hypothesis at the .01 level of significance and state that

the results are inconclusive. Therefore, group therapy cannot be recommended as an effective technique for increasing the number of activities of daily living performed by depressed people using either level of significance. The effect size for the study = $M - $ Population $M / S = 15.75 - 14 / \sqrt{7.84} = 1.75 / 2.80 = 0.63$, which is a medium to large effect.

2.
Step 1: Restate the Question as a Research Hypothesis and a Null Hypothesis about the Populations
Population 1: Depressed people who participate in group therapy
Population 2: Depressed people whose number of activities of daily living does not change

Research Hypothesis: The number of activities of daily living reported by depressed people after group therapy will be different from the number of activities of daily living reported by depressed people before group therapy.
Null Hypothesis: The number of activities of daily living reported by depressed people after group therapy will be no different from the number of activities of daily living reported by depressed people before group therapy.

Step 2: Determine the Characteristics of the Comparison Distribution
Pop $M = 0$
For ***difference scores***
$M = 5$
$S^2 = 124 / 7 = 17.71$
$S^2_M = S^2 / N = 17.71 / 8 = 2.21$
$S_M = \sqrt{S^2_M} = \sqrt{2.21} = 1.49$

The comparison distribution will be a t distribution with 7 *df*.

Step 3: Determine the Cutoff Sample Score on the Comparison Distribution at which the Null Hypothesis Will Be Rejected

The cutoff sample score for a t distribution with 7 *df* using a two-tailed test at the .05 level of significance will be ±2.365.
The cutoff sample score for a t distribution with 7 *df* using a two-tailed test at the .01 level of significance will be ±3.500.

Step 4: Determine the Sample's Score on the Comparison Distribution
$t = (M - $ Population $M) / S_M$
$= (5 - 0) / 1.4$
$= 3.36$

Step 5: Decide Whether to Reject the Null Hypothesis
Since 3.36 is more extreme than +2.365, the behavioral scientists will reject the null hypothesis at the .05 level of significance and conclude that depressed clients performed significantly more activities of daily living following participation in group therapy than they performed before therapy. Since 3.36 is not more extreme than 3.500, the behavioral scientists will fail to reject the null hypothesis at the .01 level of significance and state that the results are inconclusive. Therefore, if the behavioral scientists use the .05 level, group therapy can be recommended as an effective technique for increasing the number of activities of daily living performed by depressed people. However, the same recommendation cannot be made if the behavioral scientists use the .01 level of significance.

The effect size for the study = $M / S = 5 / \sqrt{17.71} = 5 / 4.21 = 1.19$, which is a large effect.

3.
Step 1: Restate the Question as a Research Hypothesis and a Null Hypothesis about the Populations
Population 1: Students who participate in the anxiety-reduction program
Population 2: Students whose anxiety score is 40

Research Hypothesis: The mean anxiety score of students after therapy will be less than 40.
Null Hypothesis: The mean anxiety score of students after group therapy will be equal to, or greater than, 40.

Step 2: Determine the Characteristics of the Comparison Distribution
$\mu = 40$
For *difference scores*
$M = 36.30$
$S^2 = 398.41 / 9 = 44.27$
$S^2_M = S^2 / N = 44.27 / 10 = 4.43$
$S_M = \sqrt{S^2_M} = \sqrt{4.43} = 2.10$

The comparison distribution will be a t distribution with 9 *df*.

Step 3: Determine the Cutoff Sample Score on the Comparison Distribution at which the Null Hypothesis Will Be Rejected

The cutoff sample score for a t distribution with 9 *df* using a one-tailed test at the .05 level of significance will be −1.833.
The cutoff sample score for a t distribution with 9 *df* using a one-tailed test at the .01 level of significance will be −2.822.

Step 4: Determine the Sample's Score on the Comparison Distribution
$t = (M - \text{Population } M) / S_M$
$= (36.30 - 40) / 2.10$
$= -1.76$

Step 5: Decide Whether to Reject the Null Hypothesis
Since −1.76 is not more extreme than −1.833, the psychologist will fail to reject the null hypothesis at the .05 level of significance and state that the results are inconclusive. Similarly, since −1.76 is not more extreme than −2.822, the psychologist will fail to reject the null hypothesis at the .01 level of significance and state that the results are inconclusive. Therefore, the psychologist cannot recommend the anxiety-reduction program as an effective method for reducing test anxiety at either the .05 level or the .01 level.

The effect size for the study $= M - \text{Population } M / S = 36.30 - 40 / \sqrt{44.27} = -3.70 / 6.65 = -0.56$, which is a medium effect.

Compare your explanation to the explanation provided for Problem 5(c) in Set I of the Practice Problems in the text.

4.
Step 1: Restate the Question as a Research Hypothesis and a Null Hypothesis about the Populations
Population 1: Students who participate in the anxiety-reduction program
Population 2: Students whose test anxiety does not change

Research Hypothesis: The anxiety scores of students after the anxiety-reduction program will be different from their anxiety scores before the program.
Null Hypothesis: The anxiety scores of students after the anxiety-reduction program will be no different from their anxiety scores before the program.

Step 2: Determine the Characteristics of the Comparison Distribution

Pop $M = 0$

For *difference scores*

$M = -3.9$

$S^2 = 189.90 / 9 = 20.99$

$S^2_M = S^2 / N = 20.99 / 10 = 2.10$

$S_M = \sqrt{S^2_M} = \sqrt{2.10} = 1.45$

The comparison distribution will be a t distribution with 9 df.

Step 3: Determine the Cutoff Sample Score on the Comparison Distribution at which the Null Hypothesis Will Be Rejected

The cutoff sample score for a t distribution with 9 df using a two-tailed test at the .05 level of significance = ± 2.260.
The cutoff sample score for a t distribution with 9 df using a two-tailed test at the .01 level of significance = ± 3.250.

Step 4: Determine the Sample's Score on the Comparison Distribution

$t = (M - \text{Population } M) / S_M$

$= (-3.90 - 0) / 1.45$

$= -2.69$

Step 5: Decide Whether to Reject the Null Hypothesis

Since -2.69 is more extreme than -2.260, the psychologist will reject the null hypothesis at the .05 level of significance and conclude that the anxiety-reduction program significantly reduced test anxiety. Since -2.69 is not more extreme than -3.250, the psychologist will fail to reject the null hypothesis at the .01 level of significance and state that the results are inconclusive. Therefore, if the psychologist uses the .05 level, the anxiety-reduction program can be recommended as an effective technique for decreasing the test anxiety experienced by students. However, the same recommendation cannot be made if the psychologist uses the .01 level of significance.

The effect size for the study = $M / S = -3.90 / \sqrt{20.99} = -3.90 / 4.58 = -0.85$, which is a large effect.

Compare your explanation to the explanation provided for Problem 5(c) in Set I of the Practice Problems in the text.

5.

Study	Effect Size	N	Tails	Power
(a)	Small	50	One	.40
(b)	Medium	40	One	.93
(c)	Small	40	Two	.24
(d)	Small	100	Two	.55
(e)	Medium	40	Two	.88
(f)	Large	20	Two	.93

6.

Study	Predicted Effect Size	Tails	N
(a)	Medium	One	26
(b)	Small	Two	196
(c)	Large	Two	14

Chapter 9
The *t* Test for Independent Means

Learning Objectives
After studying this chapter, you should:
- Be able to describe the logical construction of, and use of, distributions of differences between means.
- Know how to calculate the mean and variance for a distribution of differences between means.
- Know how to identify the appropriate *t* distribution for a *t* test for independent means.
- Know when and how to conduct a *t* test for independent means.
- Be able to define the normality and equality of variances assumption for the *t* test for independent means and describe their implications.
- Be able to calculate effect sizes for studies requiring a *t* test for independent means and interpret these effect sizes using Cohen's conventions.
- Be able to use power tables for the *t* test for independent means.
- Be able to use sample size tables for the *t* test for independent means.
- Be able to use the harmonic mean to estimate the power of a study for which a *t* test for independent means is the appropriate statistical test, but in which the sample sizes are unequal.
- Be able to interpret results of *t* tests for independent means as reported in research articles.

The **t test for independent means** is an appropriate statistical test when an experiment involves two samples comprised of different individuals, as is the case when an experiment involves an experimental group and a control group, but the population variances are not known. Thus, each person has only one score on the variable being measured, not two scores as was the case with the *t* for dependent means. Since the population variances must be estimated from sample data, a *t* distribution will serve as the comparison distribution. The numerator of the *t* formula will involve subtracting the mean of one group from the mean of the other group so that the comparison distribution will be a distribution of *differences* between means, not a distribution of means.

The Distribution of Differences between Means
The **distribution of differences between means** is two steps removed from the distribution of the population of individuals. The logic of constructing a distribution of differences between means is as follows. First, imagine two populations of individuals like those to be included in a study. The actual characteristics of the populations are unknown, but if the null hypothesis is true, Population M_1 = Population M_2 and the variances (S^2_1 and S^2_2) can be estimated. Using the estimated population variances and the size of the samples to be drawn from each population, the variances of each distribution of means can be computed as usual (S^2_1 / N and S^2_2 / N). A distribution of differences between means can be conceptualized by imagining that a mean is randomly selected from each distribution of means for each of the two populations, one mean is subtracted from the other, and the difference is plotted. If this process is repeated a large number of times, a distribution of differences between means will result. Since the variance of this distribution is ultimately based on the estimated variances of the two populations of individuals, the distribution can be viewed as a *t* distribution.

Key Details

1. The *t* test for independent means compares the means of two samples drawn from populations having unknown means. However, if the null hypothesis is true, the two population means are equal. Therefore, Population M_1 = Population M_2, and so the mean of the distribution of differences between means is zero.

2. In order for a *t* test for independent means to provide valid results, the assumption that the variances of the two populations of individual scores are equal must be reasonable. Although the two variances are rarely equal, the best way to identify a single variance for the distribution of differences between means is to average the two estimates to obtain the best single estimate of this distribution. The resulting average is the **pooled estimate of the population variance (S^2_{Pooled})**. If sample sizes are equal, the pooled estimate of the population variance is the average of the estimates for the two populations ($S^2_1 + S^2_2 / 2$). However, if the sample sizes are unequal, the pooled estimate of the population variance estimate is calculated as a **weighted average** that adjusts the estimate for each sample by giving

more weight to the larger sample. This weighted average is not based on the size of each sample, but rather on the number of degrees of freedom for each sample. Thus, the formula becomes
$S^2_{Pooled} = [(df_1 / df_{Total}) (S^2_1)] + [(df_2 / df_{Total}) (S^2_2)]$.

Example: Suppose that an experimenter enrolls 40 participants in a study, equally divided between the experimental and control groups. At the conclusion of the study, the estimated variance for the experimental group is 20 and the estimated variance for the control group is 50. If all 40 participants complete the study, the pooled estimate of the population variance is
$S^2_{Pooled} = S^2_1 + S^2_2 / 2 = (20 + 50) / 2 = 70 / 2 = 35$.

3. However, suppose the experimenter had enrolled 41 participants in the experimental group and 21 participants in the control group. The estimated variances remain the same. In this situation, the total number of degrees of freedom for the experimental group is $41 - 1 = 40$, and for the control group, $21 - 1 = 20$. The total number of degrees of freedom is 60. Now the pooled estimate of the population variance is
$S^2_{Pooled} = [(df_1 / df_{Total}) (S^2_1)] + [(df_2 / df_{Total}) (S^2_2)] = [(40 / 60)(20) + (20 / 60)(50)] = [(2 / 3)(20) + (1 / 3)(50)]$
$= (13.33 + 16.67) = 30$. Note that S^2_{Pooled} is between the group variances of 20 and 50, and it is closer to the variance of the larger group.

Remember that the variance for a distribution of means is the variance of the population of individual scores divided by the sample size. However, although the two populations involved when the t test for independent means is being conducted are assumed to have equal variances, the distributions of means will not have equal variances if the sample sizes are different. Therefore, the variance for each distribution of means must be calculated using the formulas $S^2_{M1} = S^2_{Pooled} / N_1$ and $S^2_{M2} = S^2_{Pooled} / N_2$.

Returning to the example with 41 participants in the experimental group and 21 in the control group, the variance for the distribution of means for the experimental group is $S^2_{M1} = S^2_{Pooled} / N_1 = 30 / 41 = 0.73$, and the variance for the distribution of means for the control group is and $S^2_{M2} = S^2_{Pooled} / N_2 = 30 / 21 = 1.43$.

4. The **variance of the distribution of differences between means** ($S^2_{Difference}$) is simply the sum of the variances of the distributions of means for the two populations $- S^2_{Difference} = S^2_{M1} + S^2_{M2}$. The standard deviation of the distribution of differences between means is the square root of the variance $- S_{Difference} = \sqrt{S^2_{Difference}}$. Returning to the example, $S^2_{Difference} = S^2_{M1} + S^2_{M2} = 0.73 + 1.43 = 2.16$, and $S_{Difference} = \sqrt{S^2_{Difference}} = \sqrt{2.16} = 1.47$.

5. Again, since the distribution of differences between means is based on estimated population variances, the distribution of differences between means for a study follows a specific t distribution. The number of degrees of freedom for this t distribution is the sum of the degrees of freedom for the two samples. Therefore, the formula is $df_{Total} = df_1 + df_2$. Using the data from the example, $df_{Total} = 40 + 20 = 60$. Reference to the t table in the text indicates that the cutoff sample t score for a one-tailed test with 60 degrees of freedom at the .05 level of significance is $+1.671$ or -1.671. For a two-tailed test, the cutoff sample score would be ± 2.001.

6. The t score for a t test for independent means is the difference between the two sample means divided by the **standard deviation of the distribution of differences between means** ($S_{Difference}$). The formula is $t = M_1 - M_2 / S_{Difference}$. Suppose that in the example, the mean for the first sample is 14 and the mean for the second sample is 10. In this example, $t = 14 - 10 / 1.43 = 4 / 1.43 = 2.80$.

Hypothesis Testing with a t Test for Independent Means
The hypothesis-testing procedure for a t test for independent means is changed for Steps 2–4. In Step 2, the comparison distribution is a distribution of differences between means. In Step 3, the number of degrees of freedom used to find the cutoff sample score is based on the degrees of freedom for two samples. In Step 4, the sample score on the comparison distribution is based on the difference between the means of two samples.

An Example of a t Test for Independent Means (Equal Sample Sizes)
A behavioral scientist is interested in determining the effect of self-defense training on the self-confidence of employees who have been transferred from a small city to a large metropolitan city. A group of 10 employees willing to be trained in self-defense is identified, and 5 are randomly assigned to a training program. The other 5

receive no special training. At the end of training, all 10 employees complete a questionnaire to assess their levels of self-confidence. The data are presented in the table included in Step 2 of the hypothesis-testing procedure. Using the .05 and .01 levels of significance, did the program make a difference in the levels of self-confidence of the two groups?

Step 1: Restate the Question as a Research Hypothesis and a Null Hypothesis about the Populations
Population 1: Employees who receive self-defense training
Population 2: Employees who do not receive self-defense training

Research Hypothesis: The self-confidence of employees who receive self-defense training will be different from the self-confidence of employees who do not receive self-defense training.
Null Hypothesis: The self-confidence of employees who receive self-defense training will be no different from the self-confidence of employees who do not receive self-defense training.

Step 2: Determine the Characteristics of the Comparison Distribution

Training Group	Deviation from M	(Deviation from $M)^2$	No Training Group	Deviation from M	(Deviation from $M)^2$
45	3.2	10.24	24	−5.20	27.04
48	6.2	38.44	34	4.80	23.04
44	2.2	4.84	29	−0.20	0.04
37	−4.8	23.04	27	−2.20	4.84
35	−6.8	46.24	32	2.80	7.84
$\Sigma = 209$	$\Sigma = 0.00$	$\Sigma = 122.80$	$\Sigma = 146.00$	$\Sigma = 0.00$	$\Sigma = 62.80$

$M_1 = 41.80; S^2_1 = 122.80 / 4 = 30.70$
$M_2 = 29.20; S^2_2 = 62.80 / 4 = 15.70$
$N_1 = 5; df_1 = N_1 - 1 = 5 - 1 = 4$
$N_2 = 5; df_2 = N_2 - 1 = 5 - 1 = 4$
$df_{total} = df_1 + df_2 = 4 + 4 = 8$

$S^2_{Pooled} = df_1 / df_{total} (S^2_1) + df_2 / df_{total} (S^2_2)$
$= 4 / 8 (30.70) + 4 / 8 (15.70) = .5 (30.70) + .5 (15.70) = 15.35 + 7.85 = 23.20$

$S^2_{M1} = S^2_{Pooled} / N_1 = 23.20 / 5 = 4.64$
$S^2_{M2} = S^2_{Pooled} / N_2 = 23.20 / 5 = 4.64$

$S^2_{Difference} = S^2_{M1} + S^2_{M2} = 4.64 + 4.64 = 9.28$
$S_{Difference} = \sqrt{S^2_{Difference}} = \sqrt{9.28} = 3.05$

The comparison distribution is a t distribution with 8 df.

Step 3: Determine the Cutoff Sample Score on the Comparison Distribution at which the Null Hypothesis Will Be Rejected
For a t distribution with 8 df, the cutoff sample score at the .05 level of significance is ±2.306
For a t distribution with 8 df, the cutoff sample score at the .01 level of significance is ±3.356

Step 4: Determine the Sample's Score on the Comparison Distribution
$t = (M_1 - M_2) / S_{Difference} = (41.80 - 29.20) / 3.05 = 12.60 / 3.05 = 4.13$

Step 5: Decide Whether to Reject the Null Hypothesis
Since 4.13 is more extreme than 2.306, the behavioral scientist will reject the null hypothesis at the .05 level of significance and accept the research hypothesis that self-defense training improves the self-confidence of employees. Similarly, 4.13 is more extreme than 3.356, so the behavioral scientist will reject the null hypothesis

at the .01 level of significance and accept the research hypothesis that self-defense training improves the self-confidence of employees.

An Example of a *t* Test for Independent Means (Unequal Sample Sizes)
Based on the success of the initial study on the effect of self-defense training on self-confidence, the behavioral scientist decided to replicate the study with a larger number of employees. The results of the second study are again presented in Step 2 of the hypothesis-testing procedure. Note that 10 participants were included in each group at the beginning of the study, but two participants in the group that did not receive training dropped out of the study.

Step 1: Restate the Question as a Research Hypothesis and a Null Hypothesis about the Populations
Population 1: Employees who receive self-defense training
Population 2: Employees who do not receive self-defense training

Research Hypothesis: The self-confidence of employees who receive self-defense training will be different from the self-confidence of employees who do not receive self-defense training.
Null Hypothesis: The self-confidence of employees who receive self-defense training will be no different from the self-confidence of employees who do not receive self-defense training.

Step 2: Determine the Characteristics of the Comparison Distribution

Training Group	Deviation from M	(Deviation from $M)^2$	No Training Group	Deviation from M	(Deviation From $M)^2$
45	3.4	11.56	38	7.75	60.06
43	1.4	1.96	27	−3.25	10.56
44	2.4	5.76	17	−13.25	175.56
32	−9.6	92.16	28	−2.25	5.06
38	−3.6	12.96	42	11.75	138.06
48	6.4	40.96	31	0.75	0.56
36	−5.6	31.36	22	−8.25	68.06
45	3.4	11.56	37	6.75	45.56
39	−2.6	6.76			
46	4.4	19.36			
$\sum = 416$	$\sum = 0.00$	$\sum = 234.40$	$\sum = 242$	$\sum = 0.00$	$\sum = 503.50$

$M_1 = 41.60; S^2_1 = 234.40 / 9 = 26.04$
$M_2 = 30.25; S^2_2 = 503.50 / 7 = 71.93$
$N_1 = 10; df_1 = N_1 - 1 = 10 - 1 = 9$
$N_2 = 8; df_2 = N_2 - 1 = 8 - 1 = 7$
$df_{Total} = df_1 + df_2 = 9 + 7 = 16$

$S^2_{Pooled} = df_1 / df_{Total} (S^2_1) + df_2 / df_{Total} (S^2_2)$
$= 9 / 16 (26.04) + 7 / 16 (71.93) = .56 (26.04) + .44 (71.93) = 46.23$

$S^2_{M1} = S^2_{Pooled} / N_1 = 46.23 / 10 = 4.62$
$S^2_{M2} = S^2_{Pooled} / N_2 = 46.23 / 8 = 5.78$
$S^2_{Difference} = S^2_{M1} + S^2_{M2} = 4.62 + 5.78 = 10.40$
$S_{Difference} = \sqrt{S^2_{Difference}} = \sqrt{10.40} = 3.22$

The comparison distribution is a *t* distribution with 16 *df*.

Step 3: Determine the Cutoff Sample Score on the Comparison Distribution at which the Null Hypothesis Will Be Rejected
For a *t* distribution with 16 *df*, the cutoff sample score at the .05 level of significance is ±2.120
For a *t* distribution with 16 *df*, the cutoff sample score at the .01 level of significance is ±2.921

Step 4: Determine the Sample's Score on the Comparison Distribution
$t = (M_1 - M_2) / S_{\text{Difference}} = (41.60 - 30.25) / 3.22 = 11.35 / 3.22 = 3.52$

Step 5: Decide Whether to Reject the Null Hypothesis
Since 3.52 is more extreme than 2.120, the behavioral scientist will reject the null hypothesis at the .05 level of significance and accept the research hypothesis that self-defense training improves the self-confidence of employees. Similarly, since 3.52 is more extreme than 2.921, the behavioral scientist will reject the null hypothesis at the .01 level of significance and accept the research hypothesis that self-defense training improves the self-confidence of employees.

Assumptions of the *t* Test for Independent Means
The *t* test for independent means has two assumptions:

1. Each of the populations of individual scores for the two groups is normally distributed. Violations of this assumption pose problems if the two population distributions are seriously skewed, and are skewed in opposite directions. Even if the population distributions are skewed, *t* test results are accurate when two-tailed tests are used and the sample sizes are not extremely small.
2. As has been indicated, the variances of the two populations of individual scores are assumed to be equal. Again, *t* tests are accurate even if the differences in the population variances are large when the sample sizes are equal.

If the population distributions are highly skewed, the variances are quite different, or both conditions are present, the *t* test for independent means can yield misleading results. Alternative tests (described in Chapter 11) may provide more valid results. In addition, computer programs like SPSS provide two types of output for the *t* test for independent means, one assuming that the variances are equal, and one assuming that they are not. The latter approach does result in lower power.

Effect Size and Power for the *t* Test for Independent Means
The effect size $= M_1 - M_2 / S_{\text{Pooled}}$, and Cohen's conventions are the same as they have been with .20 indicating a small effect, .50 indicating a medium effect, and .80 indicating a large effect. In the first of the two studies investigating the effect of self-defense training on employee self-confidence, the mean for the group that received training was 41.80, the mean for the control group was 29.20, and S^2_{Pooled} was 23.20. S_{Pooled} is equal to the square root of 23.20, which is 4.82. Therefore, the effect size $= (41.80 - 29.20) / 4.82 = 12.6 / 4.82 = 2.60$, a very large effect size. In the second of the two studies, the mean for the group that received training was 41.60, the mean for the control group was 30.25, and S^2_{Pooled} was 46.23. S_{Pooled} is equal to the square root of 46.23, which is 6.80. Therefore, the effect size $= (41.60 - 30.25) / 6.80 = 11.35 / 6.80 = 1.67$, a very large effect size as well.

The power of *t* tests for independent means can be determined during the planning stages of a study, when it is especially useful in determining the impact of sample size on the results of the statistical test. As the power table in the text indicates, one-tailed tests are more powerful than two-tailed tests, and power increases as sample size increases or as effect size increases. For example, suppose a study is being designed to compare differences between two means reflecting a medium effect size. If each group includes 20 participants, a one-tailed test at the .05 level of significance will have a power of .46. A two-tailed test at the .05 level of significance will have a power of .33. Thus, the chances that the results of the *t* tests will be statistically significant, even if the research hypothesis is true, are only 46% and 33%, respectively.

Planning Sample Size
As indicated in the preceding section, sample size determination involves effect size and power considerations, as well as consideration of the type of test to be conducted and the significance level at which the result will be evaluated. The suggested guideline of 80% power can be reached with only 20 participants per group if a large effect size is expected and the experimenters plan to use a one-tailed test and the .05 level of significance. If the experimenters plan to use a two-tailed test and the .05 level of significance, 30 participants per group are required to achieve 80% power. Note that even with 100 participants per group, 80% power cannot be obtained if a small effect size is to be detected. In this situation, the power is 41% for a one-tailed test at the .05 level and 29% for a two-tailed test at the same level.

Power When Sample Sizes Are Not Equal

Power for the t test for independent means is greatest when the number of participants in each group is equal. When sample sizes are not equal, the **harmonic mean** is used to estimate the sample size for the t test for independent means. The formula for the harmonic mean is

Harmonic mean = $[(2)(N_1)(N_2)] / [N_1 + N_2]$.

The harmonic mean is equal to the size of the sample that would exist if the unequal samples were divided into samples of equal size. For example, calculating the harmonic mean for the study that included 41 participants in the experimental group and 21 in the control group would yield:

$(2)(41)(21) / (41 + 21) = 1722 / 62 = 27.77$

Although the study included 62 participants, the study had a power equal to that of a study with approximately 56 participants if they were divided into equal groups.

Review and Comparison of the Three Kinds of t Tests

In this chapter and the preceding one, three different t tests have been described. The common factor is that the population variances must be estimated from the scores of the individuals that comprise the experimental samples, which means that the comparison distribution is a t distribution. The three t tests are:

1. The t test for one sample, in which a sample mean is compared to a known population mean.
2. The t for dependent means, in which each participant has two scores (or the participants are matched in some way).
3. The t test for independent means, in which the participants in each sample are different (independent).

The t Test for Independent Means in Research Articles

The t test for independent means is usually reported in research articles by listing the two sample means (and sometimes the standard deviations) followed by the t test results in the usual format. For example, the results for the first study describing the effects of self-defense training on employee self-confidence could be reported as follows: The mean score on the self-confidence inventory for the employees who received self-defense training was 41.80 ($SD = 5.54$), while the mean score for the employees who did not receive training was 29.20 ($SD = 3.96$); $t_{(8)} = 4.13$, $p < .01$.

Chapter Self-Tests

The test items that follow are based on the following scenario. The group of behavioral scientists that has been studying the effect of depression on the number of activities of daily living performed by depressed people is now interested in whether depressed people undergoing group therapy will perform a different number of activities than depressed people undergoing individual therapy. Therefore, the behavioral scientists have randomly selected two groups of depressed clients, one of which has undergone a 6-week group therapy program and the other 6 weeks of individual therapy. The behavioral scientists have measured the number of activities of daily living performed by both samples of depressed clients at the completion of the therapy sessions.

Understanding Key Terms in Chapter 9

Directions: Complete each statement using the word bank that follows.

Word Bank: dependent means / differences between means/ equal / harmonic mean / independent means / normal / pooled estimate / single sample / $S_{Difference}$ / $S^2_{Difference}$ / weighted average

In order to conduct the comparison between the effects of group and individual therapy, the appropriate test is a *t* test for **(1)** _____. If the behavioral scientists had matched the participants in each group on variables including age, duration of symptoms, and score on a depression inventory, the appropriate tests would be a *t* test for **(2)** _____. Finally, if the behavioral scientists wanted to compare the scores of their clients to a score on a depression inventory that divides people into clinically depressed or not clinically depressed categories, the appropriate test would be a *t* test for a **(3)** _____. Returning to the intended comparison between the means of groups undergoing group and individual therapy, the comparison distribution for their analysis will be a sampling distribution of **(4)** _____. In order to create this distribution, the behavioral scientists will have to estimate the variances of the populations of individual scores and use them to create distributions of means for each of the populations. Next, the behavioral scientists will have to combine the two distributions of means to create a single variance estimate. This combined estimate is the **(5)** _____ of the population variance. Since this estimate is adjusted to take the influence of possibly different sample sizes into account, it is a **(6)** _____. The new concepts for this distribution are **(7)** _____ and **(8)** _____. This *t* test assumes that the distributions of depression scores for both the population of depressed people undergoing group therapy and the population of depressed people undergoing individual therapy are **(9)** _____, and have **(10)** _____ variances. The power of their statistical test will be highest if the sizes of the two groups are equal. When group sizes are unequal, the **(11)** _____ provides an estimate of the power if the participants were divided into groups of equal size.

Multiple-Choice Items

1. If the behavioral scientists plan to conduct a two-tailed *t* test for independent means, the null hypothesis will be that
   A. the mean of Population I will be equal to the mean of Population 2.
   B. the mean of Population I will be different than the mean of Population 2.
   C. the mean of Population 1 will be less than the mean of Population 2.
   D. the mean of Population 1 will be greater than the mean of Population 2.

Items 2–6 are related.

The behavioral scientists are explaining the conceptual basis for the analysis they plan to conduct to an intern who understands descriptive statistics and hypothesis testing, but who does not understand the *t* test. They begin the explanation by stating that they will be making inferences about two hypothetical populations, depressed people who undergo group therapy and depressed people who undergo individual therapy.

2. Next, they explain that to conduct a *t* test for independent means,
   A. two scores are obtained from each participant in the experimental groups.
   B. the comparison distribution is a distribution of means.
   C. only two-tailed tests are possible.
   D. the variance of the populations of individual scores must be estimated.

3. The next conceptual step is that once they have determined the characteristics of the two distributions of individual scores, this information, along with the number of clients in each sample, will be used to determine
    A. the relationship between the sample distributions and the normal distribution.
    B. the characteristics of the distribution of means of the samples.
    C. the characteristics of the distribution of differences between means.
    D. the shape of the comparison distribution when the samples include infinite numbers of participants.

4. Since the calculated t is a single score, the final conceptual step is to imagine the comparison distribution as a distribution of
    A. paired variances.
    B. means.
    C. random t scores.
    D. differences between means.

5. Based on the numerator of the t formula, $(M_1 - M_2)$, the mean of the comparison distribution is
    A. $df + 2$.
    B. $df / 2$.
    C. 0.
    D. 1.

6. Conceptually, the standard deviation of this comparison distribution is the average of the variances of the distributions of means of individual depression scores of the two experimental groups. Consequently, it is called the
    A. mean estimate of the population variance.
    B. pooled estimate of the population variance.
    C. harmonic estimate of the population variance.
    D. weighted estimate of the population variance.

Items 7–12 are related.
The behavioral scientists have conducted their analysis and report that the mean number of activities performed by clients undergoing group therapy was 15.87 ($SD = 3.07$) and the mean number of activities performed by clients undergoing individual therapy was 18.35 ($SD = 3.04$); $t_{(30)} = -2.30$, $p < .05$.

7. The description of the analysis indicates that the number of participants in the study was
    A. 28.
    B. 30.
    C. 32.
    D. 34.

8. If M_1 was the mean number of activities performed by clients who underwent group therapy and M_2 was the mean number of activities performed by clients who underwent individual therapy, the t score indicates that
    A. clients who underwent individual therapy performed more activities.
    B. clients who underwent group therapy performed more activities.
    C. the means of the groups were nearly identical.
    D. the variances of the two groups were nearly identical.

9. The p value means that the behavioral scientists
    A. were measuring a large treatment effect on the number of activities performed.
    B. identified a practically significant difference in the two types of treatment.
    C. could accept a research hypothesis that treatment had an effect on the number of activities performed.
    D. could also reject the null hypothesis at the .01 level.

10. The standard deviations of the two experimental groups indicate that
    A. the effect size was large.
    B. the variances were approximately equal.
    C. the populations of individual scores were normally distributed.
    D. the study had adequate power to identify a practically significant difference between therapies.

11. If the behavioral scientists decide to replicate their study with 50 participants, they will have the most power if they divide the participants so that
   A. 25 participants receive group therapy and 25 receive individual therapy.
   B. 30 participants receive group therapy and 20 receive individual therapy.
   C. 20 participants receive group therapy and 30 receive individual therapy.
   D. 10 participants receive group therapy and 40 receive individual therapy.

12. If different numbers of participants drop out of each experimental group so that the numbers in each group are different, the behavioral scientists can estimate the power of a study that divides the remaining participants into two groups of equal size by calculating
   A. the pooled variance estimate.
   B. $S^2_{Difference}$.
   C. $S_{Difference}$.
   D. the harmonic mean.

Problems

1. The behavioral scientists have randomly selected two groups of depressed clients, one of which has undergone a 6-week group therapy program, and the other 6 weeks of individual therapy. Use the five steps of hypothesis testing to determine whether the observed differences in activities of daily living (shown in the table that follows) performed by the two groups are statistically significant at the .05 and, for practice, the .01 levels of significance. In Step 2, show all calculations. As part of Step 5, indicate which type of therapy the behavioral scientists should recommend for depressed people based on evaluation of the null hypothesis at both levels of significance and calculate the effect size. Explain what you have done to someone who is familiar with the t test for a single sample, but not with the t test for independent means.

Group Therapy	Individual Therapy
15	17
15	15
19	20
17	20
14	15
14	15
16	18
18	20

2. Although the results of the study described in Problem 1 were not statistically significant, seven of the eight depressed clients who underwent individual therapy increased the number of activities of daily living performed, and the power of the study was low. Therefore, the behavioral scientists have decided to replicate the study using a larger number of participants. They began by enrolling 20 participants in each group. However, as indicated in the table that follows, some participants did not complete the study. Use the five steps of hypothesis testing to determine whether the participants who undergo individual therapy perform more activities of daily living than participants who undergo group therapy and whether the differences are statistically significant at the .05 and, for practice, the .01 levels of significance. In Step 2, show all calculations. As part of Step 5, indicate which type of therapy the behavioral scientists should recommend for depressed people based on evaluation of the null hypothesis at both levels of significance and calculate the effect size.

Group Therapy	Individual Therapy
15	17
17	14
20	22
18	21
15	16
18	17
14	12
11	18
10	16
15	20
13	19
17	24
18	18
21	17
16	22
	20
	19

3. Six months after an industrial accident, a behavioral scientist has been asked to compare the job satisfaction of employees who participated in counseling sessions with the satisfaction of employees who chose not to participate. The scores on a job satisfaction inventory for both groups are listed in the table that follows. Use the five steps of hypothesis testing to determine whether the job satisfaction scores of the group that participated in counseling are statistically higher than the scores of employees who did not participate in counseling at the .01 level of significance. In Step 2, show all calculations. As part of Step 5, indicate whether the behavioral scientist should recommend counseling as a method to improve job satisfaction following industrial accidents based on evaluation of the null hypothesis and calculate the effect size.

Participated in Counseling	Did Not Participate in Counseling
36	37
39	35
40	36
36	33
38	30
35	38
37	39
39	35
42	32

A behavioral scientist interested in the effect of exercise on the perceptions of well-being among older adults identified 30 residents of a retirement community and divided them into two groups of 15 residents. Both groups were encouraged to walk at least 20 minutes per day. One group, however, also participated in a structured exercise program that emphasized flexibility. After 6 weeks, the behavioral scientist mailed questionnaires to the 30 residents. Responses to an item asking residents to rate their perceptions of their health on a 10-point scale on which

1 indicated "very unhealthy" and 10 indicated "very healthy" are presented in the table that follows. Use the five steps of hypothesis testing to determine whether the observed differences in health ratings of the two groups are statistically significant at the .05 level of significance. In Step 2, show all calculations. As part of Step 5, indicate whether the behavioral scientist should recommend exercise as a method to improve perceptions of health among older adults based on evaluation of the null hypothesis and calculate the effect size.

Walking and Flexibility	Walking Only
5	2
6	3
6	4
4	3
9	6
4	7
7	7
9	6
6	7
7	4
9	6
7	
4	
9	
8	

5. Determine the power of each of the following studies that is to be analyzed using a t test for independent means at the .05 level of significance.

Study	Effect Size	N	Tails
(a)	Small	10	One
(b)	Medium	30	One
(c)	Small	20	Two
(d)	Small	100	Two
(e)	Medium	40	Two
(f)	Large	20	Two

6. Determine the approximate number of participants needed for the following studies to have 80% power if a t test for independent means will be used to analyze data at the .05 level of significance. First, list the total number of participants that will need to be included in the study. Then list the number that will be assigned to each group.

Study	Effect Size	Tails
(a)	Small	2
(b)	Medium	2
(c)	Medium	1
(d)	Large	1

7. Which t test is appropriate in the following studies?
   A. Comparing the depression scores of men and women.
   B. Comparing the reading achievement scores of students who have been tutored with a mean of 100.
   C. Comparing the depression scores of disaster victims with a score that distinguishes normal depression from clinically significant depression.
   D. Comparing the depression scores of people before and after an exercise program.
   E. Comparing the reading achievement scores of students before and after a tutoring program.
   F. Comparing the reading achievement scores of boys and girls after a tutoring program.

Additional Practice: Complete any Practice Problems in Set I that your instructor has not assigned and compare your responses to those provided by the authors. Pay particular attention to the problems that require you to explain your results to someone who has never taken a course in statistics.

SPSS Applications

Application 1: *t* Test for Independent Means

Open SPSS.

Analyze the data for Problem 1. Remember that SPSS assumes that all the scores in a row are from the same participant. In this study, there are 16 participants divided into two groups of 8. Therefore, each of the 16 participants will be described by two variables, type of therapy and the number of activities of daily living performed. If "1" represents the group therapy group and "2" represents the individual therapy group, the first participant will be described by entering "1" in the top cell of the first column in the Data View window and "15" in the top cell of the second column to indicate that the participant underwent group therapy and performed 15 activities of daily living. The second participant will be described by "1" and "15," and the third by "1" and "19." When the two variables have been entered for the eight participants who underwent group therapy, repeat the process for participants who underwent individual therapy using "2" to describe their therapy group. In the Variable View window, change the first variable name to "therapy" and the second to "adl" and set the decimals for both to zero.

🖰 Analyze.
🖰 Compare means.
🖰 Independent-Samples T Test.

Since "therapy" is already selected, you can 🖰 the arrow to move the variable to the Grouping Variable(s) window.

🖰 "adl" and 🖰 the arrow to move the variable to the Test Variable(s) window.

🖰 "Define Groups" and enter "1" in the box for Group 1 and "2" in the box for Group 2.

The "Define Groups" window should look like Figure 1.

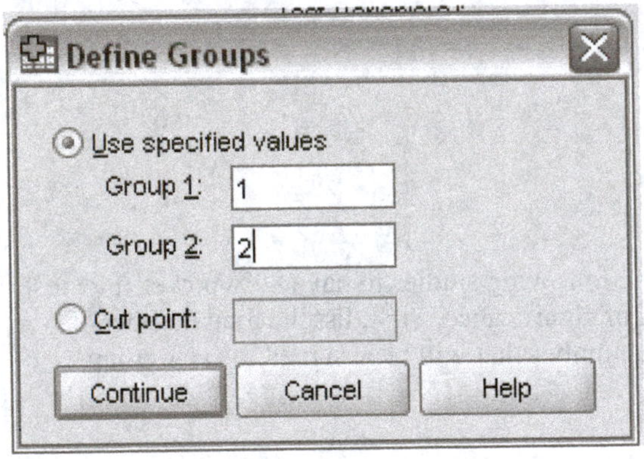

Figure 1

🖰 Continue.

The "Independent-Samples T Test" window should look like Figure 2.

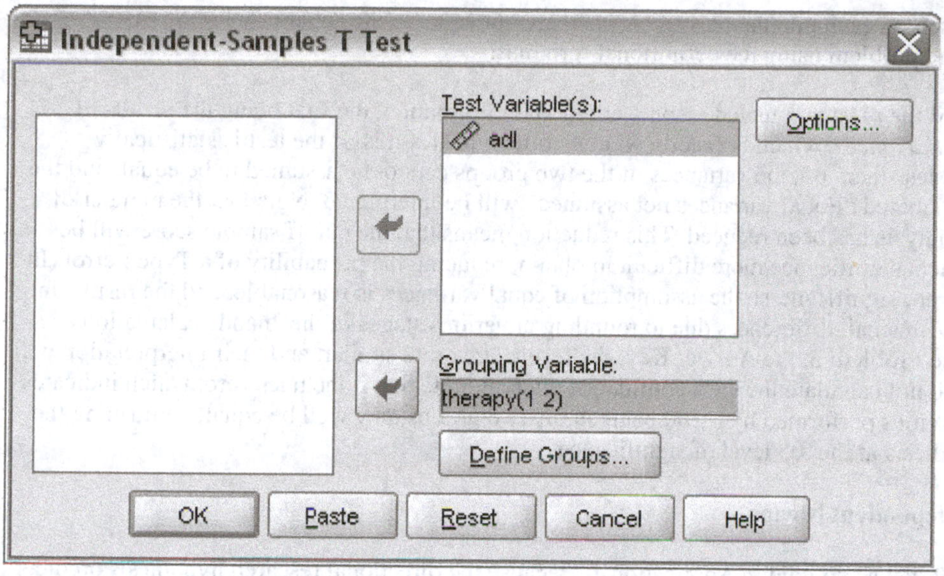
Independent-Samples T Test
Test Variable(s):
adl
Options...
Grouping Variable:
therapy(1 2)
Define Groups...
OK
Paste
Reset
Cancel
Help

Figure 2

🖱 OK.

The SPSS output should look like Figure 3 and Figure 4.

	therapy	N	Mean	Std. Deviation	Std. Error Mean
adl	1	8	16.00	1.852	.655
	2	8	17.50	2.330	.824

Figure 3

		Levene's Test for Equality of Variances		t-test for Equality of Means						
		F	Sig.	t	df	Sig. (2-tailed)	Mean Difference	Std. Error Difference	95% Confidence Interval of the Difference	
									Lower	Upper
adl	Equal variances assumed	1.167	.298	-1.426	14	.176	-1.500	1.052	-3.757	.757
	Equal variances not assumed			-1.426	13.321	.177	-1.500	1.052	-3.768	.768

Figure 4

The table in Figure 3 summarizes the data obtained during the study, including the number of participants in each therapy group, the mean and standard deviation for each group, and the standard error of the mean. This last value is the standard deviation of the distribution of means, S_M, for each group, but they are not based on the pooled variance estimate. Instead, they are based on each population variance and are not equal to the square root of S^2_M as calculated in the solution to the problem using the definitional formulas.

Figure 4 contains the results of the *t* test and includes some additional information, the first being the results of *Levene's Test for Equality of Variances*, which is exactly what its title indicates it is. If the test is statistically significant, that is, if "Sig." is less than .05, the variances of the two groups cannot be assumed to be equal, and the results of the *t* test in the row labeled "Equal variances not assumed" will be interpreted. Note that the number of degrees of freedom for this analysis has been reduced. This reduction means that the cutoff sample score will be slightly larger, making statistical significance more difficult to obtain, reducing the probability of a Type I error. In this instance, Levene's test is not significant, so the assumption of equal variances is reasonable, and the results in this row can be interpreted. With small differences due to rounding at various stages of the "hand" calculations presented in the solution to the Problem in the Answer Key, the results are quite similar, and their interpretation will be the same. Although you did not calculate the 95% confidence interval, note that it includes zero, which indicates that the mean numbers of activities performed by participants in the two groups may well be equal, confirming the failure to reject the null hypothesis at the .05 level of significance.

Application 2: *t* Test for Independent Means

Open SPSS.

Enter the data from Problem 2 just as you did in Application 1. Because the directional research hypothesis predicts that clients who undergo individual therapy will perform more activities of daily living, you may want to reverse the group numbers so that the results of the *t* test will be positive, as has been done in the results that follow. Quantitatively, the results will be identical if you do not reverse the group numbers, but the sign of *t* will be negative if the prediction is accurate.

🖱 Analyze.
🖱 Compare means.
🖱 Independent-Samples T Test.
Again, since "therapy" is already selected, you can🖱 the arrow to move the variable to the Grouping Variable(s) window.
🖱 "adl" and 🖱 the arrow to move the variable to the Test Variable(s) window.
🖱 "Define Groups" and enter "1" in the box for Group 1 and "2" in the box for Group 2.
The "Define Groups" window should look like Figure 1.
🖱 Continue.
The "Independent-Samples T Test" window should look like Figure 2.
🖱 OK.
The SPSS output should look like Figure 5 and Figure 6.

Group Statistics

	therapy	N	Mean	Std. Deviation	Std. Error Mean
adl	1	17	18.35	3.040	.737
	2	15	15.87	3.067	.792

Figure 5

Independent Samples Test

		Levene's Test for Equality of Variances		t-test for Equality of Means						
		F	Sig.	t	df	Sig. (2-tailed)	Mean Difference	Std. Error Difference	95% Confidence Interval of the Difference	
									Lower	Upper
adl	Equal variances assumed	.003	.956	2.299	30	.029	2.486	1.081	.278	4.695
	Equal variances not assumed			2.298	29.436	.029	2.486	1.082	.275	4.698

Figure 6

As in the first application, the table in Figure 5 summarizes the data obtained during the study including the number of participants in each therapy group, the mean and standard deviation for each group, and the standard error of the mean. Again, this last value is the standard deviation of the distribution of means, S_M, for each group, but they are not based on the pooled variance estimate. Instead, they are based on each population variance and are not equal to the square root of S^2_M as in the solution to the problem you calculated "by hand."

Figure 6 contains the results of the *t* test, which indicates that the results of Levene's Test are not statistically significant. Since the assumption of equal variances is reasonable, the results in this row can be interpreted. However, SPSS only provides "Sig. (2-tailed)," and the behavioral scientists stated a directional research hypothesis, which calls for a one-tailed test. The solution is to divide the two-tailed significance provided by SPSS to obtain the one-tailed significance. In this case, dividing .029 by 2 yields .015. Again, with small differences due to rounding at various stages of the "hand" calculations presented in the solution to the Problem in the Answer Key, the results are quite similar, and their interpretation will be the same.

If you want additional practice, use SPSS to analyze the data for Problem 3 and Problem 4 and compare the results to your calculations and those in the Answer Key.

Completion Items

1. independent	7. $S^2_{\text{Difference}}$
2. dependent	8. $S_{\text{Difference}}$
3. single sample	9. normal
4. differences between means	10. equal
5. pooled estimate	11. harmonic mean
6. weighted average	

Multiple-Choice Items

1. A	7. C
2. D	8. A
3. C	9. C
4. D	10. B
5. C	11. A
6. B	12. D

Problems

1.
Step 1: Restate the Question as a Research Hypothesis and a Null Hypothesis about the Populations
Population 1: Depressed people who participate in group therapy
Population 2: Depressed people who participate in individual therapy

Research Hypothesis: The number of activities of daily living reported by depressed people who undergo group therapy will be different from the number of activities of daily living reported by depressed people who undergo individual therapy.
Null Hypothesis: The number of activities of daily living reported by depressed people after group therapy will be no different from the number of activities of daily living reported by depressed people before group therapy.

Step 2: Determine the Characteristics of the Comparison Distribution
$M_1 = 16.00$; $S^2_1 = 24.00 / 7 = 3.43$
$M_2 = 17.50$; $S^2_2 = 38.00 / 7 = 5.43$
$N_1 = 8$; $df_1 = N_1 - 1 = 8 - 1 = 7$
$N_2 = 8$; $df_2 = N_2 - 1 = 8 - 1 = 7$
$df_{\text{Total}} = df_1 + df_2 = 7 + 7 = 14$

$S^2_{\text{Pooled}} = df_1 / df_{\text{Total}} (S^2_1) + df_2 / df_{\text{Total}} (S^2_2)$
$= 7 / 14 (3.43) + 7 / 14 (5.43)$
$= 1.72 + 2.72 = 4.44$

$S^2_{M1} = S^2_{\text{Pooled}} / N_1 = 4.44 / 8 = 0.56$
$S^2_{M2} = S^2_{\text{Pooled}} / N_2 = 4.44 / 8 = 0.56$

$S^2_{\text{Difference}} = S^2_{M1} + S^2_{M2} = 0.56 + 0.56 = 1.12$
$S_{\text{Difference}} = \sqrt{S^2_{\text{Difference}}} = \sqrt{1.12} = 1.06$

The comparison distribution will be a t distribution with 14 df.

Step 3: Determine the Cutoff Sample Score on the Comparison Distribution at which the Null Hypothesis Will Be Rejected
For a t distribution with 14 df, the cutoff sample score at the .05 level of significance will be ±2.145 for a two-tailed test.

For a t distribution with 14 df, the cutoff sample score at the .01 level of significance will be ±2.977 for a two-tailed test.

Step 4: Determine the Sample's Score on the Comparison Distribution
$t = (M_1 - M_2) / S_{\text{Difference}} = (16.00 - 17.50) / 1.06$
$= -1.50 / 1.06 = -1.42$ (If you reverse the means, t will be positive.)

Step 5: Decide Whether to Reject the Null Hypothesis
Since –1.42 is not more extreme than –2.145, the behavioral scientists will fail to reject the null hypothesis at the .05 level of significance and state that the results are inconclusive. Similarly, –1.42 is not more extreme than –2.977, so the behavioral scientists will fail to reject the null hypothesis at the .01 level of significance and state that the results are inconclusive. Based on these results, the behavioral scientists cannot recommend either type of therapy to increase the number of activities of daily living performed by depressed people.

The effect size for the study $= (M_1 - M_2) / S_{\text{Pooled}}$ [$S^2_{\text{Pooled}} = 4.44$ and $S_{\text{Pooled}} = \sqrt{4.44} = 2.11$]
$= (16.00 - 17.50) / 2.11 = -1.50 / 2.11 = -0.71$, which is a medium to large effect.

Compare your explanation to the explanation provided for Problem 4(c) in Set I of the Practice Problems in the text.

2.
Step 1: Restate the Question as a Research Hypothesis and a Null Hypothesis about the Populations
Population 1: Depressed people who participate in group therapy
Population 2: Depressed people who participate in individual therapy

Research Hypothesis: The number of activities of daily living reported by depressed people who undergo group therapy will be greater than the number of activities of daily living reported by depressed people who undergo individual therapy.
Null Hypothesis: The number of activities of daily living reported by depressed people after group therapy will be equal to, or less than, the number of activities of daily living reported by depressed people before group therapy.

Step 2: Determine the Characteristics of the Comparison Distribution
$M_1 = 15.87$; $S^2_1 = 131.73 / 14 = 9.41$
$M_2 = 18.35$; $S^2_2 = 147.88 / 16 = 9.24$
$N_1 = 15$; $df_1 = N_1 - 1 = 15 - 1 = 14$
$N_2 = 17$; $df_2 = N_2 - 1 = 17 - 1 = 16$
$df_{\text{Total}} = df_1 + df_2 = 14 + 16 = 30$

$S^2_{\text{Pooled}} = df_1 / df_{\text{Total}} (S^2_1) + df_2 / df_{\text{Total}} (S^2_2)$
$= 14 / 30 (9.41) + 16 / 30 (9.24)$
$= 4.39 + 4.93 = 9.32$

$S^2_{M1} = S^2_{\text{Pooled}} / N_1 = 9.32 / 15 = 0.62$
$S^2_{M2} = S^2_{\text{Pooled}} / N_2 = 9.32 / 17 = 0.55$

$S^2_{\text{Difference}} = S^2_{M1} + S^2_{M2} = 0.62 + 0.55 = 1.17$
$S_{\text{Difference}} = \sqrt{S^2_{\text{Difference}}} = \sqrt{1.17} = 1.08$
The comparison distribution will be a t distribution with 30 df.

Step 3: Determine the Cutoff Sample Score on the Comparison Distribution at which the Null Hypothesis Will Be Rejected
For a t distribution with 30 df, the cutoff sample score at the .05 level of significance will be –1.698 for a one-tailed test.
For a t distribution with 30 df, the cutoff sample score at the .01 level of significance will be –2.458 for a one-tailed test.

Step 4: Determine the Sample's Score on the Comparison Distribution
$t = (M_1 - M_2) / S_{\text{Difference}} = (15.87 - 18.35) / 1.08$
$= -2.48 / 1.08 = -2.30$ (If you reverse the means, t will be positive.)

Step 5: Decide Whether to Reject the Null Hypothesis
Since -2.30 is more extreme than -1.698, the behavioral scientists will reject the null hypothesis at the .05 level of significance and accept the research hypothesis that the number of activities of daily living reported by depressed people who undergo group therapy will be greater than the number of activities of daily living reported by depressed people who undergo individual therapy. However, -2.30 is not more extreme than -2.458, so the behavioral scientists will fail to reject the null hypothesis at the .01 level of significance and state that the results are inconclusive. Based on these results, the behavioral scientists can recommend individual therapy as a method to increase the number of activities of daily living performed by depressed people if they base their recommendation of the test of the null hypothesis at the .05 level. They cannot recommend either type of therapy to increase the number of activities of daily living performed by depressed people based on the test of the null hypothesis at the .01 level. [Remember that if you were actually conducting the study, you would select only one level of significance.]

The effect size for the study = $(M_1 - M_2) / S_{\text{Pooled}}$ [$S^2_{\text{Pooled}} = 9.32$ and $S_{\text{Pooled}} = \sqrt{9.32} = 3.05$]
$= (15.87 - 18.35) / 3.05 = -2.48 / 3.05 = -0.81$, which is a large effect.

3.
Step 1: Restate the Question as a Research Hypothesis and a Null Hypothesis about the Populations
Population 1: Employees who participate in counseling
Population 2: Employees who do not participate in counseling

Research Hypothesis: The job satisfaction of employees who participate in counseling will be higher than the job satisfaction of employees who do not participate in counseling.
Null Hypothesis: The job satisfaction of employees who participate in counseling will be the same as, or lower than, the job satisfaction of employees who do not participate in counseling.

Step 2: Determine the Characteristics of the Comparison Distribution
$M_1 = 38.00$; $S^2_1 = 40.00 / 8 = 5.00$
$M_2 = 35.00$; $S^2_2 = 68.00 / 8 = 8.50$
$N_1 = 9$; $df_1 = N_1 - 1 = 9 - 1 = 8$
$N_2 = 9$; $df_2 = N_2 - 1 = 9 - 1 = 8$
$df_{\text{Total}} = df_1 + df_2 = 8 + 8 = 16$

$S^2_{\text{Pooled}} = df_1 / df_{\text{Total}} (S^2_1) + df_2 / df_{\text{Total}} (S^2_2)$
$= 8 / 16 (5.00) + 8 / 16 (8.50)$
$= 2.50 + 4.25 = 6.75$

$S^2_{M1} = S^2_{\text{Pooled}} / N_1 = 6.75 / 9 = 0.75$
$S^2_{M2} = S^2_{\text{Pooled}} / N_2 = 6.75 / 9 = 0.75$

$S^2_{\text{Difference}} = S^2_{M1} + S^2_{M2} = 0.75 + 0.75 = 1.50$
$S_{\text{Difference}} = \sqrt{S^2_{\text{Difference}}} = \sqrt{1.50} = 1.22$

The comparison distribution will be a t distribution with 16 df.

Step 3: Determine the Cutoff Sample Score on the Comparison Distribution at which the Null Hypothesis Will Be Rejected
For a t distribution with 16 df, the cutoff sample score at the .01 level of significance will be $+2.584$ for a one-tailed test.

Step 4: Determine the Sample's Score on the Comparison Distribution
$t = (M_1 - M_2) / S_{\text{Difference}} = (38.00 - 35.00) / 1.22$
$= 3.00 / 1.22 = 2.46$ (If you reverse the means, t will be positive.)

Step 5: Decide Whether to Reject the Null Hypothesis
Since 2.46 is not more extreme than 2.584, the behavioral scientists will fail to reject the null hypothesis at the .05 level of significance and state that the results are inconclusive. Based on these results, the behavioral scientists cannot recommend counseling to increase the job satisfaction reported by employees after an industrial accident.

The effect size for the study = $(M_1 - M_2) / S_{\text{Pooled}}$ [$S^2_{\text{Pooled}} = 6.75$ and $S_{\text{Pooled}} = \sqrt{6.75} = 2.60$]
$= (38.00 - 35.00) / 2.60 = 3.00 / 2.60 = 1.05$, which is a large effect.

4.
Step 1: Restate the Question as a Research Hypothesis and a Null Hypothesis about the Populations
Population 1: Older adults who walk and participate in flexibility exercises
Population 2: Older adults who walk only

Research Hypothesis: The perception of well-being reported by people who walk and participate in flexibility exercises will be different from the perception of well-being reported by people who walk only.
Null Hypothesis: The perception of well-being reported by people who walk and participate in flexibility exercises will be no different from the perception of well-being reported by people who walk only.

Step 2: Determine the Characteristics of the Comparison Distribution
$M_1 = 6.67$; $S^2_1 = 49.33 / 14 = 3.52$
$M_2 = 5.00$; $S^2_2 = 34.00 / 10 = 3.40$
$N_1 = 15$; $df_1 = N_1 - 1 = 15 - 1 = 14$
$N_2 = 11$; $df_2 = N_2 - 1 = 11 - 1 = 10$
$df_{\text{Total}} = df_1 + df_2 = 14 + 10 = 24$

$S^2_{\text{Pooled}} = df_1 / df_{\text{Total}} (S^2_1) + df_2 / df_{\text{Total}} (S^2_2)$
$= 14 / 24 (3.52) + 10 / 24 (3.40)$
$= 1.43 + 2.04 = 3.47$

$S^2_{M1} = S^2_{\text{Pooled}} / N_1 = 3.47 / 15 = 0.32$
$S^2_{M2} = S^2_{\text{Pooled}} / N_2 = 3.47 / 11 = 0.23$

$S^2_{\text{Difference}} = S^2_{M1} + S^2_{M2} = 0.32 + 0.23 = 0.55$
$S_{\text{Difference}} = \sqrt{S^2_{\text{Difference}}} = \sqrt{0.55} = 0.74$

The comparison distribution will be a t distribution with 24 df.

Step 3: Determine the Cutoff Sample Score on the Comparison Distribution at which the Null Hypothesis Will Be Rejected
For a t distribution with 24 df, the cutoff sample score at the .05 level of significance will be ±2.064 for a two-tailed test.

Step 4: Determine the Sample Score on the Comparison Distribution
$t = (M_1 - M_2) / S_{\text{Difference}} = (6.67 - 5.00) / 0.74$
$= 1.67 / 0.74 = 2.26$ (If you reverse the means, t will be negative.)

Step 5: Decide Whether to Reject the Null Hypothesis
Since 2.26 is more extreme than 2.064, the behavioral scientist will reject the null hypothesis at the .05 level of significance and accept the research hypothesis that the perception of well-being of older adults who walk and participate in exercises to improve flexibility will be greater than the perception of well-being of older adults who walk only. Based on these results, the behavioral scientist can recommend the combination of walking and exercises to improve flexibility as a way to enhance perceptions of well-being in older adult populations.

The effect size $= (M_1 - M_2) / S_{Pooled}$ $[S^2_{Pooled} = 3.47$ and $S_{Pooled} = \sqrt{3.47} = 1.86]$
$= (6.67 - 5.00) / 1.86 = 1.67 / 1.86 = 0.90$, which is a large effect.

5.

Study	Effect Size	N	Tails	Power
(a)	Small	50	One	.11
(b)	Medium	40	One	.61
(c)	Small	40	Two	.09
(d)	Small	100	Two	.29
(e)	Medium	40	Two	.60
(f)	Large	20	Two	.69

6.

Study	Effect Size	Tails	Total N	Group N
(a)	Small	2	786	393
(b)	Medium	2	128	64
(c)	Medium	1	100	50
(d)	Large	1	40	20

7.

- A. *t* test for independent means
- B. *t* test for a single sample
- C. *t* test for a single sample
- D. *t* test for dependent means
- E. *t* test for dependent means
- F. *t* test for independent means

Chapter 10
Introduction to the Analysis of Variance

Learning Objectives
After studying this chapter, you should:
- Know when, and how to, conduct an analysis of variance.
- Be able to calculate the within-groups estimate of the population variance, the between-groups estimate of the population variance, and the F ratio.
- Be able to describe the F distribution and use an F table.
- Be able to define the normality and equality of variances assumptions underlying the analysis of variance and describe their implications.
- Be able to describe protected t tests.
- Be able to calculate effect sizes for studies requiring an analysis of variance and interpret these effect sizes using Cohen's conventions.
- Be able to use power tables for the analysis of variance.
- Be able to use sample size tables for the analysis of variance.
- Be able to describe the logic and advantages of factorial designs.
- Be able to interpret interaction effects using tables of means and graphs.
- Be able to describe the use and interpretation of two-way analysis of variance.
- Be able to interpret the results of analyses of variance as reported in research articles.

Basic Logic of the Analysis of Variance
Analysis of variance (ANOVA) may be used to compare the means of more than two groups. [Analysis of variance can be used to compare the means of two groups, but t is simpler and more straightforward.] The null hypothesis is that the means of three or more populations are equal, and the research hypothesis is that the means are unequal. Since the data being analyzed are collected from samples, the question is whether the observed differences are greater than would be expected by chance if the null hypothesis is true. While using variances to compare may seem confusing, think about the fact that a question about the way means differ can be conceptualized as a question about how the means vary. Also bear in mind that population variances can be estimated in two different ways, which will be described next.

Estimating the Population Variance from Variance within Each Sample
As was the case with the t test, population variances are estimated from sample data. Like t, analysis of variance assumes that the population variances are equal, which permits averaging estimates from each sample into a single pooled estimate called the **within-groups estimate of the population variance**. Remember that the within-groups variance is not influenced by whether the null hypothesis is true or false because it is the variance within separate populations. Thus, this variance can be attributed to chance factors like differences in the ways individuals respond to an experimental treatment or measurement error.

Estimating the Population Variance from Variation between the Means of the Samples
Since each sample mean is a number, the sample means of an experiment can be treated like the scores of individuals—that is, the mean of the means can be computed—and this mean can be used to estimate the variance of this distribution of means. The variance of this distribution of means provides another way to estimate the variance in the populations from which samples are drawn.

When the null hypothesis is true, all the populations from which samples are drawn have the same mean. However, samples drawn from identical populations will still have somewhat different means depending on the variation in the population. In addition, the greater the variation in a population, the greater the variation will be in samples drawn from the population, and the more likely the means of the samples are to be different. These expected differences between the means of samples permit calculation of the **between-groups estimate of the population variance**.

When the null hypothesis is not true, the populations have different means. The within-groups variation is still present, but since the research hypothesis is also true, the population means are different. Now variation among the means is not only due to the sources of variation that affect the within-groups estimates of the population variances, but also to the effects of the experimental treatment that have caused the population means to differ.

Comparing the Within-Groups and Between-Groups Estimates of Population Variance

Stated another way, when the null hypothesis is true, any variation among the experimental groups is attributable to variation within the groups. Therefore, the variation between groups and the variation within groups are, within the limits of sampling error, identical. Accordingly, the ratio between the two types of variance should be close to 1. However, when the research hypothesis is true, the observed variation between groups reflects both variation among individual scores and variation among means. In this situation, the between-groups variance should be larger than the within-groups variance, and their ratio should be greater than 1.

Considering the information just presented, examine the two datasets that follow.

Dataset 1: Weight loss in pounds

Exercise	Diet	Both Diet and Exercise
5	2	4
33	32	32
19	22	26
27	12	10
11	17	18
$\Sigma X = 95$	$\Sigma X = 85$	$\Sigma X = 90$
$M = 19$	$M = 17$	$M = 18$

Grand Mean = 18

Dataset 2: Weight loss in pounds

Exercise	Diet	Both Diet and Exercise
7	19	26
9	16	29
8	18	28
7	20	29
9	17	28
$\Sigma X = 40$	$\Sigma X = 90$	$\Sigma X = 140$
$M = 8$	$M = 18$	$M = 28$

Grand Mean = 18

Although the grand means of the two datasets are equal, the scores in Dataset 1 are quite variable compared to the scores in Dataset 2. Also, comparable losses are present in each group, for example, the participants whose data are entered in the first row of Dataset 1 lost 4, 2, and 5 pounds, while the participants listed in the second row lost 32, 32, and 33 pounds, respectively. On the other hand, the weight losses of participants in each group in Dataset 2 are within 2–3 pounds. Also, the group means in Dataset 1 reflect weight-loss differences of 1 pound; the group means in Dataset 2 reflect weight differences of 10 pounds. Thus, the ratio of the between-groups variance to the within-groups variance for Dataset 1 will be close to 1, but the ratio for Dataset 2 will be much larger. Concisely stated, the treatment had little effect on weight loss in the first instance, but a substantial effect in the second. This ratio is called the **F ratio**, and the question is how much larger than 1 does an *F* ratio have to be in order to reject the null hypothesis. As was the case with the *t* test, **F distributions** can be described mathematically, and **F tables** are available to determine how extreme *F* ratios must be to reject the null hypothesis.

Conducting an Analysis of Variance

In order to conduct an analysis of variance, three values must be calculated:
1. The <u>within-groups estimate of the population variance</u> is calculated using the usual method of estimating a population variance from sample data. If the sample sizes are equal, the variance estimates for the experimental groups (the samples) can be pooled by averaging. The formula is

$S^2_{\text{Within}} = (S_1^2 + S_2^2 + \ldots + S_{\text{Last}}^2) / N_{\text{Groups}}$, where

S_1^2 is the unbiased estimate of the variance of Population 1 based on the scores in the first experimental group, S_2^2 is the unbiased estimate of the variance of Population 2 based on the scores in the second experimental group, and S_{Last}^2 is the unbiased estimate of the variance of the population based on scores in the last experimental group. Remember that the value of each $S^2 = \Sigma(X - M)^2 / df$.

2. Calculating <u>the between-groups estimate of the population variance</u> requires two steps, first treating each mean as an individual number and then applying the usual formula for estimating a population variance. The formula is $S_M^2 = \sum (M - GM)^2 / df_{Between}$, where

M is the mean of each sample,

GM is the **grand mean**, that is, the overall mean of all scores or, when sample sizes are equal, the mean of the means—$GM = \sum M / N_{Groups}$, and

$df_{Between}$ is the **between-groups degrees of freedom**, that is, the number of groups minus 1 ($N_{Groups} - 1$).

The second step involves converting the estimated variance of the distribution of means to an estimate of the variance of individual scores by multiplying the variance of the distribution of means by the size of each sample. [This computation is the reverse of the earlier division of the variance of a population of individual cases by the size of the sample to obtain the variance of a distribution of means.] The formula is $S^2_{Between} = (S_M^2)(N)$.

3. The F ratio is the ratio of the between-groups estimate of the population variance to the within-groups estimate of the population variance. The formula is $F = S^2_{Between} / S_{Within}^2$.

When the F ratio has been calculated, it is compared to an F distribution to determine the probability that an F as large as the one obtained will occur if the null hypothesis is true. Since variances are squared numbers, they are always positive, and the ratio of two positive numbers cannot be less than 0. Most F ratios cluster around 1, but since the possibility of very large numbers cannot be eliminated, F distributions are skewed to the right.

Two degrees of freedom must be known to enter an **F table**.

The between-groups degrees of freedom, which is also known as the *numerator degrees of freedom*, or $df_{Between}$, is the number of groups minus 1. [$df_{Between} = N_{Groups} - 1$.]

The **within-groups degrees of freedom**, which is also known as the denominator degrees of freedom, or df_{Within}, is the sum of the degrees of freedom for all of the groups. [$df_{Within} = df_1 + df_2 + \ldots + df_{Last}$.]

Hypothesis Testing with Analysis of Variance

Suppose a health psychologist conducted a weight-loss program for morbidly obese people and obtained the data presented in the table in Step 4 of the hypothesis-testing procedure. (The table is placed in Step 4 so it will be easier to follow the calculations.) Use the five steps of hypothesis testing to determine whether there is a difference in the three weight-loss methods and whether the differences are statistically significant at the .05 and, for practice, the .01 levels of significance. In Step 4, show all calculations.

Steps of Hypothesis Testing

Step 1: Restate the question as a research hypothesis and a null hypothesis about the populations.

Population 1: People attempting to lose weight using diet alone

Population 2: People attempting to lose weight using exercise alone

Population 3: People attempting to lose weight using diet and exercise

Research Hypothesis: There will be a difference in the mean number of pounds lost by the three groups.

Null Hypothesis: There will be no difference in the mean number of pounds lost by the three groups.

Step 2: Determine the characteristics of the comparison distribution.

The study involves three groups of 10 participants each.

$df_{Between} = N_{Groups} - 1 = (3 - 1) = 2$

$df_{Within} = df_1 + df_2 + df_3 = (9 + 9 + 9) = 27$

The comparison distribution will be an F distribution with 2 and 27 df.

Step 3: Determine the cutoff sample score on the comparison distribution at which the null hypothesis should be rejected.

$F_{2,27}$ at the .05 level of significance = 3.36

$F_{2,27}$ at the .01 level of significance = 5.49

Step 4: Determine the sample's score on the comparison distribution.

Participant	Exercise	Diet	Diet and Exercise
1	21	67	78
2	54	62	50
3	26	57	55
4	21	68	62
5	28	58	56
6	57	70	77
7	52	58	71
8	37	59	53
9	26	68	79
10	47	50	69

$M_E = 36.9$
$M_D = 61.7$
$M_{D\&E} = 65.0$
$M_{Means} (GM) = 54.53$
$\Sigma(M - M)^2 = 471.85$
$S^2_M = \Sigma(M - GM)^2 / df_{Between} = 471.85 / 2 = 235.92$

$S^2_{Between} = (S^2_M)(N) = (235.92)(10) = 2359.23$

$\Sigma(X - M)^2_D = 1848.90$
$S^2_D = \Sigma(X - M)^2_D / df_D = 1848.90 / 9 = 205.43$
$\Sigma(X - M)^2_E = 370.10$
$S^2_E = \Sigma(X - M)^2_E / df_E = 370.10 / 9 = 41.12$
$\Sigma(X - M)^2_{D\&E} = 1120$
$S^2_{D\&E} = \Sigma(X - M)^2_{D\&E} / df_{D\&E} = 1120 / 9 = 124.44$

$S^2_{Within} = (124.44 + 41.12 + 205.43) / 3 = 123.67$

$F = S^2_{Between} / S^2_{Within} = 2359.23 / 123.67 = 19.08$

Step 5: Decide whether to reject the null hypothesis.
Since $F = 19.08$ is more extreme than 3.36, the psychologist will reject the null hypothesis that there is no difference among the three weight-loss methods at the .05 level of significance and conclude that the mean number of pounds lost by people using each of the three methods will be different. Since $F = 19.08$ is more extreme than 5.49, the psychologist will make the same decision at the .01 level of significance. [Remember that if you were actually conducting the study, you would use only one level of significance.]

Assumptions in the Analysis of Variance
As with the t test, analysis of variance assumes that scores in the populations are normally distributed and that the populations have equal variances. However, analysis of variance results are considered accurate when violations of its assumptions are moderate. A rule of thumb is that analysis of variance results are reasonably accurate when group sizes are equal and the largest variance estimate is no more than four to five times greater than the smallest. In the weight-loss example, the largest variance was calculated for the Diet group (205.43) and the smallest for the Exercise group (41.12). Applying the rule of thumb (205.43 / 41.12 = 4.99) indicates that while the ratio of the two variances is just within the limit, the psychologist may want to interpret the results cautiously, for example, mention this ratio in the discussion or verify the result with one of the tests described in Chapter 11.

Comparing Group Means
Rejecting the null hypothesis in an analysis of variance indicates that the population means are different. However, ANOVA does not indicate which specific population means are significantly different from each other. Considering the weight-loss example, on average the Exercise group lost 36.9 pounds, the Diet group lost 61.7 pounds, and the

Diet & Exercise group lost 65.0 pounds. The analysis of variance has indicated that there is a difference among the three means, and the most probable statistically significant difference is between the means of the Exercise and Diet & Exercise groups. The remaining questions are whether the difference between the Diet group and the Exercise group is statistically significant, which seems likely, and whether the difference between the Diet group and the Diet & Exercise group is statistically significant, which seems less likely. **Protected *t* tests** are *t* tests used to compare pairs of population means to detect those that are significantly different, and calculating *t* tests by the usual method will show that the means of the Exercise and Diet & Exercise groups are significantly different, as is the difference between the Diet group and the Exercise group. As might be expected, the difference between the Diet group and the Diet & Exercise group is not statistically significant. Such tests are considered acceptable by some statisticians because the overall ANOVA has indicated the presence of statistically significant differences between at least one pair of means. Most statisticians believe that additional protection in the form of tests like *Tukey's HSD test* is needed.

Effect Size and Power for the Analysis of Variance

The **proportion of variance accounted for (R^2)** is the measure of effect size for analysis of variance. R^2 is the proportion of the total variation of scores from the grand mean accounted for by variation between the means of groups. For example, how much of the variance in weight loss is accounted for (explained) by the different weight-loss programs? The formula is $R^2 = (S^2_{Between})(df_{Between}) / (S^2_{Between})(df_{Between}) + (S^2_{Within})(df_{Within})$. For the weight-loss example, $R^2 = (2359.23)(2) / (2359.23)(2) + (123.67)(27) = 4718.46 / 4718.46 + 3339.09 = 4718.46 / 8057.55 = 0.59$.

R^2 is also known as η^2, the Greek letter *eta* squared. R^2 can have a minimum value of 0 and a maximum value of 1, but values like the .59 obtained following the analysis of variance for the weight-loss data are rare. Therefore, Cohen's conventions for R^2 are .01 for a small effect size, .06 for a medium effect size, and .14 for a large effect size.

Tables are available for determining the power and effect size of studies in which the results are analyzed using analysis of variance. Practice using tables like those provided in the text will be provided later.

Factorial Analysis of Variance

Factorial analysis of variance is an extension of the analysis of variance procedures learned previously that permits flexible, efficient analyses by examining the effects of every possible combination of two or more variables on an outcome variable.

Basic Logic of Factorial Designs and Interaction Effects

As an example, suppose that an industrial/organizational psychologist has been hired to evaluate the effectiveness of an orientation program conducted for new employees of a large corporation as indicated by supervisory ratings after 6 weeks on the job. A secondary question is whether the program will be effective for employees who have held at least one full-time job, as opposed to employees for whom this job is their first full-time job. Therefore, the psychologist decides to randomly assign new employees to one of four groups, as shown in the table that follows:
1. Employees who attend the orientation program who have held a full-time job.
2. Employees who attend the orientation program who have never held a full-time job.
3. Employees who do not attend the orientation program who have held a full-time job.
4. Employees who do not attend the orientation program who have never held a full-time job.

		Previous Full-Time Job	
		Yes	No
Attend Orientation	Yes	Group 1	Group 2
	No	Group 3	Group 4

Thus, this **factorial research design** will enable the psychologist to examine the effects of two or more variables simultaneously by creating groups that reflect every possible combination of levels of the variables. One advantage of factorial designs is the efficiency that results from being able to examine the two variables at one time using the same participant pool, that is, without having to double the number of participants.

A second advantage is that factorial designs permit examination of the effects of combining two or more variables. For example, the psychologist will learn that employees in Groups 1 and 3 had the highest ratings, employees in Group 4 had the lowest ratings, and employees in Group 2 had intermediate ratings. In this case, the combination of attending the orientation session and having work experience appears to have had a special effect called an **interaction effect**, which occurs when the influence of one of the variables used to classify participants on the measured variable differs across the levels of the other classification variable.

The analysis of variance procedure learned earlier in the chapter is called **one-way analysis of variance** because the effect of only one variable—for example, method of weight reduction—is used to explain differences in weight loss. Since the design described in the preceding paragraph involves two potential explanatory variables—that is, attending the orientation program and previous work experience—it is a **two-way factorial research design**, and the results will be analyzed with a **two-way analysis of variance**. In the example of two-way analysis of variance, having had a full-time job and attending orientation divide employees into groups and are therefore called **grouping variables**, and they are also known as **independent variables**. In a two-way analysis, each difference between groups on one of the grouping variables is a **main effect**. In the example, the possible main effects are participation in the orientation program and prior full-time employment. Using these two variables, one interaction effect is possible. Thus, in any two-way design, experimenters can test for two possible main effects and one possible interaction effect.

Each grouping combination in a factorial design is called a **cell**, and each cell has a **cell mean**. The table that follows shows the hypothetical cell means for the orientation study.

		Previous Full-Time Job		Marginal Means
		Yes	No	
Attend Orientation	Yes	$M = 4.00$	$M = 3.33$	3.67
	No	$M = 4.00$	$M = 1.83$	2.92
Marginal Means		4.00	2.58	

Marginal means are the mean supervisory ratings for each of the grouping variables, and the four marginal means for the orientation example are shown in the preceding table. Since supervisory rating is the effect of interest in the example, it is called the **dependent variable**, or a variable considered to be an effect.

Recognizing and Interpreting Interaction Effects

Detecting interaction effects may be the primary purpose of a study. For example, the corporation may be interested in determining the usefulness of the orientation program for new employees who have prior full-time work experience. Statistically significant interaction effects can be described verbally, numerically, or graphically.

- Verbal descriptions of interaction effects can be made in terms of either variable, that is, the effect of participating in the orientation program on supervisory ratings depends on employment history, or the effect of employment history on supervisory ratings depends on participating in the orientation program.
- Numerical descriptions of interaction effects are determined by examining the pattern of differences in cell means. An interaction effect is present if the pattern of differences in one row is not the same as the difference in the other row. Equivalently, an interaction arises when the pattern of differences in one column is not the same as the difference in the other column. As will be shown later in the chapter, the interaction effect between attending the orientation program and having had a full-time job is statistically significant. Employees without previous full-time work experience who attended the orientation program received higher supervisory ratings than those who did not attend, while the supervisory ratings for employees who had previous full-time work experience were the same for employees who did and did not attend the orientation program. Such dissimilar patterns of cell means across rows or columns suggest the possibility of statistically significant interaction effects.
- Bar graphs are frequently used to depict statistically significant interaction effects. An interaction effect is indicated when the pattern of the bars in one section of the graph differs from the pattern in the other section. Main effects may also be detected from graphs in which the patterns of bars are dissimilar. For example, the statistically significant difference in supervisory ratings for employees with no previous full-

time work experience can be seen in the figure that follows. Employees who had not held a full-time job and who did not attend the orientation program had the lowest supervisory ratings, while there was little difference in the ratings for the other three groups.

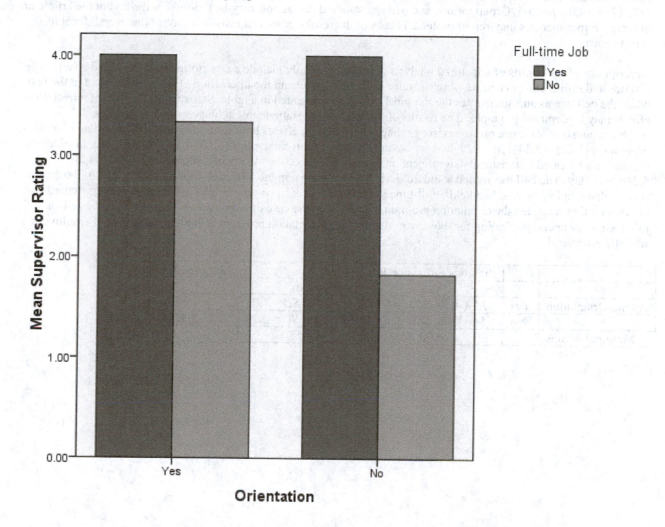

Remember that any combination of main and interaction effects can be statistically significant. As will be shown later in the chapter, both the main effects for participation in the orientation program and for having prior full-time work experience are statistically significant, as is the interaction between these two variables. However, both main effects could have been statistically significant and the interaction effect nonsignificant, or only one of the main effects and the interaction effect could have been significant.

Extensions and Special Cases of the Analysis of Variance

Three-way and higher factorial designs are straightforward extensions of two-way analysis of variance except that additional main effects and interaction effects are calculated. In the orientation example, the behavioral scientists might add educational level (for example, completed high school vs. more education) as a third variable in the design. In repeated-measures designs, participants are measured more than once, and the results are analyzed using *repeated-measures analysis of variance*. For example, supervisory ratings might be obtained after 1 month, 3 months, 6 months, and 1 year.

Analyses of Variance in Research Articles

The format for reporting one-way analysis of variance results is relatively standard and includes the F ratio, the df, and the significance level. For example, the results of the analysis of variance for the weight-loss example would be $F(2, 27) = 19.08$, $p < .05$. Group means, and perhaps standard deviations, may be reported in the text of the article or in tables. Experimenters may report protected t tests or the results of special tests that control the overall level of significance.

Descriptions of the results of a factorial analysis of variance usually include a description in the text and a table. The F ratios and information accompanying them for each main effect and the interaction effect are presented in the text, while the cell means and sometimes the marginal means are presented in a table. Statistically significant interaction effects may be depicted in graphs. The results of the orientation example might be described as follows.

A 2×2 analysis of variance on supervisory ratings showed main effects both for participating in the orientation program, $F(1,20) = 5.548$, $p = .029$, and for having had a prior full-time job, $F(1,20) = 19.795$, $p = .000$. In addition, the analysis revealed a statistically significant interaction effect between the two grouping variables, $F(1,20) = 5.548$, $p = .029$. The cell means and standard deviations are shown in the table that follows. Inspection of the means reveals that employees who had held a full-time job previously received very similar supervisory ratings, regardless of whether they attended the orientation program. However, in the case of employees who had not held a full-time job, the mean supervisory rating for those who attended the orientation program was higher than that of employees who did not attend.

		Previous Full-Time Job		Marginal Means
		Yes	No	
Attend Orientation	Yes	$M = 4.00$, $SD = 0.63$	$M = 3.33$, $SD = 1.03$	3.67
	No	$M = 4.00$, $SD = 0.63$	$M = 1.83$, $SD = 0.75$	2.92
Marginal Means		4.00	2.58	

Chapter Self-Tests

The test items that follow are based on the following scenario. The behavioral scientists studying the effects of different types of therapy on the number of activities of daily living performed by depressed people have concluded that individual therapy is more effective than group therapy in increasing the number of activities performed by their clients. Now the behavioral scientists are interested in learning how the number of hours of individual therapy affects the number of activities. Consequently, the behavioral scientists have formed three groups comprised of six clients each. Clients in Group 1 will receive 1 hour of therapy every 2 weeks, clients in Group 2 will receive 1 hour of therapy each week, and Group 3 will receive 2 hours of therapy each week.

Understanding Key Concepts in Chapter 10
Directions: Complete each statement using the word bank that follows. **You will use some words more than once.**

Word Bank: analysis of variance / between-groups estimate of the population variance / cell / cell mean /dependent variable / $df_{Between}$ / df_{Within} / F distribution / F ratio / F table / factorial analysis of variance / factorial research design / grand mean / grouping variable / independent variable / interaction effect / main effect / marginal means / one-way analysis of variance / proportion of variance accounted for / protected t tests / R^2 / $S^2_{Between}$ / S^2_{Within} / two-way analysis of variance / two-way factorial research design / within-groups degrees of freedom / within-groups estimate of the population variance

If the behavioral scientists want to compare the mean numbers of activities performed by the clients in the three groups, they will use an ANOVA, which stands for **(1)** _____. In order to calculate this statistic, the behavioral scientists will have to calculate the mean of a distribution of means that is called the **(2)** _____. Using this mean of a distribution of means, the behavioral scientists will calculate the **(3)** _____, the symbol for which is **(4)** _____. Next, they will calculate variances for each group. The average of these variances is called the **(5)** _____, the symbol for which is **(6)** _____. The test statistic, called an **(7)** _____, is equal to **(8)** _____ divided by **(9)** _____. In order to determine the statistical significance of the statistic, the behavioral scientists will use an **(10)** _____ as the basis for comparison and locate the cutoff sample score in an **(11)** _____. The behavioral scientists would locate the cutoff sample using 2 and 15 degrees of freedom, which are **(12)** _____ and **(13)** _____, respectively.

If the behavioral scientists find a statistically significant difference among the three group means, they will want to identify pairs of means that are statistically different. Since the analysis has indicated that at least one pair of means is significantly different, the behavioral scientists may determine which pair, or pairs, are significantly different using **(14)** _____. Effect size in analysis is measured as **(15)** _____, symbolized by **(16)** _____.

The test items that follow are based on the following scenario. The behavioral scientists studying the effects of different types of therapy on the number of activities of daily living performed by depressed people have concluded that more frequent therapy sessions are likely to increase the number of activities performed by their clients. Now the behavioral scientists are interested in determining the effect matching the gender of the therapist with the gender of the client on the number of activities performed. Consequently, the behavioral scientists have formed four groups comprised of five clients each. Group 1 will include women in sessions conducted by a female therapist, Group 2 will include women in sessions conducted by a male therapist, Group 3 will include men in sessions conducted by a male therapist, and Group 4 will include men in sessions conducted by a female therapist.

In the previous study, the behavioral scientists compared the mean numbers of activities performed by the clients in the three groups based on the number of therapy sessions. Since the number of therapy sessions was the only effect, they will use a **(17)** _____ analysis of variance. In the current study, the behavioral scientists may be interested in differences in the number of activities performed by depressed men and women, as well as whether the gender of the therapist has an effect on the number of activities performed. Therefore, the behavioral scientists are using a **(18)** _____, and they will analyze their data with a **(19)** _____. The effect of client gender on the number of activities is a **(20)** _____ effect, as is the effect of therapist gender. However, the behavioral scientists' primary interest may be in whether men or women respond differently to male or female therapists, which will be determined by examining the **(21)** _____. Since two variables divide the groups, the design is also called a **(22)** _____, and the appropriate analysis is a **(23)** _____. When the number of activities for each group are presented in a table, each group occupies a **(24)** _____, each of which has its own **(25)** _____. The means for male and female clients and for clients who have male therapists or female therapists are called **(26)** _____ means.

In this particular study, both the number of therapy sessions and the sex of the therapist and client are examples of an **(27)** _____, and the number of activities of daily living performed is the **(28)** _____.

Multiple-Choice Items

1. If the behavioral scientists want to compare the mean number of activities performed by clients in the three groups, they will use the
   - A. t test for independent means.
   - B. t test for dependent means.
   - C. analysis of variance.
   - D. Z test.

2. If the null hypothesis is true, the behavioral scientists can expect
   - A. the within-groups variances to be large.
   - B. the between-group variance to be large.
   - C. the ratio of the between- and within-groups variances to be approximately 10.
   - D. the within-groups variances to be small.

3. Since the sample sizes are equal, the behavioral scientists will be able to convert the estimated variance of the distribution of means to an estimate of the variance of the population of individual scores by
   - A. dividing the estimated variance of the distribution of means by the number of clients in each sample.
   - B. dividing the estimated variance of the distribution of means by the degrees of freedom in each sample.
   - C. multiplying the estimated variance of the distribution of means by the number of clients in each sample.
   - D. multiplying the estimated variance of the distribution of means by the number of degrees of freedom in each sample.

4. If the F ratio that results from an analysis of variance is statistically significant,
   - A. S^2_{Within} is larger than S^2_{Total}.
   - B. $S^2_{Between}$ is larger than S^2_{Total}.
   - C. S^2_{Within} is larger than $S^2_{Between}$.
   - D. $S^2_{Between}$ is larger than S^2_{Within}.

5. If an F ratio is not statistically significant, its value will be close to
   - A. −1.
   - B. 0.
   - C. 1.
   - D. $\sqrt{1}$.

6. In order to calculate F, the behavioral scientists will have to calculate the mean of a distribution of means, which is called the
   - A. harmonic mean.
   - B. grand mean.
   - C. ordinary mean.
   - D. pooled mean.

7. Remembering that there are six clients in each of the three groups, the number of degrees of freedom the behavioral scientists would use to locate the critical value of the statistic in a table would be
    A. 2, 15.
    B. 3, 15.
    C. 2, 18.
    D. 3, 18.

Items 8–10 are related.
8. Effect size in analysis of variance is calculated as the
    A. average difference between all possible pairs of means.
    B. proportion of variance accounted for.
    C. between-groups variance estimate divided by the within-groups standard deviation.
    D. estimated power of the study divided by the total number of degrees of freedom.

9. The effect size is also designated by
    A. F^2.
    B. R^2.
    C. N^2.
    D. Σ^2.

10. Yet another name for the effect size is
    A. alpha squared.
    B. beta squared.
    C. delta squared.
    D. eta squared.

11. If the behavioral scientists want to compare the mean numbers of activities performed by clients in three groups defined as having high, moderate, and low motivation, they will use a
    A. repeated-measures analysis of variance.
    B. 2×3 analysis of variance.
    C. one-way analysis of variance.
    D. factorial analysis of variance.

12. By examining the effects of client gender and therapist gender in the same study, the behavioral scientists are using a
    A. two-group randomized design.
    B. dichotomized design.
    C. repeated-measures design.
    D. factorial design.

13. The appropriate analysis for this study is a
    A. 1×2 analysis of variance.
    B. 2×2 analysis of variance.
    C. 2×3 analysis of variance.
    D. 2×4 analysis of variance.

14. The number of F ratios calculated in this analysis will be
    A. 1.
    B. 2.
    C. 3.
    D. 4.

15. If the clients perform more activities when their therapy is conducted by a therapist of the same gender, the behavioral scientists have detected
    A. an interaction effect.
    B. an omnibus effect.
    C. an effect of therapy.
    D. an effect of gender.

16. A statistically significant difference between the mean number of activities performed by clients who have a male therapist and clients who have a female therapist is evidence of
    A. an interaction effect.
    B. an omnibus effect.
    C. a main effect of therapy.
    D. a main effect of gender.

Use the table that follows to respond to Items 17–22

		Therapist		
		Male	Female	
Client	Male	$M = 11.0$	$M = 14.0$	$M = 12.5$
	Female	$M = 18.0$	$M = 21.0$	$M = 19.5$
		$M = 14.5$	$M = 17.5$	$M = 16.0$

17. Which of the following numbers is a cell mean?
    A. 11.0
    B. 12.5
    C. 16.0
    D. 17.5

18. Which of the following numbers is a marginal mean?
    A. 11.0
    B. 14.0
    C. 14.5
    D. 21.0

19. Which of the following numbers is the grand mean?
    A. 11.0
    B. 16.0
    C. 17.5
    D. 19.5

20. Which two means would contribute to calculation of an interaction effect?
    A. 11.0 and 18.0
    B. 12.5 and 19.5
    C. 14.0 and 21.0
    D. 14.0 and 18.0

21. The number of degrees of freedom for the effect of client gender is
    A. 1.
    B. 2.
    C. 3.
    D. 4.

22. The number of degrees of freedom for the effect of therapist gender is
    A. 1.
    B. 2.
    C. 3.
    D. 4.

23. The behavioral scientists want to see if the number of activities increases consistently during therapy or if there are some periods of decline, so they record the number of activities performed the day after the therapy session each week for 6 weeks. To determine whether the observed differences between depressed men and women were statistically significant, the behavioral scientists would use
    A. factorial analysis of variance.
    B. 2 × 3 analysis of variance.
    C. one-way analysis of variance.
    D. repeated-measures analysis of variance.

Problems

1. Remember that clients in Group 1 will receive 1 hour of therapy every 2 weeks, clients in Group 2 will receive 1 hour of therapy each week, and Group 3 will receive 2 hours of therapy each week. Use the five steps of hypothesis testing to determine whether the observed differences in the number of activities in the following table performed by the three groups are statistically significant at the .05 level of significance. Calculate the effect size for the study.

Student	Group 1	Group 2	Group 3
1	16	21	24
2	15	20	21
3	18	17	25
4	21	23	20
5	19	19	22

2. A behavioral scientist interested in the relationship between student perception of the probability of success in a statistics course and student motivation has administered an inventory designed to assess motivation in 18 students. The students have been divided into groups as follows: Students in Group 1 believe they are highly likely to succeed in the course, students in Group 2 believe they have an intermediate probability of success, and students in Group 3 believe they have little chance of success. Use the five steps of hypothesis testing to determine whether the observed differences in level of motivation in the following table are statistically significant at the .05 level of significance. Calculate the effect size for the study. Explain the results of the hypothesis-testing procedure to someone who is familiar with the t test for independent means, but not with analysis of variance.

Subject	Group 1 (High)	Group 2 (Intermediate)	Group 3 (Low)
1	9.0	3.5	4.5
2	8.5	5.5	5.5
3	6.5	6.5	6.5
4	7.0	3.5	8.0
5	8.0	4.5	5.5
6	5.5	7.0	6.0

3. Due to the increasing number of trials involving testimony by behavioral scientists, a professional organization of behavioral scientists asked judges, attorneys, jurors, and law enforcement officials to use a 10-point scale to rate the effect of such testimony on trial outcomes. The results are presented in the table that follows. Use the five steps of hypothesis testing to determine whether the observed differences in effectiveness ratings are statistically significant at the .01 level of significance. Calculate the effect size for the study.

Category	N	M	S^2
Judges	6	7.00	1.99
Attorneys	6	5.83	1.37
Jurors	6	7.83	1.37
Law Enforcement	6	3.00	3.61

4. What would be the power of the following planned studies if the experimenters plan to use analysis of variance and the .05 level of significance?

Predicted Effect Size	# of Groups	# of Participants in Each Group
Small	5	30
Medium	4	20
Medium	5	30
Large	3	30
Large	4	20

5. How many participants would need to be included in each group to have 80% power in each of the following planned studies if the experimenters plan to use analysis of variance and the .05 level of significance?

Predicted Effect Size	# of Groups
Small	5
Medium	4
Medium	5
Large	4
Large	5

6. The table of means that follows reflects the hypothetical results of a study using a factorial design to compare the level of stress reported by younger and older nontraditional students in lecture-based and computer-based courses. Assuming that any differences are statistically significant, create a bar graph like the one presented earlier with bars for course format and for student age, indicate which effects are present, and describe these effects.

		Student Age	
		Younger	Older
Course Format	Lecture-based	$M = 38$	$M = 28$
	Computer-based	$M = 28$	$M = 38$

7. The table of means that follows reflects the hypothetical results of a study using a factorial design to compare the new words learned by girls and boys in two reading programs, one using the phonics method and the other the whole-word method. Again, assuming that any differences are statistically significant, create a bar graph like the one presented earlier with bars for method and for student gender, indicate which effects are present, and describe these effects.

		Method	
		Phonics	Whole-Word
Gender	Girls	$M = 19$	$M = 15$
	Boys	$M = 16$	$M = 12$

8. The table of means that follows reflects the hypothetical results of a study using a factorial design to compare the level of anxiety reported by college students based on whether they attended a large or small high school and whether they attended a summer orientation program for incoming students. Again, assuming that any differences are statistically significant, create a bar graph like the one presented earlier with bars for method and for student gender, indicate which effects are present, and describe these effects.

		Orientation	
		Yes	No
High school	Large	$M = 20$	$M = 60$
	Small	$M = 15$	$M = 30$

Additional Practice: Complete any Practice Problems in Set I that your instructor has not assigned and compare your responses to those provided by the authors. Pay particular attention to the problems that require you to explain your results to someone who has never taken a course in statistics.

SPSS Applications

Application 1: Analysis of Variance
Open SPSS.
Analyze the data for Problem 1. Remember that SPSS assumes that all the scores in a row are from the same participant. In this study, there are 15 participants divided into three groups of five. Therefore, each of the 15 participants will be described by two variables, type of therapy and the number of activities of daily living performed. If "1" represents the group receiving individual therapy for 1 hour every 2 weeks, "2" represents the group receiving 1 hour of individual therapy each week, and "3" indicates the group receiving 2 hours of individual therapy each week, the first participant will be described by entering "1" in the top cell of the first column in the Data View window and "16" in the top cell of the second column to indicate that the participant underwent 1 hour of therapy every 2 weeks and performed 16 activities of daily living. The second participant will be described by "1" and "15," and the third by "1" and "18." When the two variables have been entered for the five participants in this group, repeat the process for participants who underwent 1 hour of individual therapy each week, using "2" to describe their therapy group. When the two variables for the five participants this group have been entered, repeat the process for Group 3, entering "3" in the first column. In the Variable View window, change the first variable name to "therapy" and the second to "adl" and set the decimals for both to zero.
〽️ Analyze.
〽️ Compare means.
〽️ One-Way ANOVA.
Since "therapy" is already selected, you can 〽️ the arrow to move the variable to the Factor window.
〽️ "adl" and 〽️ the arrow to move the variable to the Dependent List window, which instructs SPSS to conduct the analysis of variance on the number of activities performed.
The "One-Way ANOVA" window should look like Figure 1.

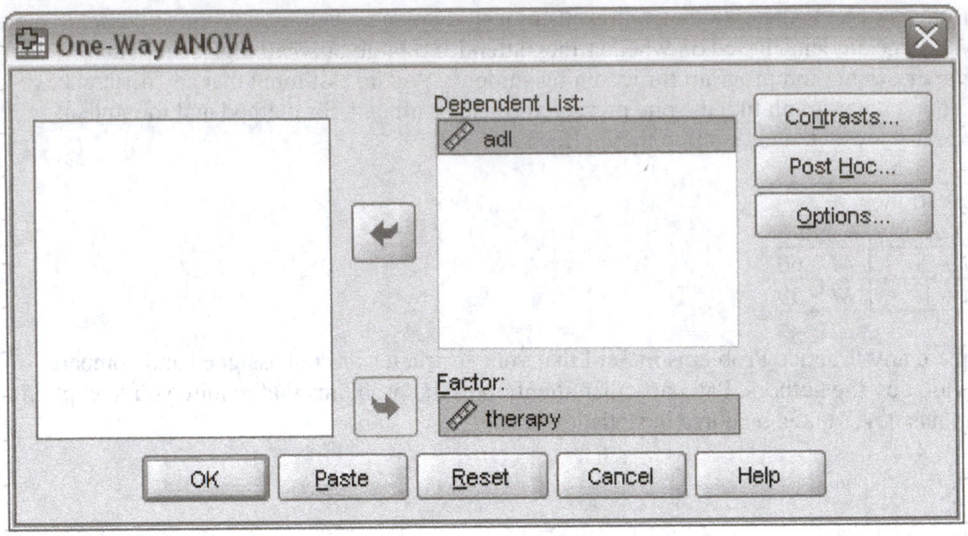

Figure 1

🖑 "Options" and click the box labeled "Descriptive" to obtain descriptive statistics.
The "Options" window should look like Figure 2.

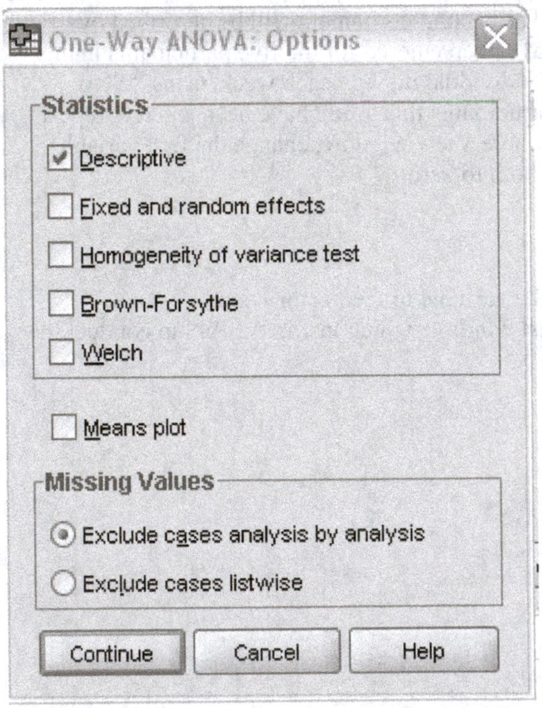

Figure 2

🖑 Continue.
🖑 OK.
The SPSS output should look like Figure 4 and Figure 5.

Descriptives

adl

	N	Mean	Std. Deviation	Std. Error	95% Confidence Interval for Mean		Minimum	Maximum
					Lower Bound	Upper Bound		
1	5	17.80	2.387	1.068	14.84	20.76	15	21
2	5	20.00	2.236	1.000	17.22	22.78	17	23
3	5	22.40	2.074	.927	19.83	24.97	20	25
Total	15	20.07	2.840	.733	18.49	21.64	15	25

Figure 4

ANOVA

adl

	Sum of Squares	df	Mean Square	F	Sig.
Between Groups	52.933	2	26.467	5.293	.022
Within Groups	60.000	12	5.000		
Total	112.933	14			

Figure 5

Comparing the descriptive statistics in Figure 4 with the means calculated in order to solve Problem 1 shows that the means are the same, and using the within-groups variances you calculated, you can verify the standard deviations. The first column in the ANOVA table in Figure 5 lists the types of population variance estimates needed for the calculation of F. Ignore the second column of the ANOVA table labeled "Sums of Squares." The third column contains the degrees of freedom for this analysis. The "Mean Square" column contains the population variance estimates $S^2_{Between}$ and S^2_{Within}, used to calculate the F ratio presented in the next column. Again, the between-groups mean square is slightly different, but the F ratio is the same. [Note that the mean squares are calculated by dividing a sum of squares by its degrees of freedom.] As you found when you solved Problem 1, the F ratio is statistically significant.

Chapter 10 Key

Completion Items

1. analysis of variance	8. $S^2_{Between}$	15. proportion of variance accounted for	22. two-way factorial research design
2. grand mean	9. S^2_{Within}	16. R^2	23. two-way factorial analysis of variance
3. between-groups estimate of the population variance	10. F disribution	17. one-way analysis of variance	24. cell
4. $S^2_{Between}$	11. F table	18. factorial research design	25. cell mean
5. within-groups estimate of the population variance	12. $df_{Between}$	19. factorial analysis of variance	26. marginal means
6. S^2_{Within}	13. df_{Within}	20. main effect	27. independent variable
7. F ratio	14. protected t tests	21. interaction effect	28. dependent variable

Multiple-Choice Items

1. C	6. B	11. C	16. D	21. A
2. A	7. A	12. D	17. A	22. A
3. C	8. B	13. B	18. C	23. D
4. D	9. B	14. C	19. B	
5. C	10. D	15. A	20. D	

Problems

1.

Subject	Group 1	Group 2	Group 3
1	16	21	24
2	15	20	21
3	18	17	25
4	21	23	20
5	19	19	22
$\sum X$	89	100	112
M	17.80	20.00	22.40
$\sum (X-M)^2$	22.80	20.00	17.20

Step 1: Restate the question as a research hypothesis and a null hypothesis about the populations.
Population 1: Depressed clients receiving 1 hour of individual therapy every 2 weeks
Population 2: Depressed clients receiving 1 hour of individual therapy every week
Population 3: Depressed clients receiving 2 hours of individual therapy every week

Research Hypothesis: There will be a difference in the mean number of activities of daily living performed by the three groups of clients based on the type of therapy each group receives.
Null Hypothesis: There will be no difference in the mean number of activities of daily living performed by the three groups of clients based on the type of therapy each group receives.

Step 2: Determine the characteristics of the comparison distribution.
The study involves three groups of five clients each.
$df_{Between} = N_{Groups} - 1 = (3 - 1) = 2$
$df_{Within} = df_1 + df_2 + df_3 = (5 - 1) + (5 - 1) + (5 - 1) = 4 + 4 + 4 = 12$
The comparison distribution will be an F distribution with 2 and 12 df.

Step 3: Determine the cutoff sample score on the comparison distribution at which the null hypothesis should be rejected.

$F_{2,12}$ at the .05 level of significance = 3.89

Step 4: Determine the sample's score on the comparison distribution.

$M_1 = 17.80$
$M_2 = 20.00$
$M_3 = 22.40$
$GM = (17.80 + 20.00 + 22.40) / 3 = 60.20 / 3 = 20.07$
$S^2_M = \Sigma(M - GM)^2 / df_{Between} = [(17.80 - 20.07)^2 + (20.00 - 20.07)^2 + (22.40 - 20.07)^2] / 3 - 1 = [(-2.27)^2 + (-0.07)^2 + (2.33)^2] / 2 = (5.15 + 0.00 + 5.43) / 2 = 10.58 / 2 = 5.29$

$S^2_{Between} = (S^2_M)(N) = (5.29)(5) = 26.45$

$\Sigma(X - M)^2_1 = 17.20$
$S^2_3 = \Sigma(X - M)^2_1 / df_1 = 17.20 / 4 = 4.30$
$\Sigma(X - M)^2_2 = 20.00$
$S^2_2 = \Sigma(X - M)^2_2 / df_2 = 20.00 / 4 = 5.00$
$\Sigma(X - M)^2_3 = 22.80$
$S^2_1 = \Sigma(X - M)^2_3 / df_3 = 22.80 / 4 = 5.70$

$S^2_{Within} = (5.70 + 5.00 + 4.30) / 3 = 15 / 3 = 5.00$

$F = S^2_{Between} / S^2_{Within} = 26.45 / 5.00 = 5.29$

Step 5: Decide whether to reject the null hypothesis.
Since $F = 5.29$ is more extreme than 3.89, the behavioral scientists will reject the null hypothesis at the .05 level of significance.

The effect size for the study = $R^2 = (S^2_{Between})(df_{Between}) / (S^2_{Between})(df_{Between}) + (S^2_{Within})(df_{Within}) = (26.45)(2) / (26.45)(2) + (5.00)(12) = 52.90 / 52.90 + 60 = 52.90 / 112.90 = 0.47$, which is a large effect.

2.

Student	Group 1 (High)	Group 2 (Intermediate)	Group 3 (Low)
1	9.0	3.5	4.5
2	8.5	5.5	5.5
3	6.5	6.5	6.5
4	7.0	3.5	8.0
5	8.0	4.5	5.5
6	5.5	7.0	6.0
ΣX	44.50	30.50	36.00
M	7.42	5.08	6.00
$\Sigma(X - M)^2$	8.71	11.21	7.00

Step 1: Restate the question as a research hypothesis and a null hypothesis about the populations.
Population 1: Students who believe they have a high probability of succeeding in the statistics course
Population 2: Students who believe they have an intermediate probability of succeeding in the statistics course
Population 3: Students who believe they have a low probability of succeeding in the statistics course

Research Hypothesis: There will be a difference in the mean motivation level of the three groups of students based on the students' perceived probability of succeeding in the statistics course.
Null Hypothesis: There will be no difference in the mean motivation level of the three groups of students based on the students' perceived probability of succeeding in the statistics course.

Step 2: Determine the characteristics of the comparison distribution.
The study involves three groups of six students each.
$df_{Between} = N_{Groups} - 1 = (3 - 1) = 2$
$df_{Within} = df_1 + df_2 + df_3 = (6 - 1) + (6 - 1) + (6 - 1) = 5 + 5 + 5 = 15$
The comparison distribution will be an F distribution with 2 and 15 df.

Step 3: Determine the cutoff sample score on the comparison distribution at which the null hypothesis should be rejected.
$F_{2,15}$ at the .05 level of significance = 3.68

Step 4: Determine the sample's score on the comparison distribution.
$M_1 = 7.42$
$M_2 = 5.08$
$M_3 = 6.00$
$GM = (7.42 + 5.08 + 6.00) / 3 = 18.50 / 3 = 6.17$
$S^2_M = \Sigma(M - GM)^2 / df_{Between} = [(7.42 - 6.17)^2 + (5.08 - 6.17)^2 + (6.00 - 6.17)^2] / 3 - 1 = [(1.25)^2 + (-1.09)^2 + (-0.17)^2] / 2$
$= (1.56 + 1.19 + 0.03) / 2 = 2.78 / 2 = 1.39$

$S^2_{Between} = (S^2_M)(N) = (1.39)(6) = 8.34$

$\Sigma(X - M)^2_1 = 8.71$
$S^2_3 = \Sigma(X - M)^2_1 / df_1 = 8.71 / 5 = 1.74$
$\Sigma(X - M)^2_2 = 11.21$
$S^2_2 = \Sigma(X - M)^2_2 / df_2 = 11.21 / 5 = 2.24$
$\Sigma(X - M)^2_3 = 7.00$
$S^2_1 = \Sigma(X - M)^2_3 / df_3 = 7.00 / 5 = 1.40$

$S^2_{Within} = (1.74 + 2.24 + 1.40) / 3 = 5.38 / 3 = 1.79$

$F = S^2_{Between} / S^2_{Within} = 8.34 / 1.79 = 4.66$

Step 5: Decide whether to reject the null hypothesis.
Since $F = 4.66$ is more extreme than 3.68, the behavioral scientist will reject the null hypothesis at the .05 level of significance.

The effect size for the study = $R^2 = (S^2_{Between})(df_{Between}) / (S^2_{Between})(df_{Between}) + (S^2_{Within})(df_{Within}) = (8.34)(2) / (8.34)(2) + (1.79)(15) = 16.68 / 16.68 + 26.85 = 16.68 / 43.53 = 0.38$, which is a large effect.

Compare your explanation to the explanation provided for Problem 3(c) in Set I of the Practice Problems in the text.

3.

Category	N	M	S^2
Judges	6	7.00	1.99
Attorneys	6	5.83	1.37
Jurors	6	7.83	1.37
Law Enforcement	6	3.00	3.61

Step 1: Restate the question as a research hypothesis and a null hypothesis about the populations.
Population 1: Judges
Population 2: Attorneys
Population 3: Jurors
Population 4: Law enforcement officials

Research Hypothesis: There will be a difference in the effectiveness of testimony by behavioral scientists based on the ratings of members of the four categories of court personnel.
Null Hypothesis: There will be no difference in the effectiveness of testimony by behavioral scientists based on the ratings of members of the four categories of court personnel.

Step 2: Determine the characteristics of the comparison distribution.
The study involves four groups of six members each.
$df_{Between} = N_{Groups} - 1 = (4 - 1) = 3$
$df_{Within} = df_1 + df_2 + df_3 + df_4 = (6 - 1) + (6 - 1) + (6 - 1) + (6 - 1) = 5 + 5 + 5 + 5 = 20$
The comparison distribution will be an F distribution with 3 and 20 df.

Step 3: Determine the cutoff sample score on the comparison distribution at which the null hypothesis should be rejected.
$F_{3,20}$ at the .01 level of significance $= 4.94$

Step 4: Determine the sample's score on the comparison distribution.
$M_1 = 7.00$
$M_2 = 5.83$
$M_3 = 7.83$
$M_4 = 3.00$
$GM = (7.00 + 5.83 + 7.83 + 3.00) / 4 = 23.66 / 4 = 5.92$
$S^2_M = \Sigma(M - GM)^2 / df_{Between} = [(7.00 - 5.92)^2 + (5.83 - 5.92)^2 + (7.83 - 5.92)^2 + (3.00 - 5.92)^2] / 4 - 1 = [(1.08)^2 + (-0.09)^2 + (1.91)^2 + (-2.92)^2] / 2 = (1.17 + 0.01 + 3.65 + 8.53) / 2 = 13.36 / 3 = 4.45$

$S^2_{Between} = (S^2_M)(N) = (4.45)(6) = 26.70$

$\Sigma(X - M)^2_1 = 10.00$
$S^2_3 = \Sigma(X - M)^2_1 / df_1 = 10.00 / 5 = 2.00$
$\Sigma(X - M)^2_2 = 6.83$
$S^2_2 = \Sigma(X - M)^2_2 / df_2 = 6.83 / 5 = 1.37$
$\Sigma(X - M)^2_3 = 6.83$
$S^2_1 = \Sigma(X - M)^2_3 / df_3 = 6.83 / 5 = 1.37$
$\Sigma(X - M)^2_4 = 18.00$
$S^2_1 = \Sigma(X - M)^2_4 / df_4 = 187.00 / 5 = 3.60$

$S^2_{Within} = (2.00 + 1.37 + 1.37 + 3.60) / 4 = 8.34 / 4 = 2.09$

$F = S^2_{Between} / S^2_{Within} = 26.70 / 2.09 = 12.78$

Step 5: Decide whether to reject the null hypothesis.
Since $F = 12.78$ is more extreme than 4.94, the organization will reject the null hypothesis at the .05 level of significance.

The effect size for the study $= R^2 = (S^2_{Between})(df_{Between}) / (S^2_{Between})(df_{Between}) + (S^2_{Within})(df_{Within}) = (26.70)(3) / (26.70)(3) + (12.78)(15) = 80.10 / 80.10 + 191.70 = 81.10 / 271.80 = 0.30$, which is a large effect.

4.

Predicted Effect Size	# of Groups	# of Participants in Each Group	Power
Small	5	30	.13
Medium	4	20	.43
Medium	5	30	.67
Large	3	30	.93
Large	4	20	.85

5.

Predicted Effect Size	# of Groups	# per Group
Small	5	240
Medium	4	45
Medium	5	39
Large	4	18
Large	5	16

6.

		Student Age		Marginal Means
		Younger	Older	
Course Format	Lecture-based	$M = 38$	$M = 28$	$M = 33$
	Computer-based	$M = 28$	$M = 38$	$M = 33$
Marginal Means		$M = 33$	$M = 33$	

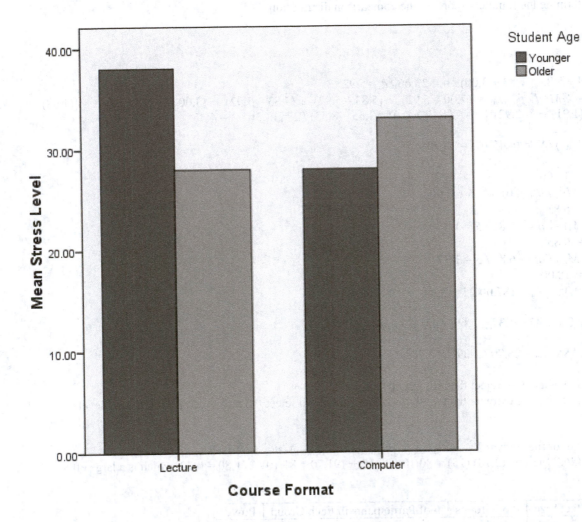

The graph with age on the horizontal axis simply reverses the order of the bars for method.

Since all marginal means are identical, no main effects are present. However, as the cell means and bar graphs indicate, an interaction effect showing that younger students experience lower levels of stress in computer-based courses, while older students experience lower levels of stress in lecture-based courses.

7.

		Method		Marginal Means
		Phonics	Whole-Word	
Gender	Girls	$M = 19$	$M = 15$	$M = 17$
	Boys	$M = 16$	$M = 12$	$M = 14$
Marginal Means		$M = 17.5$	$M = 13.5$	

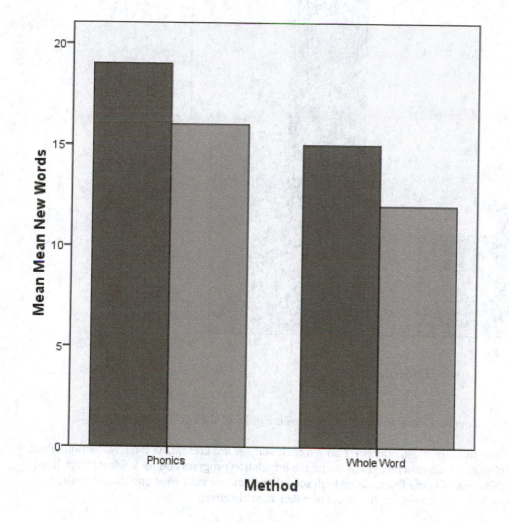

The graph with gender on the horizontal axis simply reverses the order of the bars for method.

Since all marginal means are different, main effects for both format and age are present. However, as the differences between cell means and bar graphs indicate, no interaction effect is present. Each combination learns the number of new words expected by knowing the level of each variable separately, that is, the difference between the cell means for each row and each column is three.

8.

		Orientation		Marginal Means
		Yes	No	
High school	Large	$M = 20$	$M = 60$	$M = 40.0$
	Small	$M = 15$	$M = 30$	$M = 22.5$
Marginal Means		$M = 17.5$	$M = 45.05$	

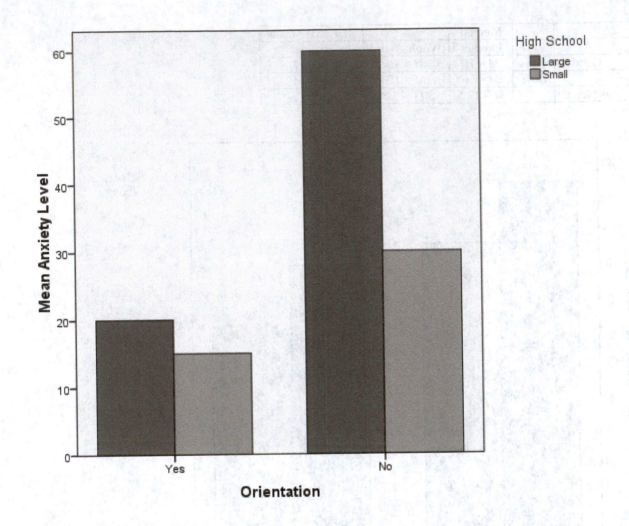

The graph with high school on the horizontal axis simply reverses the order of the bars for orientation.

Since all marginal means are different, main effects for both format and age are present, as is an interaction effect. The level of anxiety is higher for students who did not attend the orientation program and for students from large high schools, but the combination of being from a large high school and being unable to attend the orientation program is greater than would be expected from the effect of either variable alone.

Chapter 11
Chi-Square Tests and Strategies When Population Distributions Are Not Normal

Learning Objectives
After studying this chapter, you should:
- Know how to conduct a chi-square test for goodness of fit and interpret the results.
- Know how to conduct a chi-square test for independence and interpret the results.
- Be able to define the assumptions underlying the chi-square tests.
- Know how to calculate the effect size for chi-square tests for independence.
- Know how to use tables to estimate power for chi-square tests for independence.
- Know how to use tables to estimate sample sizes for chi-square tests for independence.
- Know when data transformations are appropriate.
- Know how to use the square-root transformation.
- Know how rank-order tests are conducted.
- Be able to interpret the results of chi-square tests, data transformations, and rank-order tests as reported in research articles.

Types of Chi-Square Tests
Chi-square tests are appropriate when analyzing *nominal variables*—variables in which the values represent categories. The purpose of the chi-square tests is to determine whether the observed frequencies of people falling into particular categories are significantly different from the numbers of people who would be expected to fall into these categories based on the null hypothesis, or on some theoretical basis. A **chi-square test for goodness of fit** is conducted when the observed frequencies of a single nominal variable are being compared to a known or theoretical distribution. In other words, they answer questions about how well an observed frequency distribution of a nominal variable fits an expected pattern of frequencies. A **chi-square test for independence** is conducted when the observed frequencies of two (or more) nominal variables, each with two or more categories, are being compared to the frequencies that would be expected by chance. Thus, it is a hypothesis-testing procedure used to determine the distribution of frequencies across the categories of one nominal variable that are unrelated to (independent of) the distribution across categories of a second nominal variable.

In chi-square tests, the **observed frequency** is the number of people actually in a particular category, while the **expected frequency** is the number of people in a category if the null hypothesis is true. Thus, hypothesis testing using chi-square tests involves determining whether the differences between the observed frequencies and the expected frequencies are greater than would be expected by chance. The formula for the **chi-square statistic (χ^2)** will make the logic of the tests clear.

$\chi^2 = \Sigma \, [(O - E)^2 / E]$ where
O represents the observed frequency in a category,
E represents the expected frequency in a category, and
Σ indicates the results of the operations in the brackets should be summed across all categories.

As has been the case with other tests, a distribution called the **chi-square distribution** reflects the distribution of the chi-square statistic when the statistic is due to chance. The shape of a particular chi-square distribution depends on the number of degrees of freedom, which is one less than the number of categories. Thus, the formula for determining the number of degrees of freedom for a chi-square test of goodness of fit is $df = N_{Categories} - 1$. [Remember that all chi-square distributions are skewed to the right because the chi-square statistic cannot be less than zero, but it can be very large.] Once the chi-square statistic has been calculated and the number of degrees of freedom has been determined, a cutoff sample score on the comparison distribution can be determined by consulting a **chi-square table**, and this cutoff score can be used to make a decision about the null hypothesis.

An Example
As an example of the chi-square test for goodness of fit, a group of behavioral scientists conducting group therapy sessions for people suffering from posttraumatic stress disorder is interested in the effects of the disorder on sleep patterns. A review of the research on the topic indicates that the behavioral scientists can expect 45% of the participants in their therapy sessions to experience insomnia, 15% to experience hypersomnia (excessive sleepiness),

10% to experience parasomnias (for example, nightmares), and 30% to experience no sleep disorders. If 60 people are attending therapy sessions, the expected frequencies would be 9 people experiencing hypersomnia, 27 experiencing insomnia, 6 experiencing a parasomnia, and 18 experiencing no sleep disorder. When surveyed, 6 people reported experiencing hypersomnia, 26 reported experiencing insomnia, 14 reported experiencing a parasomnia, and 14 reported experiencing no sleep disorder. The steps of hypothesis testing for conducting the chi-square test for goodness of fit would be as follows.

Steps of Hypothesis Testing

Step 1: Restate the question as a research hypothesis and a null hypothesis about the populations.
Population 1: People experiencing posttraumatic stress disorder like those participating in group therapy.
Population 2: People experiencing posttraumatic stress disorder who are experiencing sleep disorders in proportion to the percentages of disorders reported in previous research.

Research hypothesis: The distributions of people over categories of sleep disorders in the two populations are different.
Null hypothesis: The distributions of people over categories of sleep disorders in the two populations are no different.

Step 2: Determine the characteristics of the comparison distribution.
Since the behavioral scientists are interested in three types of sleep disorders and have included a category of people who are not experiencing any disorder, the analysis involves four categories. Applying the formula $df = N_{categories} - 1$, the comparison distribution is a chi-square distribution with 3 degrees of freedom.

Step 3: Determine the cutoff sample score on the comparison distribution at which the null hypothesis should be rejected.
At the .05 level of significance, the cutoff sample chi-square with 3 degrees of freedom is 7.815.

Step 4: Determine the sample's score on the comparison distribution.
Applying the formula for chi-square yields
$$\chi^2 = \Sigma \left[(O - E)^2 / E \right]$$
$$= \Sigma \left[(6 - 9)^2 / 9 \right] + \left[(26 - 27)^2 / 27 \right] + \left[(14 - 6)^2 / 6 \right] + \left[(14 - 18)^2 / 18 \right]$$
$$= \Sigma \left[(-3)^2 / 9 \right] + \left[(-1)^2 / 27 \right] + \left[(8)^2 / 6 \right] + \left[(-4)^2 / 18 \right]$$
$$= \Sigma \left[(9 / 9) + (1 / 27) + (64 / 6) + (16 / 18) \right]$$
$$= \Sigma \left[1.00 + 0.04 + 10.67 + 0.22 \right]$$
$$= 11.93$$

Step 5: Decide whether to reject the null hypothesis.
The chi-square statistic for the sample of 11.93 is more extreme than the cutoff sample chi-square of 7.815. Therefore, the behavioral scientists will reject the null hypothesis, accept the research hypothesis, and conclude that the types of sleep disorders experienced by participants in their therapy sessions are different from those experienced by participants in previous studies.

Chi-square Tests for Independence
The most common use of chi-square involves two nominal variables, each having two or more categories. For example, suppose the behavioral scientists expanded their study of sleep disorders by adding 20 participants and analyzed the types of disorders experienced based on whether a participant acquired posttraumatic stress disorder through exposure to combat or to a natural disaster. In this situation, a *chi-square test for independence* would be the appropriate analysis.

The table that follows is called a **contingency table**. These tables are used to show the distributions of two (or more) nominal variables and include the frequencies of the combinations of the variables in addition to the total frequencies. [This table is a 2 × 4 contingency table.]

Traumatic Event	Sleep Disorder Hypersomnia	Insomnia	Parasomnias	None	Total
Combat	4	11	17	8	40
Disaster	8	20	8	4	40
Total	12	31	25	12	80

The question to be answered by this analysis is whether there is any relation between the traumatic event that precipitated posttraumatic stress disorder and the type of sleep disorder experienced. If no relation is present, the proportion of people experiencing each type of sleep disorder will be the same, regardless of which type of traumatic event precipitated the posttraumatic stress disorder. (The reverse statement, that sleep disorders experienced by people who experienced combat or a disaster will be the same, is also true.) **Independence** is the term used to describe the situation in which there is no relation between the two variables.

In order to conduct a chi-square test for independence, the differences between the observed and expected frequencies for each combination of categories must be calculated. Each combination is reflected in one **cell** of the contingency table. Each expected frequency is based on the premise that the two variables are independent—that there is no relation between the variables. In the example, 50% of the people experienced combat and 50% experienced a disaster. Therefore, this same 50–50 division should be true for each of the four sleep disorders. To determine the expected frequency for any cell, compute each row's percentage of the total number of participants. Next, multiply its row percentage by the total number of participants in its column for each cell. As a formula, $E = (R / N)(C)$ where
E = the expected frequency for a particular cell,
R = the number of participants in the row containing the cell,
N = the total number of participants in the analysis, and
C = the number of participants in the column containing the cell. [This formula is especially useful when the row percentages are not equal.]
The expected frequencies for the example analysis are shown in parentheses.

Traumatic Event	Sleep Disorder Hypersomnia	Insomnia	Parasomnias	None	Total
Combat	4 (6.0)	11 (15.5)	17 (12.5)	8 (6.0)	40 (50%)
Disaster	8 (6.0)	20 (15.5)	8 (12.5)	4 (6.0)	40 (50%)
Total	12	31	25	12	80

The chi-square statistic is then calculated as before. However, the number of degrees of freedom is equal to the number of rows minus 1 multiplied by the number of columns minus 1. As a formula,
$df = (N_{Rows} - 1)(N_{Columns} - 1)$.

The steps of hypothesis testing for conducting the chi-square test for independence would be as follows.

Steps of Hypothesis Testing

Step 1: Restate the question as a research hypothesis and a null hypothesis about the populations.
Population 1: People experiencing posttraumatic stress disorder like those participating in group therapy.
Population 2: People experiencing posttraumatic stress disorder for whom having experienced combat or a disaster is independent of the type of sleep disorder they are experiencing.

Research Hypothesis: The types of sleep disorders reported by people who experienced combat are different from the disorders reported by people who experienced disasters.
Null Hypothesis: The types of sleep disorders reported by people who experienced combat are the same as the disorders reported by people who experienced disasters.

Step 2: Determine the characteristics of the comparison distribution.
Since the behavioral scientists have identified two groups of participants based on experiencing combat or a disaster, and have included three types of sleep disorders and a category of people who are not experiencing any disorder, the comparison distribution is a chi-square distribution with 3 degrees of freedom; $df = (N_{Rows} - 1)(N_{Columns} - 1)$ $= (2 - 1)(4 - 1) = (1)(3) = 3$.

Step 3: Determine the cutoff sample score on the comparison distribution at which the null hypothesis should be rejected.
At the .05 level of significance, the cutoff sample chi-square with 3 degrees of freedom is 7.815.

Step 4: Determine the sample's score on the comparison distribution.
Applying the formula for chi-square yields
$$\chi^2 = \Sigma\,[(O - E)^2 / E]$$
$$= \Sigma\,[(4 - 6)^2 / 6] + [(11 - 15.5)^2 / 15.5] + [(17 - 12.5)^2 / 12.5] + [(8 - 6)^2 / 6] + [(8 - 6)^2 / 6] + [(20 - 15.5)^2 / 15.5]$$
$$+ [(8 - 12.5)^2 / 12.5] + [(4 - 6)^2 / 6]$$
$$= \Sigma\,[(-2)^2 / 6] + [(-4.5)^2 / 15.5] + [(4.5)^2 / 12.5] + [(2)^2 / 6] + [(2)^2 / 6] + [(4.5)^2 / 15.5] + [(-4.5)^2 / 12.5] + [(-2)^2 / 6]$$
$$= \Sigma\,[(4 / 6) + (20.25 / 15.5) + (20.25 / 12.5) + (4 / 6) + (4 / 6) + (20.25 / 15.5) + (20.25 / 12.5) + (4 / 6)]$$
$$= \Sigma\,[0.67 + 1.31 + 1.62 + 0.67 + 0.67 + 1.31 + 1.62 + 0.67]$$
$$= 8.54$$

Step 5: Decide whether to reject the null hypothesis.
The chi-square statistic for the sample of 8.54 is more extreme than the cutoff sample chi-square of 7.815. Therefore, the behavioral scientists will reject the null hypothesis, accept the research hypothesis, and conclude that the types of sleep disorders experienced by participants whose posttraumatic stress disorder was precipitated by combat are different from the sleep disorders experienced by participants whose posttraumatic stress disorder was precipitated by a disaster.

Assumptions for Chi-Square Tests
Chi-square tests are not restricted by the assumptions that variables be normally distributed in populations or that they have equal variances when comparisons are to be made. However, no score can be related to any other score. Said another way, scores must be independent of all other cases. For example, chi-square would be inappropriate for comparing the proportions of sleep disorders experienced by the 80 people before and after some number of therapy sessions.

Effect Size and Power for Chi-Square Tests for Independence
Chi-square can be used to calculate the degree of association between two nominal variables. When chi-square is calculated from a 2 × 2 contingency table, the measure of association is the **phi coefficient**. The formula is

$\Phi = \sqrt{\chi^2 / N}$. Phi can have values from 0 to 1 and be interpreted like a correlation coefficient. Cohen's conventions for Φ are the same as those for r,
- .10 indicates a small effect,
- .30 indicates a medium effect, and
- .50 indicates a large effect.

Suppose the behavioral scientists identified 40 people experiencing posttraumatic stress disorder and obtained the data in the following table about the number who reported a sleep disorder and who did not report a sleep disorder. (Again, the expected frequencies are included in parentheses.)

	Sleep Disorder		
Traumatic Event	Yes	No	Total
Combat	14 (10.0)	6 (10.0)	20 (50%)
Disaster	6 (10.0)	14 (10.0)	20 (50%)
Total	20	20	40

$$\chi^2 = \Sigma [(O - E)^2 / E]$$
$$= \Sigma [(14 - 10)^2 / 10] + [(6 - 10)^2 / 10] + [(6 - 10)^2 / 10] + [(14 - 10)^2 / 10]$$
$$= \Sigma [(4)^2 / 10] + [(4)^2 / 10] + [(4)^2 / 10] + [(4)^2 / 10]$$
$$= \Sigma [(16 / 10) + (16 / 10) + (16 / 10) + (16 / 10)]$$
$$= \Sigma [1.60 + 1.60 + 1.60 + 1.60]$$
$$= 6.40$$

$\Phi = \sqrt{\chi^2 / N} = \sqrt{6.40 / 40} = \sqrt{0.16} = 0.40$, which is a medium to large effect size.

The extension of phi to larger contingency tables is **Cramer's Φ**. The only difference from phi is that the denominator involves multiplying N by the number of degrees of freedom for the variable with fewer categories. In the case of the analysis of the 2 × 4 table described earlier, $\chi^2 = 8.54$ and the traumatic event category had only $1df$ (2 – 1). Therefore, Cramer's $\Phi = \sqrt{\chi^2 / (N)(df_{Smaller})} = \sqrt{8.54 / (80)(1)} = \sqrt{8.54 / 80} = \sqrt{.11} = .33$, which is a medium effect size. Remember that Cohen's effect size conventions for Cramer's Φ depend on the number of degrees of freedom for the variable with the fewest categories. When one variable has two categories, the effect size conventions are the same as the conventions for phi. When the smallest number of categories is three or more, a table like Table 11-7 on page 384 in the text should be used.

Power and Sample Size for Chi-Square Tests for Independence
The power for a chi-square test for independence can be determined by referring to tables like Table 11-8 on page 385 in the text. For example, with a medium effect size, 100 participants would be needed to obtain 85% power if the analysis involved a 2 × 2 contingency table at the .05 level of significance. If only 50 participants had been included in the study in which the association between the two types of traumatic events and the four types of sleep disorders was determined, the power would have been 40% to detect a medium effect size at the .05 level of significance. The power would have increased to 71% if 100 participants had been included.

Table 11-9 on page 386 in the text can be used to determine the approximate number of participants needed to achieve 80% power for small, medium, and large estimated effect sizes at the .05 level of significance. For example, if the behavioral scientists had anticipated a medium effect size between the type of traumatic event (combat or natural disaster) and the presence or absence of a sleep disorder, they would have needed to plan to obtain responses from 87 participants to achieve 80% power. If the behavioral scientists had anticipated a medium effect size when determining the association between the two types of traumatic events and the four types of sleep disorders, they would have needed to plan to obtain responses from 121 participants to obtain 80% power.

Strategies for Hypothesis Testing When Distributions Are Not Normal
Assumptions in the Standard Hypothesis-Testing Procedures
As has been indicated, many standard hypothesis-testing procedures (*t* tests and analysis of variance) require that variables in populations
- be normally distributed and
- have equal variances.

The results of these tests are still reasonably accurate when violations of these assumptions are not serious. However, when distributions are clearly not normal or variances are clearly unequal, errors in interpreting the results of these tests are likely. Such situations may arise when a sample distribution has a floor or ceiling effect, or when one or more outliers are present.

Data Transformations
When characteristics of sample scores indicate that the population from which the sample was drawn may not be normally distributed, a **data transformation**, such as taking the square root of each score, may be performed to make the characteristics of the sample more like those of a normal distribution. The advantage of these transformations is that they permit the use of familiar statistical tests. Transformations are justified when they are applied to all scores in a dataset, not just to the scores in a particular group, because the order of the scores does not change.

Commonly used data transformations include:

- The **square-root transformation** is used to reduce the skew of a distribution that is skewed to the right (a positively skewed distribution).
- The *log transformation*, taking the logarithm of each score, is also used to reduce the skew of a distribution that is skewed to the right, but its effect is stronger than the square-root transformation.
- The *inverse and arcsine transformations* are also used.

Rank-Order Methods

A **rank-order transformation** provides another way to deal with the potential problems caused by non-normal distributions. Using this transformation involves changing the scores in a dataset to ranks, which results in a rectangular distribution instead of a normal distribution. Scores from any distribution can be transformed into ranks and analyzed using statistical methods called **rank-order tests**, or **distribution-free tests**. Such tests are also called **nonparametric tests** because they do not require estimation of population values (parameters) like the variance. Tests that do require estimation of population values, for example, *t* tests and analysis of variance, are called **parametric tests**. (Rank-order tests that correspond to the parametric tests presented in the text are presented in Table 11-13 on page 375.)

The basic logic of rank-order tests involves ranking all scores from lowest to highest, regardless of the group in which a score is found, adding the ranks in the group with the lower scores, and comparing the sum with a cutoff sample score from a table appropriate for the statistical test being used. The null hypothesis of a rank-order test is that the ranks of the experimental groups are equal.

The advantage of data transformations is that they permit use of familiar parametric tests. However, not all datasets can be adequately modified by transformation. On the other hand, while rank-order methods can be applied to any dataset,

- these tests may not be familiar,
- rank-order methods for complex analyses are not available,
- the logic does not hold when large numbers of scores have tied ranks, and
- the original dataset is distorted, which results in loss of information.

With respect to Type I and Type II errors, parametric tests are as good as, or better than, any of the alternatives when the assumptions of the test are met. When the assumptions of parametric tests are not met, the comparative advantages of data transformations and rank-order tests are not clear.

Chi-Square Tests in Research Articles

Experimenters generally report the observed frequencies for each category or cell, the degrees of freedom, the total number of participants, the chi-square statistic, and the level of significance. For example, the results of the chi-square test for goodness of fit between the proportions of people experiencing posttraumatic stress disorder in the behavioral scientists' group therapy sessions and the proportions reported in previous research might be reported as $\chi^2 (3, N = 60) = 11.93, p < .05$. A report of the 2×4 chi-square test for independence examining the independence of the four types of sleep disorders based on whether a participant acquired posttraumatic stress disorder through exposure to combat or to a natural disaster would begin with a description of the categories followed by the results of the chi-square test, $\chi^2 (3, N = 80) = 8.54, p < .05$. Reports may or may not include an estimate of effect size, but these estimates can be calculated from the information given.

Data transformations are typically described just before the description of the statistical analysis in the Results section. Rank-order tests are described in the same way as the parametric tests presented earlier.

Chapter Self-Tests

The test items that follow are based on the following scenario. A group of behavioral scientists conducting sessions for students to help them learn to deal with conflicts more effectively has administered an inventory that will indicate whether a student deals with conflict primarily by responding aggressively, manipulatively, passively, or assertively.

Understanding Key Terms in Chapter 11

Directions: Using the word bank that follows, complete each statement.
Word Bank: cell / chi-square distribution / chi-square statistic / chi-square table / chi-square test for goodness of fit / chi-square test for independence / chi-square tests / contingency table / Cramer's phi / data transformation / distribution-free tests / expected frequency / independence / nonparametric tests / observed frequency / parametric tests / phi coefficient / rank-order tests / rank-order transformation / square-root transformation / χ^2

If the behavioral scientists are interested in determining whether the distribution of students across the four ways of dealing with conflict agrees with the distribution the behavioral scientists expect, the behavioral scientists will conduct a **(1)** _____. If the behavioral scientists are also interested in determining whether students who have been suspended from school use different methods of conflict resolution than students who have not been suspended, they will conduct a **(2)** _____. The general name for tests used when one or more variables are nominal is the **(3)** _____. When conducting these tests, the behavioral scientists will first determine the number of students who use each of the four methods of dealing with conflict. This number is the **(4)** _____, and it will be compared to the number of students that would be expected to use each method if the null hypothesis is true. This latter number is the **(5)** _____. When the difference between these two types of numbers is weighted and summed across all the categories in a particular analysis, the result is a **(6)** _____ which is symbolized by **(7)** _____. In order to determine whether their result could have occurred by chance, the behavioral scientists will use a **(8)** _____. To identify the appropriate cutoff sample score, the behavioral scientists will refer to a **(9)** _____.

In order to be sure that the numbers of students in any category, or combination of categories, as well as the total numbers of students across categories, is clear, the behavioral scientists will organize their data in a **(10)** _____. If the behavioral scientists find that 10 of 40 students primarily respond to conflict aggressively, 10 manipulatively, 15 passively, and 5 assertively, each number will be shown in a **(11)** _____. If the behavioral scientists conduct a test to see if there is any relationship between being suspended from school and the method of conflict resolution, they will be conducting a test of **(12)** _____ between the two variables. If the behavioral scientists have conducted an analysis to see if there is an association between being suspended from school and responding either assertively or passively to a particular type of conflict, they can estimate their effect size using the **(13)** _____. If the behavioral scientists have conducted an analysis to see if there is an association between being suspended from school and all four ways of responding to a particular type of conflict, they can estimate their effect size using **(14)** _____.

The previous analyses using the *t* tests and analysis of variance assumed that the variables being compared were normally distributed in the population and had equal variances. Therefore, these tests are called **(15)** _____. Since the outlying scores observed by the psychologists are high scores, the distributions of scores are skewed to the right. Due to the nature of their data, the psychologists decide to adjust the scores so that the distributions appear more like normal distributions by making a **(16)** _____. With a dataset that is skewed to the right, an adjustment that often works well is a **(17)** _____. If the psychologists arrange the scores in order from lowest to highest, they will be making a **(18)** _____. One advantage of this adjustment is that the psychologists could use the familiar statistical tests used earlier. Alternatively, the adjustment would permit the use of different tests called **(19)** _____. Since the transformation results in a rectangular distribution, the psychologists do not need to estimate values like the population variance. Therefore, these tests are called **(20)** _____. Since the shape of the score distribution does affect the results of the analysis, these tests are also called **(21)** _____.

Multiple-Choice Items

1. Which pair of variables would the behavioral scientists analyze using a chi-square test?
   A. Anxiety and self-esteem scores
   B. GPA and class rank
   C. Conflict-resolution style and self-esteem
   D. Being suspended from school and conflict-resolution style

2. In which of the following situations would the behavioral scientists conduct a chi-square test for goodness of fit?
   A. If they want to determine whether there is an association between method of conflict resolution and having been suspended from school.
   B. If they want to determine whether the same proportions of students use each method of conflict resolution.
   C. If they want to determine whether the method of conflict resolution and academic success are independent.
   D. If they have used Cramer's Φ to estimate the effect size of the chi-square test.

3. If the behavioral scientists find that there is no association between the method of conflict resolution and academic success,
   A. the variables are said to be independent.
   B. the analysis will yield a chi-square statistic much larger than 1.00.
   C. the analysis will have a large effect size.
   D. the variables will be contingent on each other.

4. Chi-square distributions are
   A. rectangular.
   B. symmetrical.
   C. skewed to the left.
   D. skewed to the right.

5. Values of the chi-square statistic
   A. can be negative.
   B. are normally distributed.
   C. can be very large.
   D. are unweighted.

Items 6–12 are based on the following scenario and table.
The behavioral scientists have surveyed a group of 20 students referred for causing behavior problems and obtained the following results.

Conflict Resolution			
Suspension from School	Assertive	Other	Total
Yes	1 (3.5)	9 (6.5)	10 (50%)
No	6 (3.5)	4 (6.5)	10 (50%)
Total	7	13	20

6. This type of table is called a
   A. frequency table.
   B. grouped frequency table.
   C. chi-square table.
   D. contingency table.

7. The square in the table indicating that one student who used assertive methods of conflict resolution had been suspended from school is an example of
   A. a cell.
   B. a contingency.
   C. an observed frequency.
   D. an expected frequency.

8. In the square in the table indicating that nine students who used other methods of conflict resolution had been suspended for school, 9 is the
   A. cell mean.
   B. expected frequency.
   C. observed frequency.
   D. partial chi-square.

9. In the same square, 6.5 is the
   A. cell mean.
   B. expected frequency.
   C. observed frequency.
   D. partial chi-square.

10. The value of 6.5 was obtained using
   A. $(R / C)(N)$.
   B. $(N / R)(C)$.
   C. $(R / C)(R)$.
   D. $(R / N)(C)$.

11. The effect size for this table should be estimated by calculating
   A. X.
   B. B.
   C. Φ.
   D. η.

12. If the category labeled "Other" is expanded to show the three methods of conflict resolution it includes, the effect size should be estimated by calculating
   A. Cramer's Φ.
   B. Cramer's X.
   C. Pearson's B.
   D. Pearson's X.

Items 13–14 are related.
13. The psychologists have examined a frequency distribution of their data and note that the distribution appears to be slightly skewed to the right. The general term for the adjustment they can make to reduce the skew so that the distribution is more like a normal distribution is called
   A. an arcsine transformation.
   B. a data transformation.
   C. an inverse transformation.
   D. a square-root transformation.

14. A more specific adjustment they can make to reduce the skew so that the distribution is more like a normal distribution is called
   A. an arcsine transformation.
   B. an inverse transformation.
   C. a log transformation.
   D. a square-root transformation.

Items 15–18 are related.
15. Another alternative available to the psychologists is to arrange the scores in order from the lowest to the highest, in which case, they will be making
   A. an arcsine transformation.
   B. a rank-order transformation.
   C. a log transformation.
   D. an inverse transformation.

16. The assumptions of the tests the psychologists have used previously are not applicable because the resulting distribution is
    A. only slightly skewed.
    B. bimodal.
    C. normal.
    D. rectangular.

17. The hypothesis-testing procedures based on this type of adjustment are called
    A. reflective tests.
    B. parametric tests.
    C. nonparametric tests.
    D. error-free tests.

18. Another name for these hypothesis-testing procedures is
    A. parametric tests.
    B. distribution-free tests.
    C. inverse tests.
    D. error-free tests.

19. The hypothesis-testing procedures the psychologists have used previously depend on assumptions about the characteristics of the population distribution and are called
    A. reflective tests.
    B. nonparametric tests.
    C. error-free tests.
    D. parametric tests.

Problems

1. The table that follows includes the primary method of conflict resolution used by 20 students.

Method	Aggressive	Manipulative	Passive	Assertive
N of Students	8	2	2	8

(a) Following the five steps of hypothesis testing, conduct the appropriate chi-square test to determine whether the observed frequencies are significantly different from the frequencies expected by chance at the .05 level of significance. (b) Explain your response to someone who has never had a course in statistics.

2. Next, the behavioral scientists categorized the students based on the primary method of conflict resolution used and whether the student had been suspended from school for misbehavior. These data are presented in the table that follows.

		Method			
Suspended	Aggressive	Manipulative	Passive	Assertive	Total
Yes	7	1	1	1	10
No	1	1	1	7	10
Total	8	2	2	8	20

(a) Following the five steps of hypothesis testing, conduct the appropriate chi-square test to determine whether the observed frequencies are significantly different from the frequencies expected by chance at the .05 level of significance. (b) Calculate the effect size. (c) Explain your response to someone who has never had a course in statistics.

3. Believing that assertiveness is the most effective method of conflict resolution, the behavioral scientists categorized students so that the aggressive, manipulative, and passive categories were combined. These data are presented in the table that follows.

Conflict Resolution

Suspension from School	Assertive	Other	Total
Yes	1	9	10
No	6	4	10
Total	7	13	20

(a) Following the five steps of hypothesis testing, conduct the appropriate chi-square test to determine whether the observed frequencies are significantly different from the frequencies expected by chance at the .05 level of significance. (b) Calculate the effect size.

4. A school psychologist interested in the attentiveness of kindergarten children asked teachers to place children in one of three categories: very attentive, normally attentive, and generally inattentive. The teacher ratings are shown in the following table.

Rating	Very Attentive	Normally Attentive	Generally Inattentive
N of Students	16	24	20

Following the five steps of hypothesis testing and using the .05 level of significance, conduct the chi-square test that would enable the psychologist to determine whether more children were placed in any one category than would be expected by chance.

5. The school psychologist then divided the students into groups of older and younger students. (a) Following the five steps of hypothesis testing and using the .05 level of significance, conduct the chi-square test that would enable the psychologist to determine whether age and attentiveness are independent. (b) Calculate the effect size.

Age	Attentiveness Very Attentive	Normally Attentive	Generally Inattentive	Total
Younger	9	14	7	30
Older	7	10	13	30
Total	16	24	20	60

6. What is the effect size for the studies included in the table that follows?

Study	N	Chi-square	Design
(a)	60	12.00	2×2
(b)	80	12.00	2×4
(c)	60	12.00	3×3
(d)	80	12.00	2×2
(e)	120	12.00	2×2

7. What is the power of the planned studies listed in the table that follows at the .05 level of significance?

Study	Predicted Effect Size	Design	N
(a)	Medium	2×2	50
(b)	Large	2×4	50
(c)	Small	3×3	100
(d)	Medium	2×2	100
(e)	Large	2×2	200

8. Approximately how many participants would be needed for each of the studies in the table that follows to have 80% power at the .05 level of significance?

Study	Predicted Effect Size	Design
(a)	Medium	2×3
(b)	Large	2×4
(c)	Small	3×3
(d)	Large	2×5
(e)	Large	3×3

9. Calculate a square-root transformation, rounding each square root to one decimal place, on the scores below and explain the effect of the transformation on the scores.
(a) Stress scores: 30, 34, 71, 36, 62
(b) Anxiety scores: 36, 58, 39, 41, 38
(c) Attentiveness ratings: 8, 10, 2, 9, 7

10. Make a rank-order transformation of each of the five datasets that follow.
(a) Stress scores: 30, 34, 71, 36, 62
(b) Self-esteem scores: 36, 34, 35, 39, 33
(c) Depression scores: 10, 12, 15, 8, 11, 12, 7, 14, 8
(d) Anxiety scores: 36, 58, 39, 41, 38
(e) Attentiveness ratings: 8, 10, 2, 9, 7

11. A psychologist divided a group of 12 students into two groups of six students each. One group underwent a training program designed to help them view their surroundings in more creative ways, while the second group heard a lecture about creative thinking. After the sessions, the students in the two groups made the following scores on a creativity test.
Training Group: 16, 14, 15, 17, 16, 24
Lecture Group: 10, 12, 14, 11, 13, 18
(a) What is the most likely reason that a data transformation may clarify analysis of this dataset? (b) Conduct a t test for independent means on the actual creativity scores. (c) Transform the data using a square-root transformation and conduct a t test for independent means on the transformed data. (d) Transform the data using a rank-transformation and conduct a t test for independent means on the transformed data. (e) Compare the results of the three analyses. (f) Explain what you have done to someone who is familiar with the t test for independent means, but not with data transformations.

12. A behavioral scientist interested in the effects of three methods of treating test anxiety has randomly assigned five students to a group that will receive counseling, five students to a group that will be taught to use a relaxation technique, and five students to a group that will be taught to use the relaxation technique in the rooms where they take tests. The test anxiety scores for the three groups at the conclusion of the study follow.
Counseling: 30, 29, 24, 26, 22
Relaxation: 27, 25, 28, 20, 16
Relaxation in setting: 23, 20, 21, 19, 12
(a) What is the most likely reason that a data transformation may clarify analysis of this dataset? (b) Conduct an analysis of variance using the actual scores. (c) Transform the data using a square-root transformation and conduct an analysis of variance on the transformed data. (d) Transform the data using a rank-transformation and conduct an analysis of variance on the transformed data. (e) Compare the results of the three analyses. (f) Explain what you have done to someone who is familiar with analysis of variance but not with data transformations.

Additional Practice: Complete any Practice Problems in Set I that your instructor has not assigned and compare your responses to those provided by the authors. Pay particular attention to the problems that require you to explain your results to someone who has never taken a course in statistics.

SPSS Applications

Application 1: Chi-Square Test for Goodness of Fit
Open SPSS.

A dataset based on Problem 1 is shown in Figure 1. Remember that SPSS assumes that all the scores in a row are from the same participant. In this study, there are 20 students, some of whom have been suspended for misbehavior. The primary conflict-resolution style used by each student is also entered. [Ignore the first variable in this analysis.] When you have entered the data for all 20 students, move to the Variable View window and change the first variable name to "suspend" and the second to "style." You can enter "Suspended" and "Resolution Style," or similar labels in the Label column for clarity if you wish. Set the number of decimals for both variables to zero.

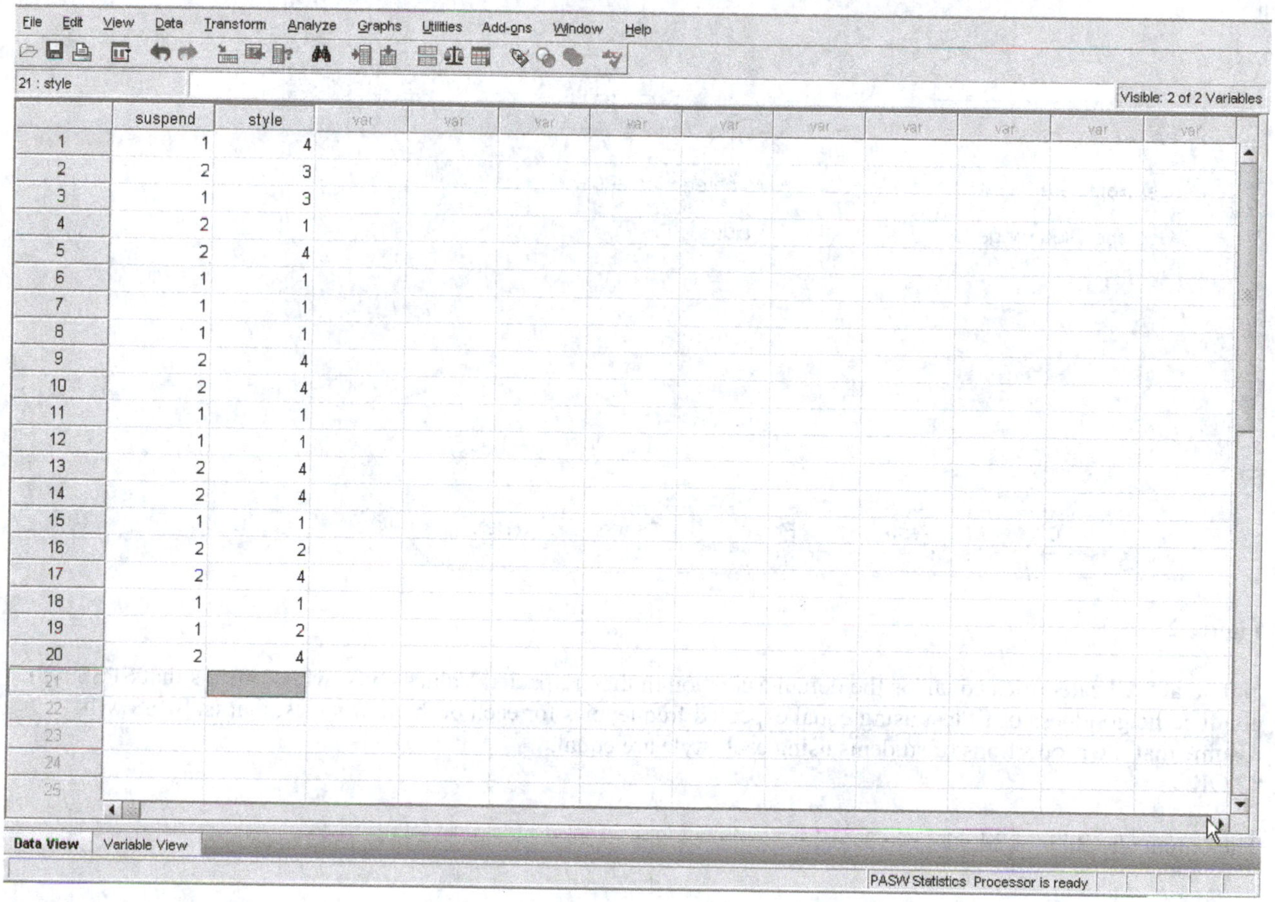

	suspend	style
1	1	4
2	2	3
3	1	3
4	2	1
5	2	4
6	1	1
7	1	1
8	1	1
9	2	4
10	2	4
11	1	1
12	1	1
13	2	4
14	2	4
15	1	1
16	2	2
17	2	4
18	1	1
19	1	2
20	2	4

Figure 1

🖰 Analyze.

🖰 Non-Parametric Tests and 🖰 Chi-Square.

🖰 the variable "style" and then 🖰 the arrow next to the box labeled "Test Variable List" to indicate that the chi-square test for goodness of fit should be conducted on the conflict-resolution style variable.

The Chi-Square Test window should look like Figure 2.

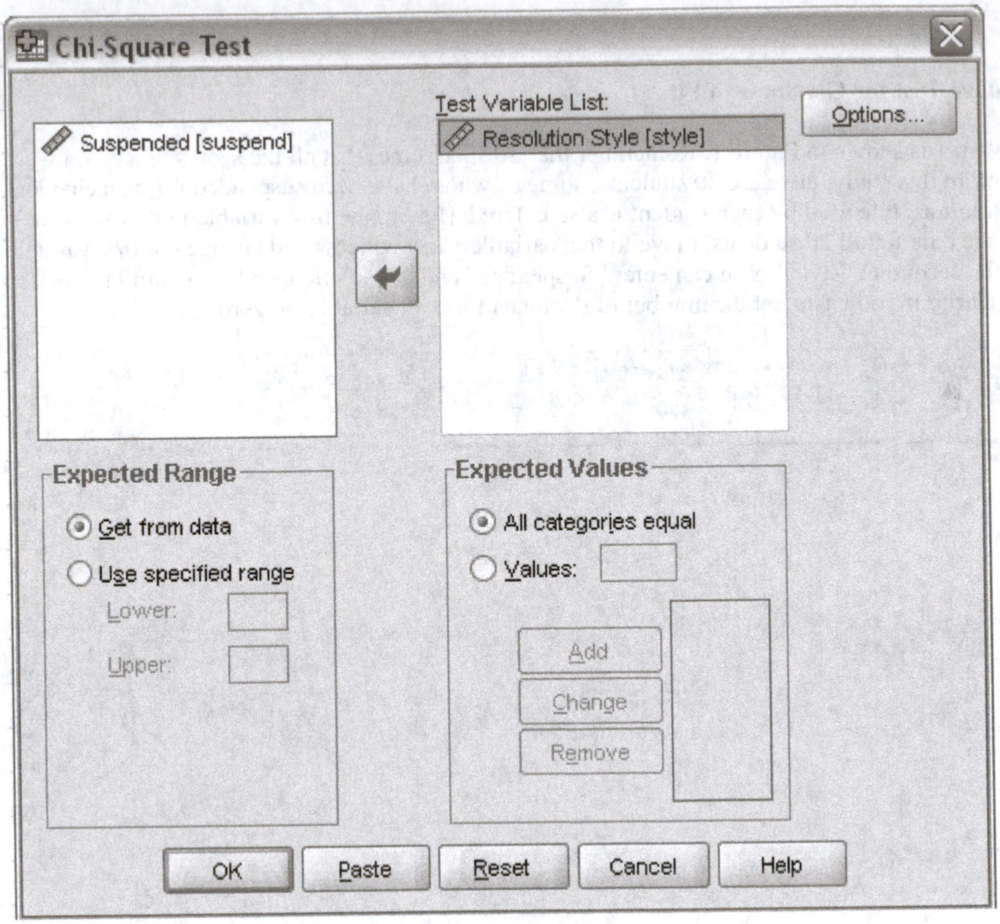

Figure 2

Note that "All categories equal" is the default selection in the "Expected Values" box, which means that SPSS will conduct the goodness of fit test using equal expected frequencies for each of the four styles, that is, SPSS will assume that the proportions of students using each style are equal.
🖱 OK.

The output should look like Figure 3.

Chi-Square Test

Frequencies

Resolution Style

	Observed N	Expected N	Residual
1	8	5.0	3.0
2	2	5.0	-3.0
3	2	5.0	-3.0
4	8	5.0	3.0
Total	20		

Test Statistics

	Resolution Style
Chi-Square	7.200[a]
df	3
Asymp. Sig.	.066

a. 0 cells (.0%) have expected frequencies less than 5. The minimum expected cell frequency is 5.0.

Figure 3

The first table includes the observed frequencies, the expected frequencies, and in the column labeled "Residual," the difference between the observed and expected frequencies. The second table includes the chi-square statistic, the number of degrees of freedom, and the exact significance level. The exact significance level of .066 is greater than .05, confirming the decision you made using the steps of hypothesis testing for Problem 1—the null hypothesis that the conflict-resolution styles are used equally by students cannot be rejected.

Since you will use the dataset in the next application, you may leave it open, save it, or access it from the "Open an existing data source" window when you open SPSS.

Application 2: Chi-Square Test for Independence
Open SPSS.
Now you can use SPSS to analyze the data for Problem 2, adding the variable "suspend" to the analysis. Remember that in this problem, we were interested in whether there was an association between conflict-resolution style and having been suspended from school for misbehavior. Since the analysis will involve two nominal variables, the appropriate test is a chi-square test for independence.

🖱 Analyze.
🖱 Descriptive Statistics and 🖱 Crosstabs.
Since "suspend" is already selected, 🖱 the arrow next to the box labeled "Rows."
🖱 the variable "style" and 🖱 the arrow next to the box labeled "Columns."
The Crosstabs window should look like Figure 4.

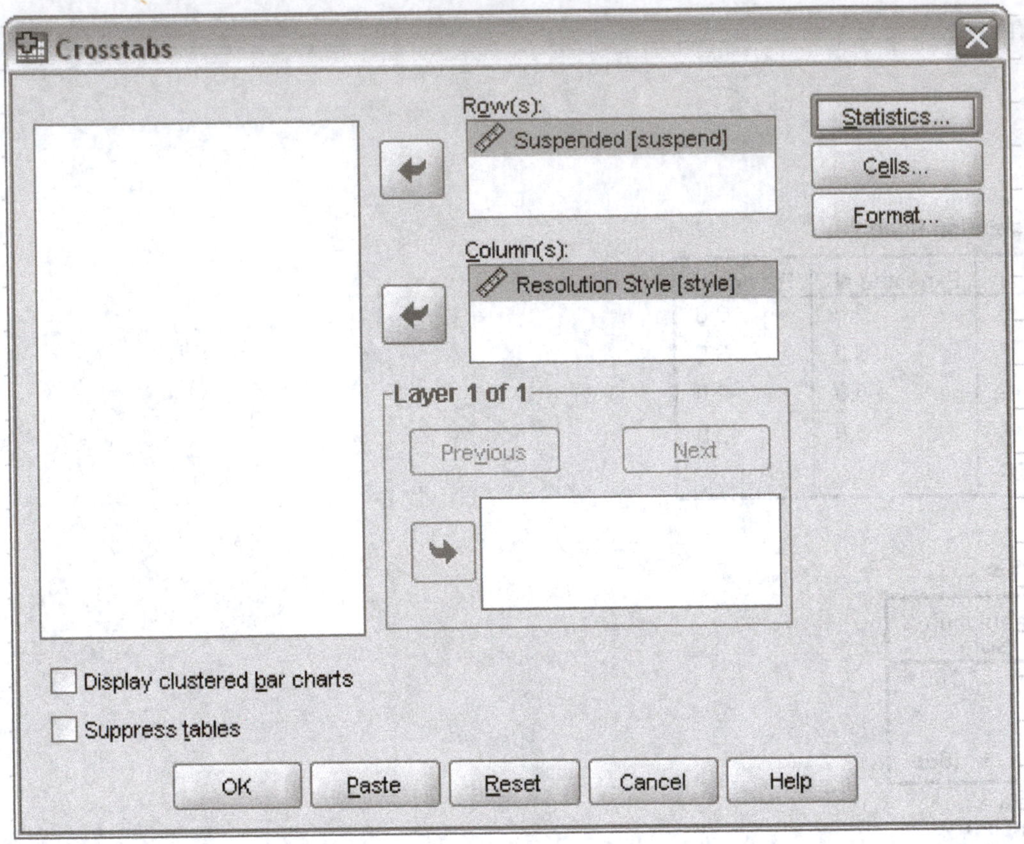

Figure 4

🖱 "Statistics" and 🖱 the box labeled "Chi-square."
The Crosstabs: Statistics window should look like Figure 5.

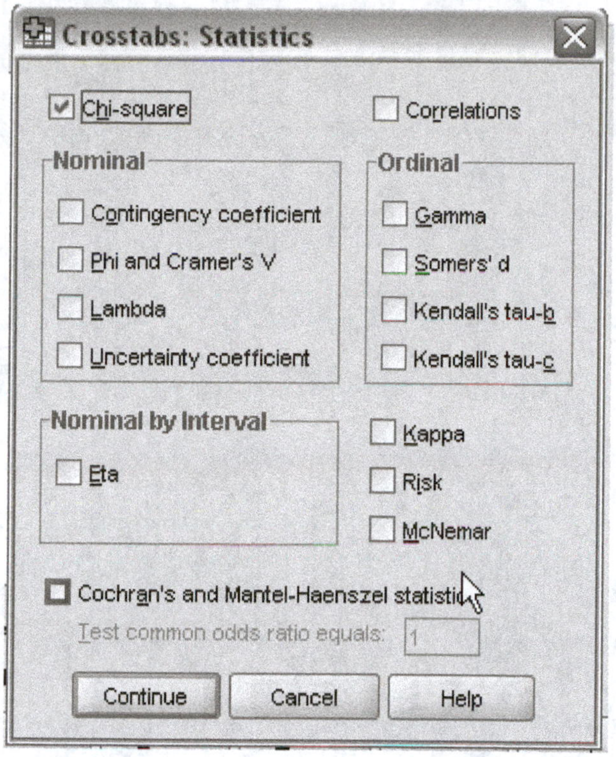

Figure 5

🖰 Continue.

🖰 "Cells" and 🖰 the box labeled "Expected."

The Crosstabs: Cell Display window should look Figure 6.

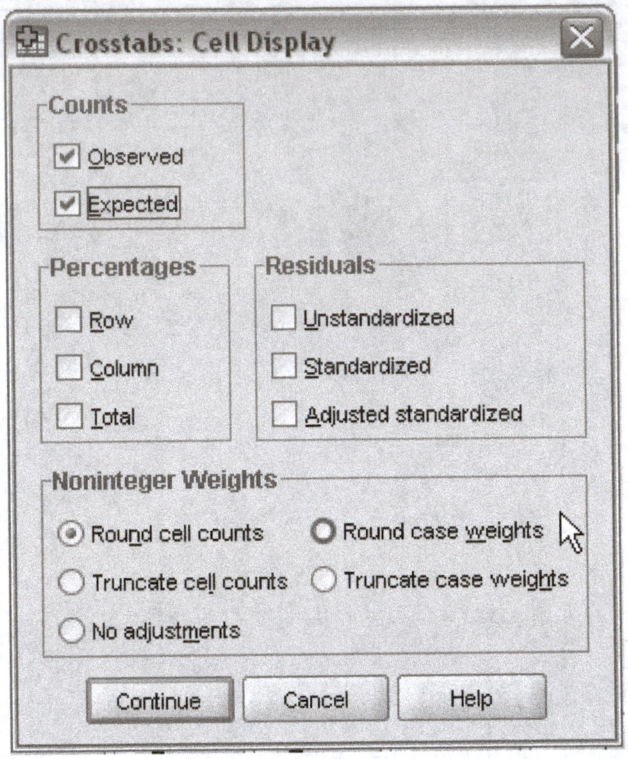

Figure 6

Continue.
OK.

The output should look like Figure 7.

Crosstabs

Case Processing Summary

	Cases					
	Valid		Missing		Total	
	N	Percent	N	Percent	N	Percent
Suspended * Resolution Style	20	100.0%	0	.0%	20	100.0%

Suspended * Resolution Style Crosstabulation

			Resolution Style				Total
			1	2	3	4	
Suspended	1	Count	7	1	1	1	10
		Expected Count	4.0	1.0	1.0	4.0	10.0
	2	Count	1	1	1	7	10
		Expected Count	4.0	1.0	1.0	4.0	10.0
Total		Count	8	2	2	8	20
		Expected Count	8.0	2.0	2.0	8.0	20.0

Chi-Square Tests

	Value	df	Asymp. Sig. (2-sided)
Pearson Chi-Square	9.000[a]	3	.029
Likelihood Ratio	10.124	3	.018
Linear-by-Linear Association	8.319	1	.004
N of Valid Cases	20		

a. 8 cells (100.0%) have expected count less than 5. The minimum expected count is 1.00.

Figure 7

The first table indicates how many students have data for each of the two variables, and would indicate if any students were missing data for any variable. The second table is the contingency table for the two variables. Requesting "Expected" in the Crosstabs: Cell Display window caused SPSS to print both the observed and expected frequencies. The first line in the third table presents the same Pearson chi-square you calculated when you solved Problem 2, and the exact significance level of .029 confirms the decision to reject the null hypothesis and accept the research hypothesis that there is an association between primary conflict-resolution style and suspension from school for misbehavior.

Application 3: Data Transformations and Rank-Order Tests

Open SPSS.

Analyze the data for Problem 11. Remember that SPSS assumes that all the scores in a row are from the same participant. In this study, there are 12 participants divided into two groups of six students, each having a score on a creativity test. Although the variable labeled "group" is not necessary for the data transformation, it will be used later in the application, so enter these data as well. When you have entered the data for all 12 students, move to the Variable View window and change the first variable name to "group" and the second to "creat." You can enter "Group" and "Creativity" in the Label column for clarity. Set the number of decimals for both variables to zero. The SPSS data editor window should look like Figure 8.

	group	creat
1	1	16
2	1	14
3	1	15
4	1	17
5	1	16
6	1	24
7	2	10
8	2	12
9	2	14
10	2	11
11	2	13
12	2	18

Figure 8

↰ Transform.

↰ Compute Variable.

Type the name of the new variable "sqrtcvty" in the "Target Variable" box.

Type "sqrt(creat)" in the "Numeric Expression" box to indicate that SPSS will take the square root of each score and create a new variable called "sqrtcvty."

The "Compute Variable" window should look like Figure 9.

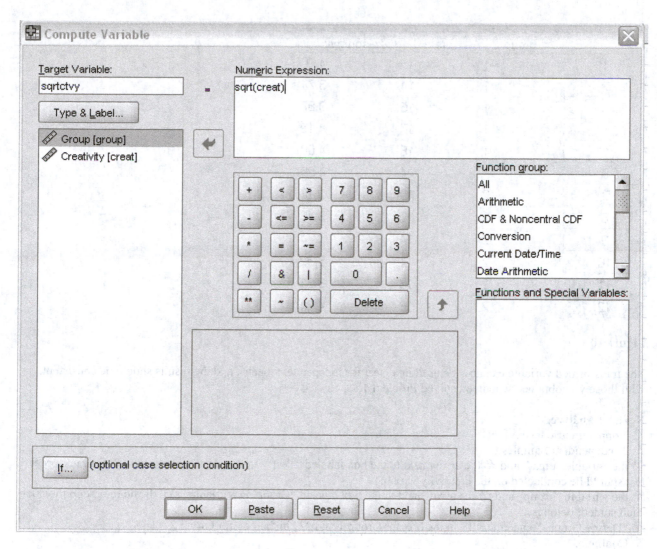

Figure 9

🖱 OK.

Now the SPSS data editor window should look Figure 10.

	group	creat	sqrtctvy
1	1	16	4.00
2	1	14	3.74
3	1	15	3.87
4	1	17	4.12
5	1	16	4.00
6	1	24	4.90
7	2	10	3.16
8	2	12	3.46
9	2	14	3.74
10	2	11	3.32
11	2	13	3.61
12	2	18	4.24

Figure 10

The transformed variable can now be used in a *t* test for independent means, and the results should be consistent with those you obtained when you solved Problem 4.

Next, ⊕ Analyze.
⊕ Nonparametric tests.
⊕ 2 Independent Samples.
⊕ the variable "creat" and ⊕ the arrow next to the box labeled "Test Variable List" to indicate that the rank-order test should be conducted on the creativity variable.
⊕ the variable "group" and ⊕ the arrow next to the box labeled "Grouping Variable" to indicate the group to which each student belongs.
⊕ "Define Groups" and enter "1" in the box for Group 1 and "2" in the box for Group 2.
⊕ Continue.
The "Two-Independent-Samples Tests" window should look like Figure 11.

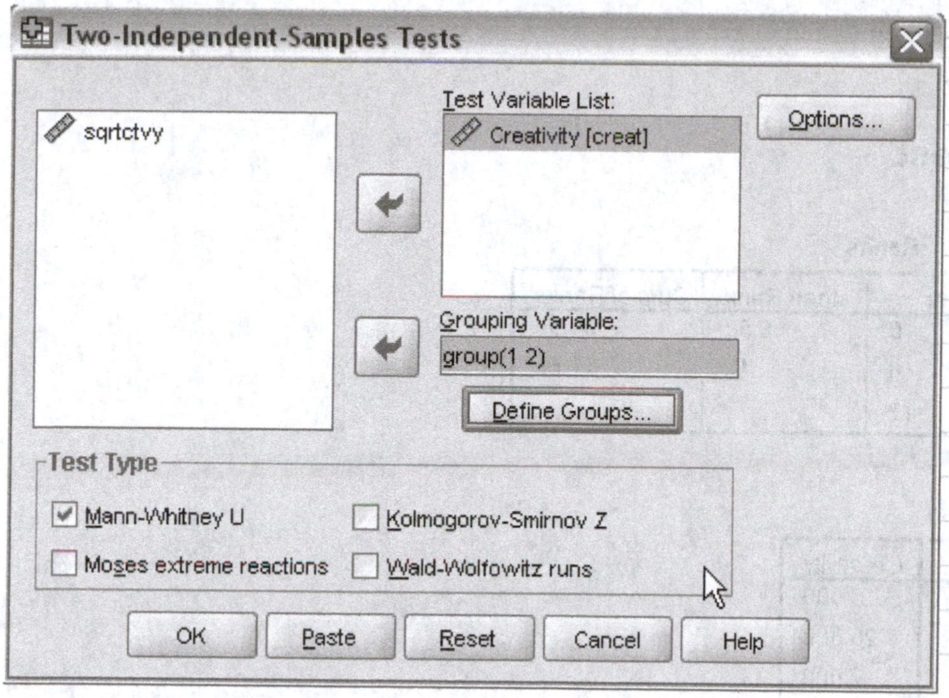

Figure 11

🖰 OK.

The output window should look like Figure 12.

NPar Tests

Mann-Whitney Test

Ranks

	Group	N	Mean Rank	Sum of Ranks
Creativity	1	6	8.58	51.50
	2	6	4.42	26.50
	Total	12		

Test Statistics[b]

	Creativity
Mann-Whitney U	5.500
Wilcoxon W	26.500
Z	-2.009
Asymp. Sig. (2-tailed)	.045
Exact Sig. [2*(1-tailed Sig.)]	.041[a]

a. Not corrected for ties.

b. Grouping Variable: Group

Figure 12

The output indicates that a NPar Test (nonparametric test) was conducted. If you remember, the box for the Mann–Whitney U Test was checked in the "Two-Independent-Samples Tests" window. Notice that the Test Statistics box includes results for the Mann–Whitney U test and the Wilcoxon rank-sum test, which give mathematically equivalent results, as well as a value for Z. Note that the mean ranks presented in the Ranks table are the same as those you calculated when you solved Problem 4, and you would make the same decision to reject the null hypothesis that you made on the basis of the t test for independent means you conducted.

Completion Items

1. chi-square test for goodness of fit	8. chi-square distribution	15. parametric tests
2. chi-square test for independence	9. chi-square table	16. data transformation
3. chi-square tests	10. contingency table	17. square-root transformation
4. observed frequency	11. cell	18. rank-order transformation
5. expected frequency	12. independence	19. rank-order tests
6. chi-square statistic	13. phi coefficient	20. nonparametric tests
7. χ^2	14. Cramer's phi	21. distribution-free tests

Multiple-Choice Items

1. D	5. C	9. B	13. B	17. C
2. B	6. D	10. D	14. D	18. B
3. A	7. A	11. C	15. B	19. D
4. D	8. C	12. A	16. D	

Problems

1.
The appropriate test would be a chi-square test for goodness of fit.

Steps of Hypothesis Testing
Step 1: Restate the question as a research hypothesis and a null hypothesis about the populations.
Population 1: The population of students using methods of conflict resolution like those observed by the behavioral scientists.
Population 2: The population of students who use each method of conflict resolution equally.

Research Hypothesis: The distributions of people over methods of conflict resolution in the two populations are different.
Null Hypothesis: The distributions of people over methods of conflict resolution in the two populations are no different.

Step 2: Determine the characteristics of the comparison distribution.
Since the behavioral scientists are interested in four methods of conflict resolution, the comparison distribution is a chi-square distribution with 3 degrees of freedom ($df = N_{categories} - 1 = 4 - 1 = 3$).

Step 3: Determine the cutoff sample score on the comparison distribution at which the null hypothesis should be rejected.
At the .05 level of significance, the cutoff sample chi-square with 3 degrees of freedom is 7.815.

Step 4: Determine the sample's score on the comparison distribution.
Applying the formula for chi-square yields
$\chi^2 = \Sigma [(O - E)^2 / E]$
$= \Sigma [(8 - 5)^2 / 5] + [(2 - 5)^2 / 5] + [(2 - 5)^2 / 5] + [(8 - 5)^2 / 5]$
$= \Sigma [(3)^2 / 5] + [(-3)^2 / 5] + [(-3)^2 / 5] + [(3)^2 / 5]$
$= \Sigma [(9 / 5) + (9 / 5) + 9 / 5) + (9 / 5)]$
$= \Sigma [1.80 + 1.80 + 1.80 + 1.80]$
$= 7.20$

Step 5: Decide whether to reject the null hypothesis.
The chi-square statistic for the sample of 7.20 is not more extreme than the cutoff sample chi-square of 7.815. Therefore, the behavioral scientists cannot reject the null hypothesis and must state that their results are inconclusive. Thus, despite the differences in observed frequencies, the behavioral scientists cannot conclude that

the distribution of methods of conflict resolution used by the students in their sample is different from the distribution of the population of students like those in the sample.
(b) Compare your explanation to the explanation provided for Problem 2 in Set I of the Practice Problems in the text.

2.
The appropriate test would be a chi-square test for independence.

Steps of Hypothesis Testing
Step 1: Restate the question as a research hypothesis and a null hypothesis about the populations.
Population 1: Students for whom the primary method of conflict resolution is associated with being suspended from school for misbehavior or not being suspended.
Population 2: Students for whom the primary method of conflict resolution is independent of being suspended from school for misbehavior or not being suspended.

Research Hypothesis: The primary methods of conflict resolution used by students who have been suspended from school are different from the methods of students who have not been suspended.
Null Hypothesis: The primary methods of conflict resolution used by students who have been suspended from school are no different from the methods of students who have not been suspended.

Step 2: Determine the characteristics of the comparison distribution.
The behavioral scientists have identified two groups of students based on whether or not students have been suspended from school for misbehavior and the students' use of one of four methods of conflict resolution. Therefore, the comparison distribution is a chi-square distribution with 3 degrees of freedom; $df = (N_{Rows} - 1)(N_{Columns} - 1) = (2 - 1)(4 - 1) = (1)(3) = 3$.

Step 3: Determine the cutoff sample score on the comparison distribution at which the null hypothesis should be rejected.
At the .05 level of significance, the cutoff sample chi-square with 3 degrees of freedom is 7.815.

Step 4: Determine the sample's score on the comparison distribution.
Applying the formula for chi-square yields
$\chi^2 = \Sigma [(O - E)^2 / E]$
$= \Sigma [(7 - 4)^2 / 4] + [(1 - 1)^2 / 1] + [(1 - 1)^2 / 1] + [(1 - 4)^2 / 4] + [(1 - 4)^2 / 4] + [(1 - 1)^2 / 1]$
$+ [(1 - 1)^2 / 1] + [(7 - 4)^2 / 4]$
$= \Sigma [(3)^2 / 4] + [(0)^2 / 1] + [(0)^2 / 1] + [(-3)^2 / 4] + [(-3)^2 / 4] + [(0)^2 / 1] + [(0)^2 / 1]$
$+ [(3)^2 / 4]$
$= \Sigma [(9 / 4) + (0 / 1) + (0 / 1) + (9 / 4) + (9 / 4) + (0 / 1) + (0 / 1) + (9 / 4)]$
$= \Sigma [2.25 + 0.00 + 0.00 + 2.25 + 2.25 + 0.00 + 0.00 + 2.25]$
$= 9.00$

Step 5: Decide whether to reject the null hypothesis.
The chi-square statistic for the sample of 9.00 is more extreme than the cutoff sample chi-square of 7.815. Therefore, the behavioral scientists will reject the null hypothesis, accept the research hypothesis, and conclude that the primary methods of conflict resolution used by students who have been suspended from school for misbehavior are different from the primary methods used by students who have not been suspended.
(b) Cramer's $\Phi = \sqrt{\chi^2 / (N)(df_{Smaller})} = \sqrt{9.00 / (20)(1)} = \sqrt{9.00 / 20} = \sqrt{.45} = .67$, which is a large effect size.
(c) Compare your explanation to the explanation provided for Practice Problem 4 in Set I of the Practice Problems in the text.

3.
The appropriate test would be a chi-square test for independence.

Steps of Hypothesis Testing
Step 1: Restate the question as a research hypothesis and a null hypothesis about the populations.
Population 1: Students for whom the primary method of conflict resolution is associated with being suspended from school for misbehavior or not being suspended.
Population 2: Students for whom the primary method of conflict resolution is independent of being suspended from school for misbehavior or not being suspended.

Research Hypothesis: The primary methods of conflict resolution used by students who have been suspended from school are different from the methods of students who have not been suspended.
Null Hypothesis: The primary methods of conflict resolution used by students who have been suspended from school are no different from the methods of students who have not been suspended.

Step 2: Determine the characteristics of the comparison distribution.
The behavioral scientists have identified two groups of students based on whether or not students have been suspended from school for misbehavior and the students' use of either assertiveness or one of the other three methods of conflict resolution. Therefore, the comparison distribution is a chi-square distribution with 1 degree of freedom; $df = (N_{Rows} - 1)(N_{Columns} - 1) = (2 - 1)(2 - 1) = (1)(1) = 1$.

Step 3: Determine the cutoff sample score on the comparison distribution at which the null hypothesis should be rejected.
At the .05 level of significance, the cutoff sample chi-square with 1 degree of freedom is 3.841.

Step 4: Determine the sample's score on the comparison distribution.
Applying the formula for chi-square yields
$$\chi^2 = \Sigma \left[(O - E)^2 / E \right]$$
$$= \Sigma \left[(1 - 3.5)^2 / 3.5 \right] + \left[(9 - 6.5)^2 / 6.5 \right] + \left[(6 - 3.5)^2 / 3.5 \right] + \left[(4 - 6.5)^2 / 6.5 \right]$$
$$= \Sigma \left[(2.5)^2 / 3.5 \right] + \left[(2.5)^2 / 6.5 \right] + \left[(2.5)^2 / 3.5 \right] + \left[(-2.5)^2 / 6.5 \right]$$
$$= \Sigma \left[(6.25 / 3.5) + (6.25 / 6.5) + (6.25 / 3.5) + (6.25 / 6.5) \right]$$
$$= \Sigma \left[1.79 + 0.96 + 1.79 + 0.96 \right]$$
$$= 5.50$$

Step 5: Decide whether to reject the null hypothesis.
The chi-square statistic for the sample of 5.50 is more extreme than the cutoff sample chi-square of 3.841. Therefore, the behavioral scientists will reject the null hypothesis and conclude that there is an association between using assertiveness as the primary method of conflict resolution as opposed to using one of the other three methods.

(b) $\Phi = \sqrt{\chi^2 / N} = \sqrt{5.50 / 20} = \sqrt{0.28} = 0.52$, which is a large effect size.

4.
The appropriate test would be a chi-square test for goodness of fit.

Steps of Hypothesis Testing
Step 1: Restate the question as a research hypothesis and a null hypothesis about the populations.
Population 1: The population of students whose attentiveness is like those rated by their teachers.
Population 2: The population of students whose attentiveness is equally distributed among the three categories.

Research Hypothesis: The distributions of students across categories of attentiveness in the two populations are different.
Null Hypothesis: The distributions of students across categories of attentiveness in the two populations are no different.

Step 2: Determine the characteristics of the comparison distribution.
Since the teachers placed students in three categories based on attentiveness, the comparison distribution is a chi-square distribution with 2 degrees of freedom ($df = N_{categories} - 1 = 3 - 1 = 2$).

Step 3: Determine the cutoff sample score on the comparison distribution at which the null hypothesis should be rejected.

At the .05 level of significance, the cutoff sample chi-square with 2 degrees of freedom is 5.992.

Step 4: Determine the sample's score on the comparison distribution.

Applying the formula for chi-square yields

$\chi^2 = \Sigma \left[(O-E)^2 / E \right]$
$= \Sigma \left[(16-20)^2 / 20 \right] + \left[(24-20)^2 / 20 \right] + \left[(20-20)^2 / 20 \right]$
$= \Sigma \left[(-4)^2 / 20 \right] + \left[(4)^2 / 20 \right] + \left[(0)^2 / 20 \right]$
$= \Sigma \left[(16 / 20) + (16 / 20) + (0 / 20) \right]$
$= \Sigma \left[0.80 + 0.80 + 0.00 \right]$
$= 1.60$

Step 5: Decide whether to reject the null hypothesis.

The chi-square statistic for the sample of 1.60 is not more extreme than the cutoff sample chi-square of 5.992. Therefore, the behavioral scientists cannot reject the null hypothesis and must state that their results are inconclusive. The results do not indicate that the distribution of students across categories of attentiveness is different from the distribution that would be expected by chance.

5.
The appropriate test would be a chi-square test for independence.

Steps of Hypothesis Testing

Step 1: Restate the question as a research hypothesis and a null hypothesis about the populations.

Population 1: Students whose attentiveness depends on age.
Population 2: Students for whom attentiveness is independent of age.

Research Hypothesis: The attentiveness of older students is different from the attentiveness of younger students.
Null Hypothesis: The attentiveness of older students is no different from the attentiveness of younger students.

Step 2: Determine the characteristics of the comparison distribution.

Since the behavioral scientists have identified groups of older and younger students based on one of three levels of attentiveness, the comparison distribution is a chi-square distribution with 2 degrees of freedom
$df = (N_{\text{Rows}} - 1)(N_{\text{Columns}} - 1) = (2-1)(3-1) = (1)(2) = 2$.

Step 3: Determine the cutoff sample score on the comparison distribution at which the null hypothesis should be rejected.

At the .05 level of significance, the cutoff sample chi-square with 2 degrees of freedom is 5.992.

Step 4: Determine the sample's score on the comparison distribution.

Applying the formula for chi-square yields

$\chi^2 = \Sigma \left[(O-E)^2 / E \right]$
$= \Sigma \left[(9-8)^2 / 8 \right] + \left[(14-12)^2 / 12 \right] + \left[(7-10)^2 / 10 \right] + \left[(7-8)^2 / 8 \right] + \left[(10-12)^2 / 12 \right]$
$+ \left[(13-10)^2 / 10 \right]$
$= \Sigma \left[(1)^2 / 8 \right] + \left[(2)^2 / 12 \right] + \left[(-3)^2 / 10 \right] + \left[(-1)^2 / 8 \right] + \left[(-2)^2 / 12 \right] + \left[(3)^2 / 10 \right]$
$= \Sigma \left[(1 / 8) + (4 / 12) + (9 / 10) + (1 / 8) + (4 / 12) + (9 / 10) \right]$
$= \Sigma \left[0.13 + 0.33 + 0.90 + 0.13 + 0.33 + 0.90 \right]$
$= 2.72$

Step 5: Decide whether to reject the null hypothesis.

The chi-square statistic for the sample of 2.72 is not more extreme than the cutoff sample chi-square of 5.992. Therefore, the behavioral scientists cannot reject the null hypothesis and must state that the results are inconclusive regarding the association of age and attentiveness.

(b) Cramer's $\Phi = \sqrt{\chi^2 / (N)(df_{\text{Smaller}})} = \sqrt{2.72 / (60)(1)} = \sqrt{2.72 / 60} = \sqrt{.05} = .21$, which is a small to medium effect size.

6.

Study	N	Chi-square	Design	Effect Size
(a)	60	12.00	2 × 2	0.45
(b)	80	12.00	2 × 4	0.39
(c)	60	12.00	3 × 3	0.32
(d)	80	12.00	2 × 2	0.39
(e)	120	12.00	2 × 2	0.32

7.

Study	Predicted Effect Size	Design	N	Power
(a)	Medium	2 × 2	50	.56
(b)	Large	2 × 4	50	.86
(c)	Small	3 × 3	100	.11
(d)	Medium	2 × 2	100	.85
(e)	Medium	2 × 4	200	.96

8.

Study	Predicted Effect Size	Design	N
(a)	Medium	2 × 3	107
(b)	Large	2 × 4	44
(c)	Small	3 × 3	1,194
(d)	Large	2 × 5	48
(e)	Large	3 × 3	48

9. Square roots

Study					
(a)	5.5	5.8	8.4	6.0	7.9
(b)	6.0	7.6	6.2	6.4	6.2
(c)	1.4	2.6	2.8	3.0	3.2

In each case, the distribution of scores appears more likely to have come from a normal distribution because the values of the outliers are more like the values of the other scores.

10.
The responses below list the rank of score in the dataset followed by the raw score.
(a) 1-30, 2-34, 3-36, 4-62, 5-71
(b) 1-33, 2-34, 3-35, 4-36, 5-39
(c) 1-7, 2.5-8, 2.5-8, 4-10, 5-11, 6.5-12, 6.5-12, 8-14, 9-15
(d) 1-36, 2-38, 3-39, 4-41, 5-58
(e) 1-2, 2-7, 3-8, 4-9, 5-10

11.
(a) Both groups include potential outliers.
(b) Cutoff sample t, 10 df, $p < .05$, two-tailed $= \pm 2.228$. Training Group: $M = 17.00$, $S^2 = 12.80$; Lecture Group: $M = 13.00$, $S^2 = 8.00$; $S^2_{Pooled} = 10.40$; $S_{Difference} = 1.86$; $t = 2.15$; Do not reject the null hypothesis.
(c) Training Group: 3.32, 3.74, 3.87, 4.12, 4.00, 4.90; Lecture Group: 3.16, 4.00, 3.74, 3.46, 3.61, 4.24
Cutoff sample t, 10 df, $p < .05$, two-tailed $= \pm 2.228$. Training Group: $M = 3.99$, $S^2 = .28$; Lecture Group: $M = 3.70$, $S^2 = .15$; $S^2_{Pooled} = .21$; $S_{Difference} = .27$; $t = 1.09$; Do not reject the null hypothesis.
(d) Training Group: 8.5, 5.5, 7.0, 10.0, 8.5, 12.0; Lecture Group: 1.0, 3.0, 5.5, 2.0, 4.0, 11.0
Cutoff sample t, 10 df, $p < .05$, two-tailed $= \pm 2.228$. Training Group: $M = 8.58$, $S^2 = 5.14$; Lecture Group: $M = 4.42$, $S^2 = 12.84$; $S^2_{Pooled} = 8.99$; $S_{Difference} = 1.73$; $t = 2.41$; Reject the null hypothesis.
The rank-order transformation adjusted the potential outliers in each group so that the distributions more closely resembled normal distributions and the variances were more nearly equal. [Compare your explanation to the explanation provided for Problem 10 in Set I of the Practice Problems in the text.]

12.
(a) The group learning the relaxation technique in the setting includes a potential outlier, and each of the other two groups includes one student with a relatively low score.

(b) Cutoff sample F 2, 12 df, $p < .05 = 3.89$. Counseling: $M = 26.20$, $S^2 = 11.20$; Relaxation: $M = 23.20$, $S^2 = 25.70$; Relaxation is setting: $M = 19.00$, $S^2 = 17.50$; $S^2_{Between} = 64.40$; $S^2_{Within} = 18.33$; $F = 3.07$; Do not reject the null hypothesis.

(c) Counseling: 5.48, 5.39, 4.90, 5.10, 4.69; Relaxation: 5.20, 5.00, 5.29, 4.47, 4.00; Relaxation in setting: 4.80, 4.47, 4.58, 4.36, 3.46. Cutoff sample F 2, 12 df, $p < .05 = 3.89$. Counseling: $M = 5.11$, $S^2 = .108$; Relaxation: $M = 4.79$, $S^2 = .296$; Relaxation is setting: $M = 4.33$, $S^2 = .263$; $S^2_{Between} = .760$; $S^2_{Within} = .222$; $F = 3.42$; Do not reject the null hypothesis.

(d) Counseling: 15.0, 14.0, 9.0, 11.0, 7.0; Relaxation: 12.0, 10.0, 13.0, 4.5, 2.0; Relaxation in setting: 8.0, 4.5, 6.0, 3.0, 1.0. Cutoff sample F 2, 12 df, $p < .05 = 3.89$. Counseling: $M = 11.20$, $S^2 = 11.20$; Relaxation: $M = 8.30$, $S^2 = 23.20$; Relaxation is setting: $M = 4.50$, $S^2 = 7.25$; $S^2_{Between} = 56.45$; $S^2_{Within} = 13.88$; $F = 4.07$; Reject the null hypothesis.

Inspection of the ranked data shows the influence of the two potential outliers in the dataset. Neither the analysis of the actual scores nor of the data following the square-root transformation was statistically significant. However, following the rank-order transformation, the distributions more closely resembled normal distributions, and the analysis revealed the statistically significant difference indicated by the general consistency of the scores in the three groups. [Compare your explanation to the explanation provided for Problem 11 in Set I of the Practice Problems in the text.]

Chapter 12
Applying Statistical Methods in Your Own Research Project

Learning Objectives
After studying this chapter, you should:
- Be able to select a statistical test as part of designing a research study using a decision tree.
- Know the difference between between-subjects and within-subjects research designs.
- Know the analysis options when two or more outcome variables are measured.
- Know how to enter scores into a computer and check their accuracy.
- Be able to plan to collect useful data from computer or Internet methods.
- Be able to select a method for handling missing values.
- Be able to check for normal distributions and identify outliers.
- Know the frequently used methods for handling outliers.
- Know how to develop a systematic plan for conducting statistical analyses to answer the primary questions of a research study.
- Know the major parts of a research report and their primary contents.

Selecting a Statistical Test
Once a research question has been identified, the next step is to identify a specific research plan to answer the question, and one of the first tasks is to identify the statistical analysis that will be used. Failure to identify the analysis may mean that no methods will be available to analyze the data collected, or the methods may not be ideal. Advance identification of the analysis is also necessary in determining the number of participants needed in a study and the power of the study.

When scores are measured on an equal-interval scale, the initial question involves determining whether the study is designed to detect differences between or among means or to identify associations among variables. A decision tree like the one in Figure 12-1 in the text can be useful in making such decisions. If the focus is on differences between means, the number of means will determine whether a *t* test or analysis of variance is used, and once this determination is made, a decision about whether to use a **between-subjects design**, or a *within-subjects design*, will need to be made. In other words, will the experimental groups be comprised of different people, or will measurements be made on the same people on two or more occasions.

If a study focuses on associations or predictions, a decision will need to be made about whether the interest is only in the former, or whether predictions will be made. If predictions are to be made, the number of predictor variables will determine whether bivariate or multivariate regression will be used.

If the scores are to be categories, or nominal variables, then the chi-square tests for goodness of fit or independence are available. However, if people can be included in more than one category on any variable, or if the contingency tables can be three- or more-way, then advanced analysis procedures will be required, and it may be easier to redesign a study so that equal-interval variables are measured. Remember that if a nominal variable has only two categories, or can be divided into two categories, arbitrary numbers can be assigned, and the variable can be treated as if it is equal-interval. This method does not work when more than two categories are possible, and it should not be used when one of the categories would have a wide majority of the participants.

When a study involving more than one criterion or outcome variable is planned, several analyses are possible.
- One solution is to analyze each outcome variable separately.
- A second method is to combine multiple outcome measures into a single overall measure. However, since high scores may be of interest on some variables and low scores on others, the scores on all variables may be converted to *Z* scores before combining them.
- A third approach is to use **multivariate statistical tests** that analyze all the outcome variables simultaneously. However, these are advanced procedures.

Determining the power and sample size for a study involves several considerations.

- First, determining the power of a study requires identifying the statistical test.
- Second, estimate the effect size by either considering prior research results or deciding on the size of the effect that would be meaningful.
- Power tables like those in the text can be used, or tables for more advanced or unusual procedures may be found in texts or computer programs.
- Tables are available for determining the sample size needed for 80% power, and if the number of participants is too large to be practical, one of the methods described in Chapter 7 may be used to change the power of the study.
- Finally, the study itself may be modified.

Conducting the Study

When planning data-gathering procedures, remember to:

- Design questionnaires or data recording sheets so that entering scores into a computer will be easy.
- Store the questionnaires or data recording sheets in a safe place.
- Record all important information that is not provided by participants on each questionnaire or data recording sheet.

Entering Scores into the Computer

- Determine how to use the spreadsheet format in SPSS, or any other computer program, and enter the variables in the same order as they are recorded on the questionnaire or data recording sheet.
- Use meaningful variable names that are short enough to make easy use of the spreadsheet. Variable names that are too long make the spreadsheet so wide that scrolling across columns can become laborious.
- Enter participant scores directly and let the program combine variables, do any calculations necessary, or create number codes for variables originally entered as words or letters, for example, converting "male" or "female" to "1" or "2."
- If possible, enter all the data at one time, saving frequently and noting any unusual scores and decisions made about how to enter (or delete) them in the dataset. Always save multiple copies of the dataset in more than one location.
- Double-check the data, at least for a portion of the participants. It is preferable to have another person perform this process for a portion of the participants.

Conducting Research Using Computerized and Internet Methods

- Be sure data are collected accurately and that the format is understandable.
- Be sure the data include information like the time and date of collection and information that will permit matching with other records like paper-and-pencil questionnaires, recorded interviews, physical measures, and so forth.

Data Screening

Use a computer program (for example, *Descriptive Statistics, Descriptives* in SPSS) to

- Get a summary of each variable in the study.
- Make sure that the number of cases matches the number of participants.
- Ensure that the maximum and minimum scores do not indicate a typing error.
- Verify that the mean and standard deviation are reasonable.

Use *Descriptive Statistics, Frequencies* to perform the same function for nominal variables or for variables with only a few possible values.

Missing values may be present because a participant did not respond, observers missed a behavior, a recording device failed, or data are lost. The best practice is to leave blank cells for missing scores. The data file can be printed to locate missing values. Computer programs like SPSS exclude participants who have missing values on any variable in an analysis, so consideration should be given to replacing missing values with individual means or group means, or to creating new variables so that these additions can be tracked.

Checking for normal distributions can be accomplished by selecting the "Skewness" option in "*Descriptive Statistics*" in SPSS. Since 0 indicates perfect normality, a histogram should be created for any variable that has a skewness value more extreme than ±1 to see if the distribution looks seriously skewed. If the variable is seriously skewed, the data can be transformed or a rank-order method of analysis can be used.

Most extreme skewness is caused by outliers, which can be detected by looking for long tails or separated scores in histograms or by using the computer to calculate Z scores. Z scores more extreme than ±3 may be considered outliers. After making sure that an outlier is not due to a data entry error, an experimenter can

- Exclude the participant if the participant is not part of the population to which you want to generalize your results.
- Use a rank-order method of analysis.
- Recode the score so that it is just higher than the next lower score.

Whatever is done should be described in the research report.

Once the data have been carefully screened, become familiar with the data by reviewing overall and group descriptive statistics, graphs, and patterns of correlations. Review the original analysis plan, or develop a systematic analysis plan and test the hypotheses that will answer the questions that led to the study. Review all computer output carefully to be sure that

- All intended variables were included.
- All participants were included.
- The intended analysis was conducted.

Once the major results are available, explore them to identify unexpected findings. Remember that findings from exploratory analyses may be due to chance because when many analyses are conducted, some will be significant due to chance. Exploratory results should be clearly identified in the results section of the research report and considered tentative.

Most research reports include the following sections.

- The *Introduction* includes prior research.
- The *Methods* may include some results including information about the participants and reliability analyses conducted on the questionnaires or other data collection instrument used in the study.
- The rest of the results are included in the *Results* section, which typically begins with presentation of descriptive statistics, followed by the analyses conducted to test the hypotheses of the study, and concluding with exploratory findings. Each analysis should be described completely following the examples in the sections of each chapter dealing with the ways the results of various tests are reported in research articles.
- The *Discussion* includes a summary of the major conclusions, describes how the results relate to larger issues the study was designed to address, presents limitations of the study, and suggests implications for future research.

There are no Chapter Self-Tests for this chapter.

There are no SPSS applications for this chapter.

Web Chapter W1
Overview of the Logic and Language of Behavioral and Social Sciences Research

Learning Objectives
After studying this chapter, you should:
- Be able to describe a true experiment.
- Be able to define the basic terms used in describing experiments.
- Be able to describe the various methods for enrolling participants and assigning them to groups in experiments.
- Be able to differentiate the several types of research designs including matched-group, repeated-measures, correlational, and single-subject designs.
- Be able to describe the sources of bias including placebo, Hawthorne, and experimenter effects that can affect experimental results.
- Be able to describe the concept of sample representativeness and the roll of random sampling in obtaining representative samples.
- Know the types of measurements made in social science research.
- Be able to distinguish reliability and validity and define the types of each.

The goal of research in the behavioral and social sciences is to test a theory or the effectiveness of a practical application. Well-planned research results in unambiguous conclusions that apply to a variety of other situations. Less well-planned research, even if the results are consistent with predictions, may be subject to alternative interpretations or apply only in specific situations. Most behavioral and social scientists think about the logic of research in terms of an ideal approach, so that actual studies are evaluated in terms of the ways they do and do not reach this ideal. The ideal is a "true experiment."

The Traditionally Ideal Research Approach
The True Experiment
The **true experiment** is the standard against which all other methods are compared. Replace the general hypothesis that "Changing the level of X causes a change in the score on Y" with an example hypothesis stating that "Participation in a self-help group designed to teach coping skills (X) will reduce the level of stress (Y) perceived by college students." A true experiment to explore this topic would systematically vary participation in a self-help group, keeping everything else the same, and measure the effect of participation on perceived stress. For example, in a true experiment, one group of students might attend a counseling session once a week for 6 weeks. Another initially identical group of students would not attend such counseling sessions. Theoretically, the only difference between the two groups is participation in the counseling sessions. Therefore, if the students who participate in counseling report lower scores on a stress inventory, their scores can be attributed to the counseling. (If they have higher scores, then *that* effect would also have to be attributed to the counseling.)

Basic Terminology of the Experiment
The **experimental group** is the group in which the level of X is changed. The **control group** is the group in which X is kept at normal levels. The individuals in research studies are called **participants**. The variable that is systematically changed, or X (participation in self-help counseling) is called the **independent variable**. The procedure of systematically changing the independent variable is sometimes called an **experimental manipulation** or *manipulating the independent variable*. The variable that is supposed to change as a result of the study, or Y (score on a stress inventory) is called the **dependent variable**. Participants are selected from a **population** of all the people on earth of the type being studied. A **sample** includes the particular participants selected to be in a study. Thus, the four key characteristics of an ideal research design are that:
1. The participants in the experimental and control groups are identical.
2. The experimental and control groups are exposed to identical situations (*except* for manipulation of the independent variable).
3. The sample perfectly represents the intended population.
4. The measurement of the dependent variable is completely accurate and appropriate for what it is supposed to be measuring.

Equivalence of Participants in Experimental and Control Groups

The equivalence of participants in the experimental and control groups usually is the main issue in deciding whether the conclusions of a study are unambiguous. For example, suppose the level of stress perceived by students selected to participate in counseling was different from the level of students who did not participate in counseling. Determining the meaning of any differences in stress between the two groups at the end of the study would be difficult. The difference could be due either (a) to the manipulation of the independent variable (participating in self-counseling or not) or (b) to initial differences in student levels of perceived stress. To avoid such ambiguous results, researchers try to obtain equivalent experimental and control groups using one of five strategies: random assignment to groups, matched-group design, repeated-measures research design, correlational research design, and single-subject research.

Random Assignment to Groups

Random assignment to groups is the most likely procedure to create two identical groups of participants. For example, if 60 students were available to participate in the counseling experiment, each student could be assigned to either the experimental group or the control group by flipping a coin. The two groups of 30 participants created in this way would not be identical, but at least there will be no *systematic* difference between them. In behavioral and social science research, the term "random" means using a strictly random procedure, not haphazardly selecting people for the two groups. Haphazard selection is likely to produce unintended systematic differences. For example, suppose students selected for the counseling study were selected from students living in campus housing, while students living off campus served as the control group. The two groups might differ because students living on campus might be less likely to have a full- or part-time job. On the other hand, suppose students selected to participate in counseling are volunteers who have sought help from the counseling center, while the control group consists of students in a social science class who are willing to complete a stress inventory. In this case, the students in the experimental and control groups might be quite different.

The purpose of random assignment is to eliminate such initial systematic differences between groups, so that any differences in the dependent variable after the experiment can only be due either to the manipulation of the independent variable or to the random assignment. True random processes follow the laws of probability. Therefore, hypothesis-testing procedures covered in the text are based on the probability that any observed differences in a study could have been due to the random assignment. If the statistical analysis indicates that this probability is unlikely, then the only reasonable remaining explanation is that manipulation of the independent variable caused the difference. This is the basic logic behind the statistical analysis of results of experiments, and is the reason that random assignment and statistical methods are so important in behavioral and social science research.

Matched-Group Designs

In some situations, random assignment to groups is impractical. For example, ethics may require that all students who seek the services of a counseling center to help them reduce stress be enrolled in a program. Thus, the question becomes how the program can be shown to be the cause of reductions in stress. One method is the **matched-group research design**. For example, the experimental group may consist of students who have sought help from the counseling center at one university, and the control group of students at another university who have high stress levels, but for whom the self-help counseling program is not available. Every member of this control group could be matched to a member of the experimental group on variables such as age, socioeconomic status, gender, primary source of stress, and so forth.

Matched-group designs are better than having no control group, and if both groups are tested before and after the experiment, the matched-group design can lead to reasonably unambiguous results. Called a *matched-group pretest–posttest design*, this design is an example of a *quasi-experimental design*, which is any design that reasonably approximates a true experiment, but that does not include random assignment. However, no matter how well matched two groups may be, and even when pretesting and posttesting are used, researchers can never know that no systematic initial differences between the groups existed. Indeed, in most cases, lack of random assignment means that there *are* systematic initial differences between groups. The self-help counseling program may be possible at one university because of the number of counselors available, while the university supplying the control group may have too few counselors to offer such a program.

Repeated-Measures Research Designs

A **repeated-measures research design** (or *within-subjects research design*) creates two identical groups by testing the same people twice. The students in the counseling example could be tested before and after the 6-week program. The *single-group pretest–posttest design* is the simplest repeated-measures design and, as the name implies, involves testing a single group of individuals twice, once before and once after an experimental treatment. This design is weak because observed changes have many possible alternative explanations. For example, the initial testing can change a participant so that when tested again, the participant is different due to the testing and not to the experimental treatment. In addition, the passage of time produces changes that may mask true experimental effects. For example, some students in the counseling could resolve health or relationship problems during the 6-week experiment, resulting in reduced stress independent of the counseling program.

Due to these potential weaknesses, the single-group pretest–posttest design is considered a *preexperimental design*. However, such designs may be useful during initial exploratory studies, and conclusions drawn from such studies are tentative. Additional studies using stronger designs like quasi-experimental or true experimental designs should be conducted.

Repeated-measures designs can be applied in laboratory settings in such a way that they become true experiments. Suppose that students are taught to use a relaxation technique to reduce stress. The students' stress might be measured when relaxation is practiced just before a simulated discussion with a professor about poor performance (the experimental condition), and then when the technique is not practiced before another simulated discussion (the control condition). A problem with this approach, however, is that students will be familiar with the situation the second time, creating a *practice effect* or *carryover effect*. If both simulations occur during the same counseling session, students could be tired by the time they perform the second task, creating a *fatigue effect*. **Counterbalancing**, in which half the participants are tested first in one condition and the other half of the participants are tested first in the other condition, is one method for counteracting these effects. Ideally, the order of treatments is determined by random assignment.

Correlational Research Designs

A **correlational research design** is used to determine whether an association between two variables exists in a group of people without any experimental manipulation. For example, a counselor conducting one of the self-help groups might use a correlational design to investigate the relationship between stress and anxiety among students in the group, which would most likely reveal that students reporting high levels of stress tend to report high levels of anxiety. Although the correlational design is often the best design available in some circumstances, and is consequently widely used, it is a weak design in that its results are open to alternative explanations besides "*X* caused *Y*." For example, if stress and anxiety are significantly correlated, is it because stress causes anxiety, anxiety causes stress, or some third variable like parental pressure is causing both stress and anxiety? Thus, an advantage of true experiments over correlational studies is that the independent variable is manipulated in the former so that its effect on the dependent variable can be observed. Despite their limitations, correlational designs may be useful in exploratory studies or when random assignment is impossible.

Single-Subject Research

Single-subject research involves examination of a single group, organization, or individual using the *case study* or *participant observation* approaches. Such research is not experimental, but these methods are used to provide a rich understanding of complex topics in many behavioral and social sciences. Such research also may be useful in exploratory studies conducted prior to investing in experimental designs. Statistics are not usually used because the pattern of results should be so clear that statistics are unnecessary.

The advantages and disadvantages of the major research designs are presented in Table W1-1.

Equivalence of Circumstances for Experimental and Control Groups

Ideal studies involve both identical groups and testing in identical circumstances. Despite the difficulties in achieving these goals, experimenters can maximize equivalence by practices like conducting experiments in isolated locations to minimize external influences that might make one experimental session different from another. Experimenters can also standardize the sessions as much as possible, for example, by tape-recording instructions to participants. However, special problems such as the placebo effect, the Hawthorne effect, and experimenter effects may influence the equivalence of circumstances in behavioral and social science research, particularly applied research.

Placebo effects reflect the influence of a participant's expectation or motivation to do well on experimental results. **Hawthorne effects** reflect the influence of the attention the participant receives and of the participant's reaction to being a participant. For example, if students in the control group report lower levels of stress simply because they know they are part of a study dealing with stress, they are demonstrating a placebo effect. If students in the experimental group report lower levels of stress simply because of the attention they receive from the counselors, and not because the sources of their stress have become less intense, they are demonstrating the Hawthorne effect.

The best solution to these problems is to conduct a study in which both groups receive some treatment that is perceived to be helpful, but only one group actually receives a treatment consisting of more than attention and raised expectations. However, setting up a control condition that is perceived to be helpful but is not is often impossible or unethical in the behavioral and social sciences. An actual placebo may be appropriate in a *double-blind procedure*, in which neither the participants nor the experimenters know of any participant's group assignment.

Experimenter effects, including *experimenter bias*, are the unintended influences of an experimenter on a study. For example, in the stress study, the counselors conducting sessions for the experimental group may want the treatment to be effective to the point that they develop a predisposition to see more improvement in the students attending the counseling sessions than actually occurs. Even independent observers are subject to this type of bias. Using *blind conditions of testing*, in which the experimenter is unaware of a participant's group membership, is a potential solution to this problem.

Representativeness of the Sample
A third requirement of an ideal study is that the sample of participants should accurately represent the population to which the results are to be applied. Such representativeness is called **generalizability** or *external validity*. (*Internal validity* refers to the equivalence of the experimental and control groups and equivalence of circumstances.) For example, some people will respond to mail surveys and others will not, and systematic differences between these two types of respondents are a reasonable expectation. Similarly, people who volunteer to participate in an experiment may differ from those who do not.

Random sampling is the optimal method for ensuring that a sample is representative of its population. Random sampling involves listing all members of the population to which the results will be generalized, and then using a random procedure (such as selecting participants using a random number table) to select a sample from this population. Such a sample is called a *probability sample* because every member of the population being studied has an equal probability of being included in the study sample.

Measurement
The fourth condition required for an ideal study is that the measures be accurate and appropriate. The three main kinds of measures used in behavioral and social science research include:
1. **Self-report measures**, such as questionnaires or interviews
2. *Observational* or **behavioral measures**, such as rating scales or counts of various behaviors
3. **Physiological measures**, such as hormone levels, heart rate, or blood flow in a particular brain area

All three kinds of measurement are evaluated mainly in terms of their reliability and validity.

Reliability
The **reliability** of a measure is its accuracy or consistency. For example, a participant in behavioral or social science research responding to the same questionnaire on different days may have a different score. Such score variation may be due to poorly worded questions or incorrect recording, like misplacing responses on a spreadsheet. Observational measures may be unreliable because observers may disagree, and physiological measures often vary from moment to moment.

The three types of reliability are:
1. **Test–retest reliability**, in which the same group is tested twice
2. **Internal consistency**, in which scores on half the questions may be compared to scores on the other half
3. **Interrater reliability**, which is the degree of agreement between observers

The types of reliability are summarized in Table W1-2.

Validity

The **validity** of a measure refers to whether it actually measures what it claims to measure. (The word *validity* is also applied to entire studies, as in internal validity and external validity, when it refers to the appropriateness and breadth of the conclusions that can be drawn from the results.) A measure that is not reliable cannot be valid. However, even if a measure is reliable, it may not necessarily be valid for measuring what it is intended to measure. In addition, a reliable measure may not be valid because it is actually measuring the respondents' tendency to try to make a good impression, to say yes, or to demonstrate some other **response bias**. One way to address the problem of trying to make a good impression is to include a *social desirability scale*, sometimes called a *lie scale*. When a participant's score on such a scale is high, the researcher may choose not to include that participant's responses. Alternatively, scores on a social desirability scale may be used in a statistical procedure, such as partial correlation or an analysis of covariance, to adjust the person's score on the full measure.

Validity is more difficult to assess than reliability. Methods for estimating validity include:
1. **Content validity**, based on whether the content of the measure appears to cover all the aspects of the variable to be measured, is usually determined by the judgment of the researcher or other experts. There are, however, more systematic means of evaluating the validity of a measure.
2. **Criterion-related validity** involves special studies in which scores on the measure are compared to some other likely indicator of the same variable. One type of criterion-related validity is *predictive validity*, or how well scores on the measure predict future behavior. *Concurrent validity* is useful for comparing scores on one measure with scores on another measure of the same attribute.

These types of validity are summarized in Table W1-3.

Another type of validity is *construct validity*, which may include criterion-related validity and sometimes content validity. However, textbooks on psychological measurement disagree on an accurate definition.

Chapter Self-Tests
Understanding Key Terms in Web Chapter W1

The completion items that follow are based on the following scenario. In response to student expressions of a sense of uneasiness and decreased self-confidence following a series of assaults on a university campus, a group of behavioral scientists from several disciplines has decided to collaborate on a study to see if self-defense training will increase student self-confidence.

Directions: Using the word bank that follows, complete each statement.

Word Bank: behavioral measures / content validity / control group / correlational research design / counterbalancing / criterion-related validity / dependent variable / experimental group / experimental manipulation / experimenter effects / generalizability / Hawthorne effects / independent variable / internal consistency / interrater reliability / matched-group research design / participants / physiological measures / placebo effects / population / random assignment to groups / random sampling / reliability / repeated-measures research design / response bias / sample / self-report measures / single-subject research / test–retest reliability / true experiment / validity

In their review of earlier studies, the behavioral scientists identify an inventory that has been used to measure self-confidence in several studies. The scientists' review of prior research also indicates that the inventory has provided useful data when it was completed by people in studies, in which case the inventory was being used as a **(1)** _____. The scientists also plan to have students keep a journal in which they record places and situations that make them uneasy and rate the intensity of their unease during the course of the study. In addition, students will periodically wear heart rate monitors so that their ratings of unease can be correlated with their heart rate at that time. The journals and intensity ratings are examples of **(2)** _____ and the heart rate data are one of a number of **(3)** _____ that could be made. If a study is conducted to see if there is an association between the heart rates of students and their rankings of their unease, the study would be using a **(4)** _____.

The behavioral scientists obtained a copy of the inventory and the technical manual that accompanied it. As they reviewed the manual, they looked for evidence that scores on the inventory were consistent, which is evidence of the inventory's **(5)** _____. The scientists found that some evidence of consistency was obtained by testing the same people on two occasions, which provided an estimate of **(6)** _____. Another type of evidence of consistency was provided by comparing scores on one half of the inventory with scores on the other half, which provided an estimate of **(7)** _____. Finally, evidence that observers could complete the inventory after observing people in certain situations with a high degree of agreement between or among observers was presented to provide evidence of **(8)** _____.

The behavioral scientists also reviewed the manual to be sure that the inventory actually measured self-confidence, or for evidence of the inventory's **(9)** _____. The manual indicated that the inventory had been reviewed by a panel of other investigators familiar with aspects of self-confidence and agreed that the inventory covered the important behaviors related to self-confidence, which indicated that the inventory had **(10)** _____. The scientists also found the results of studies that indicated that scores on the inventory could be used to predict how people would respond in situations requiring self-confidence, and that the inventory was correlated with several other inventories designed to measure self-confidence. The results of these studies provided evidence of the inventory's **(11)** _____. The scientists also found that the inventory included a social desirability scale that would help them identify students who were trying to appear more self-confident than they actually were, or whose answers to questions on the inventory were demonstrating **(12)** _____.

As the behavioral scientists continued to design their study, they discussed the method that would provide the best evidence that self-defense training would actually increase self-confidence and agreed that the standard against which all other research methods are compared is the **(13)** _____. In order to implement this method, the scientists first had to identify the students who would be enrolled in the study. Due to time and financial constraints, not all students can be included in the initial study. Therefore, all the students enrolled at the university would be considered the **(14)** _____ from which a

(15) _____ of 50 students would be drawn. Although traditionally referred to as participants, some behavioral sciences like psychology currently refer to people enrolled in studies as
(16) _____.

The next step was to divide the 50 students into two groups, one that would receive the self-defense training, the
(17) _____, and one that would not receive the training, the
(18) _____. The selective administration of the self-defense training is referred to as
(19) _____, and means that self-defense training is the **(20)** _____, and self-confidence is the **(21)** _____. If the 50 students are divided into two groups of 25 students each by flipping a coin, the scientists have used **(22)** _____. An important requirement of any study is that the sample of people being studied accurately represents the population to which the results of the study are to be applied. This representativeness is called **(23)** _____, and the best way to ensure that a sample has this representativeness is to use a method that every member of the population has an equal probability of being selected for the sample. The method is known as **(24)** _____.

In case the option of having an untreated group at the university was considered untenable, one of the scientists agreed to see if a colleague would identify a similar group of students from a university that had experienced similar assaults. If this group from another university was used, the scientists would be using a **(25)** _____. The scientists also discussed the possibility of selecting a group of 30 students and measuring their self-confidence before and after self-defense training, which would be a
(26) _____. Since students would be familiar with the inventory, raising the possibility of practice or carryover effects, the scientists decided that if they had to use this design, 15 students would complete the inventory and immediately enter the training program, completing inventory at the end of training and again 6 weeks later. The other 15 students would complete the inventory at the beginning of the study and again after 6 weeks. However, these students would not undergo the training program until after the second administration of the inventory. They would then undergo self-defense training and
retake the inventory at the end of training. This practice is known as **(27)** _____. Finally, several scientists wanted to identify a student experiencing a very low level of self-confidence for intense study. These scientists would be conducting **(28)** _____.

Another aspect of the behavioral scientists' planning involved consideration of potential problems that might bias the results of their studies, one being a possible increase in self-confidence attributable simply due to students expecting to experience an increase as a result of participating in the self-defense training program. Such expectations or motivation to do well are called **(29)** _____. The scientists also considered the possibility that students might exhibit an increase in self-confidence simply due to the attention they receive because they are participating in a study. Such biasing effects are called
(30) _____. Finally, the scientists discussed ways to ensure that their view that self-defense training would be an effective way to increase self-confidence under the current circumstances did not cause them to evaluate students in the program more favorably than the results merited. Such sources of bias are called **(31)**
_____.

Multiple-Choice Items

The multiple-choice items that follow are based on the following scenario. A group of behavioral scientists is planning studies to investigate the effects of different methods of instruction on the attitudes of high school freshmen toward teachers in a large school system.

1. The standard against which the behavioral scientists judge the adequacy of any of their research designs is
    A. random assignment.
    B. a true experiment.
    C. a matched-group research design.
    D. counterbalancing.

One of the first steps the scientists take is to consider various ways to measure attitudes.

2. If freshmen are asked to complete questionnaires at various times during the school year, they are completing
    A. behavioral measures.
    B. criterion measures.
    C. physiological measures.
    D. self-report measures.

3. If outside observers rate student behaviors to assess their attitudes at various times during the school year, they are completing
    A. behavioral measures.
    B. criterion measures.
    C. physiological measures.
    D. self-report measures.

4. If health personnel are asked to measure the heart rates and respiration rates of freshmen before certain learning tasks at various times during the school year, they are completing
    A. behavioral measures.
    B. criterion measures.
    C. physiological measures.
    D. self-report measures.

The scientists have identified consistency as a primary attribute of any scale or inventory they select for their studies.

5. The measurement term that is synonymous with consistency is
    A. counterbalancing.
    B. reliability.
    C. sampling.
    D. validity.

6. If the evidence of consistency is provided by correlating the scores of people measured at two different times, the method is called
    A. equivalent forms reliability.
    B. internal consistency.
    C. interrater reliability.
    D. test–retest reliability.

7. If the evidence of consistency is provided by correlating the scores on one half of the test with scores on the other half, the method is called
    A. equivalent forms reliability.
    B. internal consistency.
    C. interrater reliability.
    D. test–retest reliability.

8. If the evidence of consistency is provided by comparing the scores of two or more observers of student behavior, the method is called
    A. equivalent forms reliability.
    B. internal consistency.
    C. interrater reliability.
    D. test–retest reliability.

The scientists also want to be sure that any scale or inventory they select for their studies actually measures attitudes toward teachers.

9. The extent to which a test or inventory measures what it is designed to measure is called
    A. counterbalancing.
    B. reliability.
    C. sampling.
    D. validity.

10. If the items on an inventory appear to cover all the important aspects of attitudes toward teachers, the inventory is said to have
    A. content validity.
    B. criterion-related validity.
    C. internal consistency.
    D. response bias.

11. If the scores on an inventory can be used to predict student attitudes toward teachers prior to being exposed to a different method of instruction, the inventory is said to have
    A. content validity.
    B. criterion-related validity.
    C. internal consistency.
    D. response bias.

12. If the inventory includes a subscale designed to identify freshmen who are attempting to have more favorable attitudes toward teachers than they actually do because they believe negative attitudes are undesirable, the subscale is designed to detect
    A. content validity.
    B. criterion-related validity.
    C. internal consistency.
    D. response bias.

13. All high school freshmen in the school system would be the
    A. population.
    B. sample.
    C. participants.
    D. control group.

14. If the scientists decide to select 100 freshmen from several different schools in the system to be taught using more individualized methods, these freshmen will comprise a
    A. population.
    B. criterion group.
    C. control group.
    D. sample.

15. The best method for ensuring that a sample is representative of the population of all freshmen in the school system is
    A. matched-pairs.
    B. random sampling.
    C. correlation.
    D. counterbalancing.

16. Having a representative sample for a study helps ensure that the results of the study will have
    A. reliability.
    B. validity.
    C. generalizability.
    D. internal consistency.

17. For this particular study, these 100 freshmen will also comprise
    A. the control group.
    B. a random sample.
    C. an experimental manipulation.
    D. the experimental group.

18. An additional 100 freshmen from the same schools in the system who will be taught by more traditional methods will comprise
    A. the control group.
    B. a random sample.
    C. an experimental manipulation.
    D. the experimental group.

19. If the results of the study are published in a psychology journal, freshmen could also be called
    A. participants.
    B. subjects.
    C. variables.
    D. scores.

20. In these studies, the instructional method will be
    A. the independent variable.
    B. the dependent variable.
    C. a measure of content validity.
    D. a self-report measure.

21. Subjecting different groups of freshmen to different instructional methods is called
    A. control.
    B. random sampling.
    C. experimental manipulation.
    D. self-report.

22. Student attitude will be
    A. the independent variable.
    B. the dependent variable.
    C. a measure of content validity.
    D. a self-report measure.

23. Although difficult in educational settings, the best way to create identical groups of freshmen would be by
    A. random assignment to groups.
    B. creating matched pairs of students.
    C. including students who volunteered for the study.
    D. basing group assignment on physiological measures.

24. If the groups of freshmen in different schools were created by selecting freshmen so that their ages were equal and there were equal numbers of males and females in each group, the scientists would be using a
   A. true experiment.
   B. repeated-measures research design.
   C. matched-pairs research design.
   D. correlational research design.

25. If the scientists expect student attitudes to change over time, they can use a
   A. true experiment.
   B. repeated-measures research design.
   C. matched-pairs research design.
   D. correlational research design.

26. In another study, team teaching was to be compared to traditional instruction in a single school. In this study, half the freshmen in the school were assigned to be in team-taught classes for one grading period and in a traditional class for the next grading period. The order of instructional method was reversed for the remaining freshmen. This method is called
   A. counterbalancing.
   B. test–retesting.
   C. random sampling.
   D. internal consistency.

27. If the scientists want to see if there is a relationship between grades and attitudes, they will use a
   A. true experiment.
   B. repeated-measures research design.
   C. matched-pairs research design.
   D. correlational research design.

28. One scientist has identified five freshmen who made low grades in middle school and plans to monitor their attitudes as they are exposed to different methods of instruction throughout the school year. This scientist is conducting
   A. test–retesting.
   B. correlational research.
   C. single-subject research.
   D. counterbalancing.

29. Halfway through the school year, the scientists interview a sample of freshmen and discover that the students expect to have better attitudes because they know the schools want them to make better grades. This is an example of
   A. experimenter effects.
   B. placebo effects.
   C. Hawthorne effects.
   D. multivariable effects.

30. These same interviews reveal that many freshmen in the team-teaching and individualized instruction approaches are making better grades because they believe they are receiving more attention from their teachers. This is an example of
   A. experimenter effects.
   B. placebo effects.
   C. Hawthorne effects.
   D. multivariable effects.

31. If a team of outside observers reports that the attitudes they observe are not as favorable as those reported by the scientists, the outside observers are reporting evidence of
    A. experimenter effects.
    B. placebo effects.
    C. Hawthorne effects.
    D. multivariable effects.

Web Chapter W1 Key

Completion Items

1. self-report measures	16. participants	31. experimenter effects
2. behavioral measures	17. experimental group	
3. physiological measures	18. control group	
4. correlational research design	19. experimental manipulation	
5. reliability	20. independent variable	
6. test–retest reliability	21. dependent variable	
7. internal consistency	22. random assignment to groups	
8. interrater reliability	23. generalizability	
9. validity	24. random sampling	
10. content validity	25. matched-group research design	
11. criterion-related validity	26. repeated-measures research design	
12. response bias	27. counterbalancing	
13. true experiment	28. single-subject research	
14. population	29. placebo effects	
15. sample	30. Hawthorne effects	

Multiple-Choice Items

1. B	16. C	31. A
2. D	17. D	
3. A	18. A	
4. C	19. A	
5. B	20. A	
6. D	21. C	
7. B	22. B	
8. C	23. A	
9. D	24. C	
10. A	25. B	
11. B	26. A	
12. D	27. D	
13. A	28. C	
14. D	29. B	
15. B	30. C	

Web Chapter W2
Making Sense of Advanced Statistical Procedures in Research Articles

Learning Objectives
After studying this chapter, you should:

- Know how to interpret the results of advanced statistical procedures that explore relationships (hierarchical and stepwise multiple regression, partial correlation, multilevel modeling, factor analysis, and causal modeling) reported in research articles.
- Know how to interpret the information about the reliability of tests and measures reported in research articles.
- Know how to interpret the results of advanced statistical procedures that compare groups (analysis of covariance and multivariate analysis of variance) reported in research articles.
- Know how to read the results of unfamiliar statistical techniques reported in research articles.

A Brief Review of Multiple Regression
Regression is the prediction aspect of correlation, and multiple regression is used to predict a score on a criterion variable using two or more predictor variables. A multiple regression prediction rule includes a regression coefficient for each predictor so that a person's score on each predictor variable is multiplied by the regression coefficient for the variable. When Z scores have been calculated, the regression coefficients are *standardized* and called *standardized regression coefficients* or *betas* (βs).

The formula for a regression equation including three predictor variables is Predicted $Z_Y = (\beta_1)(Z_{X1}) + (\beta_2)(Z_{X2}) + (\beta_3)(Z_{X3})$.

The accuracy of a prediction rule is indicated by R^2, or the proportion of variance accounted for. Multiple regression provides the statistical significance of R^2 and of the regression coefficient for each predictor variable.

Hierarchical and Stepwise Multiple Regression
Hierarchical multiple regression involves entering predictor variables, or groups of predictor variables, in a particular sequence, often based on theory or prior research. The effectiveness of each added variable or group of variables is determined by the amount each increases R^2. **Stepwise multiple regression**, or simply stepwise regression, begins by identifying the predictor variable that accounts for most of the variance in the criterion variable, that is, the predictor that yields the largest R^2. If the R^2 is not significant, the analysis ends. If the R^2 is significant, the predictor variable that, in combination with the initial predictor variable, results in the greatest increase in R^2 is added to the equation. If the combined variables result in a significant R^2, the next variable that, in combination with the first two, contributes to R^2 is added. The process continues until no more predictor variables are left, or until no remaining variable increases R^2 significantly. The difference between the two methods is that hierarchical regression enters predictor variables in an order specified by the experimenter, while the computer program controls the order of variable entry in stepwise regression. Therefore, stepwise regression is useful in reducing a large number of variables in exploratory studies, or in applied studies in which accurate prediction is more important than theoretical considerations.

Partial Correlation
Partial correlation is used to determine the correlation between two variables while **holding constant, partialing out, controlling for,** or **adjusting for** the influence of one or more additional variables. (The latter four terms are used synonymously.) The result is a **partial correlation coefficient** that can have values between −1 and +1.

Reliability
Reliability refers to the consistency or stability of a measure like an achievement test or a personality inventory.

- **Test–retest reliability** is estimated by administering the same measure to the same group on two different occasions.
- **Split-half reliability** is estimated by correlating responses on one half of a test or inventory (the odd-numbered items) with responses on the other half of the test or inventory (the even-numbered items). If participants are responding consistently, the correlation should be high.

- The way items are divided into halves can result in inaccurate correlation coefficients when using the split-half method. A more general method called **Cronbach's alpha** (α) is the equivalent of dividing a test or inventory into all possible split-halves, calculating the correlation for each split, and determining the average of all splits. Since alpha provides a measure of how well items on a test or inventory assesses a common characteristic, it provides an **internal consistency reliability** coefficient.

Reliability is an important concern when a new test or inventory is being developed.

Multilevel Modeling
Multilevel modeling is an advanced type of regression analysis used when people are grouped in ways that could affect the pattern of scores. The variables in the analysis that reflect the people in each grouping are called **lower-level variables**, and the variables that reflect the grouping as a whole are called **upper-level variables**. **Hierarchical linear modeling (HLM)** is the most common name for these methods.

Factor Analysis
When large numbers of variables have been measured in a group of people, **factor analysis** may be used to identify groups of these variables that have high correlations with each other, but low correlations with other variables. Each group of variables is called a **factor**, and correlation between a variable and its factor is its **factor loading**. Variables have loading on each factor, but high loadings on only one. While loadings can range from -1 to $+1$, only loadings of $\pm.30$ or more are considered to be meaningful. While the calculations used in the several methods of factor analysis are objective, naming factors is subjective.

Causal Modeling
Causal modeling methods are used to determine whether the pattern of correlations among variables confirms a theory about which variables are causing which.
- The results of a **path analysis** are included in a diagram in which an arrow indicates the **path**, or cause-and-effect relationship between pairs of variables. The strength of the causal relationship, controlling for the influence of any other variables that may have arrows indicating paths to the same variable, is indicated by a **path coefficient**, which can be interpreted like a standardized regression coefficient.
- In **mediational analysis**, the purpose is to determine whether a third variable, the mediator variable, explains the causal relationship between two other variables.
- **Structural equation modeling** is an extension of path analysis with the advantage that a **fit index** can be calculated to indicate how well the observed correlations correspond to those hypothesized by the experimenter. While higher values indicate better fit for most indexes, for the RMSEA (root mean square error of approximation), a smaller number indicates a better fit. A second advantage of structural equation modeling is that combinations of variables can be combined into a **latent variable** that, while not actually measured, can be used to approximate a construct of interest to the experimenter.

The results of causal modeling procedures are subject to the same limits on interpretation that are true for correlation.

Procedures that Compare Groups
Statistical tests used to compare groups involve two types of variables. An independent variable defines group membership, for example, the experimental and control groups, especially when the groups are created by random assignment. [Tests like two-way analysis of variance include at least two independent variables.] A dependent variable reflects the effect of the experimental treatment.
- **Analysis of covariance (ANCOVA)** is an analysis of variance in which the effects of the experimental treatment on the dependent variable are adjusted to partial out or hold constant the effects of one or more variables that may influence the effect of the treatment, but that are of no interest in a particular study. Each of these unwanted variables is called a covariate. The results of ANCOVA are interpreted like an analysis of variance except that adjusted means are reported when the dependent variable is described.
- Multivariate statistics are procedures that involve more than one dependent variable, so **multivariate analysis of variance (MANOVA)** is an analysis of variance involving more than one dependent variable. The result is still an F ratio, and if the multivariate F ratio is statistically significant, separate univariate

analyses of variance are conducted for each dependent variable to determine which are contributing to the significant multivariate result.

- **Multivariate analysis of covariance (MANCOVA)** is an analysis of covariance with more than one dependent variable.

How to Read Results Involving Unfamiliar Statistical Techniques

Even experienced experimenters encounter unfamiliar statistical methods in research articles. In such cases, the basic intent of the analysis can usually be determined. First, examine the p value(s), which should clarify the pattern of results that is being considered significant. Next, look for an indication of the degree of association or the size of the difference. If the purpose of the analysis and the interpretation of the results is still unclear, refer to a more advanced statistics text or consult someone who has taken more advanced courses. New statistical methods are being developed constantly, such as analyses called computer-intensive methods, so you should expect to have to learn new techniques.

The statistical techniques discussed in this chapter are summarized in Table W2-6.

Chapter Self-Tests

The test items that follow are based on the following scenario. The psychologists studying depression have measured a number of additional variables so that they can study a variety of influences on the depression they observe among their clients by conducting more complex analyses of association, and by making more detailed comparisons between and among groups.

Understanding Key Terms in Web Chapter W2
Directions: Using the word bank that follows, complete each statement.

Word Bank: adjusting for / analysis of covariance / controlling for / covariate / Cronbach's alpha / factor / factor analysis / factor loading / fit index / hierarchical linear modeling / hierarchical multiple regression / holding constant / internal consistency reliability / latent variable / lower-level modeling / mediational analysis / multilevel modeling / multivariate analysis of covariance / multivariate analysis of variance / multivariate statistics / partial correlation / partial correlation coefficient / partialing out / path / path analysis / path coefficient / reliability / split-half reliability / stepwise multiple regression / structural equation modeling / test–retest reliability / upper-level modeling

Some of the first analyses the psychologists want to conduct involve determining variables that will help them predict depression. A review of their clients' files reveals that the psychologists have recorded information about or measured 20 variables for each client that may predict depression. In order to perform an exploratory analysis that will reduce the number of potential predictor variables to a more manageable number, the psychologists might use **(1)** _____. This first initial analysis identifies five significant predictor variables including anxiety, stress, marital satisfaction, job satisfaction, and age. If the psychologists begin their second analysis by entering anxiety and stress as a first group of predictor variables, then adding marital and job satisfaction as a second group, and concluding by entering age, examining the increase in R^2 at each stage, they have conducted a **(2)** _____. Based on the results of this analysis, the psychologists want to examine the relationship between stress and depression over and above the influence anxiety. An appropriate analysis in this situation is **(3)** _____. In this analysis, the psychologists are said to be **(4)** _____, **(5)** _____, **(6)** _____, or **(7)** _____ anxiety, and the resulting statistic is called a **(8)** _____.

Another advanced procedure that is used when people are grouped in ways that could affect the pattern of scores is **(9)** _____. The variables that reflect the grouping as a whole are called **(10)** _____, and the variables that reflect the people in each grouping are called **(11)** _____. The most common name for these methods is **(12)** _____.

Having reviewed the previous research on stress, the psychologists have selected a relatively brief inventory that can be used to measure a person's functioning on any given day in terms of anxiety, stress, and depression. In their review of research articles, the psychologists identified 30 statements that described behaviors and emotions reflecting the three variables of interest. The statistical procedure that would permit reduction of these 90 statements to an inventory comprised of 24–30 items is **(13)** _____. After this reduction, the group of statements that the psychologists labeled as measuring one of the three variables of interest is called a **(14)** _____, and the correlation of a statement describing a characteristic associated with anxiety with the larger group of statements reflecting anxiety is called a **(15)** _____.

Having developed a 24-item inventory, the psychologists are now concerned about the consistency or stability of client scores, that is, with the inventory's **(16)** _____. If the psychologists administer the inventory to a group of 50 people on two occasions separated by 2 weeks and calculate the correlation between the two sets of scores, they have calculated the **(17)** _____. If the psychologists divide the inventory by separating the odd-numbered and even-numbered items and correlate the scores resulting from this division of items, they have calculated the **(18)** _____. On the other hand, the psychologists might use a method that yields the average correlation of possible divisions of the inventory into two equal sets of items. This measure is called **(19)** _____, and is a measure of **(20)** _____.

Having identified a set of variables that predict development of depression, the psychologists are interested in developing models that will enable them to test whether patterns of correlations among sets of variables can be predicted by a specific theory about which variables are causing other variables. If the psychologists present the results in a diagram in which variables are connected by arrows, they have conducted a **(21)** _____. Each arrow represents a **(22)** _____, and the correlation that summarizes the relationship between variables connected by arrows is a **(23)** _____. If the psychologists want to see if the relationship between stress and depression is due to an intervening variable like anxiety or perceived health status, they would use **(24)** _____. However, the psychologists are expanding their analysis to obtain an overall measure of how well their model agrees with their theory. In this case, they can use **(25)** _____. The number that summarizes the agreement between the model and the theory is a **(26)** _____. An additional advantage of this method is that it will allow the psychologists to combine variables like job and marital satisfaction to provide an overall estimate of general satisfaction with life without actually measuring such a broad variable. This overall estimate is called a **(27)** _____.

Having examined these associations, the psychologists are now interested in comparing groups. If the psychologists decide to control for anxiety as part of their comparison of groups, they will use **(28)** _____. In this analysis, anxiety is a **(29)** _____. Due to the many correlations between and among variables the psychologists have observed, they decide to conduct some analyses involving two or more dependent variables. The procedures used in these analyses are called **(30)** _____. If the psychologists want to compare both stress and depression simultaneously for the two groups described above, they would conduct a **(31)** _____, and if they wanted to make the same comparison while controlling for anxiety, they would conduct a **(32)** _____.

Multiple-Choice Items

1. Based on theoretical considerations, the psychologists want to examine the effects of stress and anxiety on depression over and above demographic variables. Therefore, the psychologists first enter age, sex, and occupation as a group. Next, they enter stress and anxiety as a group. This statistical procedure is
    A. multivariate regression.
    B. multiple regression.
    C. hierarchical regression.
    D. stepwise regression.

2. If the psychologists' statistical analysis is considered to be controversial because they entered 10 independent variables into a regression model and permitted a computer algorithm to determine which were statistically significant, they used
    A. multivariate regression.
    B. multiple regression.
    C. hierarchical regression.
    D. stepwise regression.

3. If the psychologists want to determine the association between anxiety and depression while adjusting for the level of stress, they would use
    A. multiple regression.
    B. partial correlation.
    C. bivariate correlation.
    D. stepwise regression.

4. Another term for the adjustment described in Item 4 is
    A. partialing out.
    B. internal consistency.
    C. factor loading.
    D. fit index.

Items 5–7 are related.
The psychologists are interested in the consistency and stability of the scores on the inventories they use to measure anxiety, stress, and depression.

5. The general term used to describe the consistency and stability of inventories like these is
    A. internal consistency.
    B. factor loading.
    C. reliability.
    D. partialing.

6. If the psychologists assess consistency by administering one of the inventories to the same people after a certain amount of time has elapsed and correlating the two sets of scores, they are estimating
    A. internal consistency reliability.
    B. interrater reliability.
    C. split-half reliability.
    D. test–retest reliability.

7. If the psychologists calculate Cronbach's alpha, they will obtain an estimate of
    A. internal consistency reliability.
    B. interrater reliability.
    C. split-half reliability.
    D. test–retest reliability.

8. An advanced type of regression analysis that handles research situations in which people are grouped in some way that could affect the pattern of scores is
    A. multilevel modeling.
    B. multiple regression.
    C. partial correlation.
    D. factor analysis.

9. If an educational psychologist wants to investigate the relationships among stress, pressure at school, and family pressure but is concerned that the way students are assigned to courses may affect the pattern of scores on the scales used to measure the variables, the psychologist could use
    A. multivariate analysis of variance.
    B. partial correlation.
    C. factor analysis.
    D. hierarchical linear modeling.

Items 10–14 are related.
Having measured a large number of variables, the psychologists are considering statistical procedures that will allow them to examine relationships among all these variables.

10. The method that involves examining correlations between pairs of variables to see which ones are correlated and which are not is called
    A. mediational analysis.
    B. partial correlation.
    C. factor analysis.
    D. path analysis.

11. If the psychologists apply this procedure and identify a group of variables that have high correlations with others and define the group "General Satisfaction," they are defining a
    A. path.
    B. constant.
    C. fit.
    D. factor.

12. If the psychologists examine patterns of correlations between variables to identify causal relationships, they are using
    A. mediational analysis.
    B. partial correlation.
    C. factor analysis.
    D. path analysis.

13. The cause-and-effect connections between variables are shown by arrows, which are called
    A. loadings.
    B. paths.
    C. steps.
    D. adjustments.

14. If the psychologists want to demonstrate that the relationship between anxiety and depression may be due to the influence of perceived stress, they can use
    A. mediational analysis.
    B. partial correlation.
    C. factor analysis.
    D. path analysis.

Items 15–17 are related.
15. If the psychologists want an overall measure of agreement between their theory about the causes of depression and the correlations they have observed, they can use
    A. mediational analysis.
    B. partial correlation.
    C. structural equation modeling.
    D. path analysis.

16. The measure of agreement in this analysis is called a
    A. factor loading.
    B. covariate.
    C. latent variable.
    D. fit index.

17. A variable that is not actually measured, but that is approximated by a combination of several variables in the analysis, is a
    A. factor loading.
    B. covariate.
    C. latent variable.
    D. fit index.

Items 18–22 are related.
18. If the psychologists want to control for the anxiety level of these men and women, they would use
    A. structural equation modeling.
    B. analysis of variance.
    C. analysis of covariance.
    D. multivariate analysis of variance.

19. Anxiety level would be called a
    A. factor loading.
    B. covariate.
    C. latent variable.
    D. fit index.

20. For any analysis including more than one dependent variable, the psychologists will need to use
    A. structural equation modeling.
    B. factor analysis.
    C. fit indexes.
    D. multivariate statistics.

21. If the psychologists want to compare the depression inventory and stress inventory scores of men and women in group therapy based on their marital status (married vs. unmarried) in the same analysis, they will use
    A. multivariate analysis of variance.
    B. multivariate analysis of covariance.
    C. structural equation modeling.
    D. mediational analysis.

22. If the psychologists want to compare the depression inventory and stress inventory scores of men and women in group therapy based on their marital status (married vs. unmarried) in the same analysis and while partialing out the effects of anxiety inventory scores, they will use
    A. multivariate analysis of variance.
    B. multivariate analysis of covariance.
    C. structural equation modeling.
    D. mediational analysis.

Problems

1. A social scientist has developed a theoretical model of perceived quality of life that includes seven predictor variables. (a) Which type of multiple regression would the scientist be using if the seven independent variables were analyzed in a step-by-step manner to identify the subset of predictor variables that account for the most variance in the criterion variable? (b) Which type of multiple regression would the scientist be using if a group of variables including age, gender, and marital status were entered first, followed by scores on a job satisfaction scale and the number of years the person has been in the same job, and finally by scores on inventories measuring opinions about health and general well-being? (c) How is R^2 used in each method? (d) Explain both methods to someone who is familiar with ordinary multiple regression.

2. The psychologist studying attentiveness in kindergarten children has collected the following data from each child: age in months, gender, intelligence, achievement, and attentiveness ratings. (a) What statistical procedure would the psychologist use to determine the association between attentiveness and achievement while holding the effect of intelligence constant? (b) Explain the method to someone who is familiar with correlation and multiple regression, but not with this method. (c) What statistical procedure would the psychologist use to address the possibility that sex is an intervening variable in the hypothesized causal relationship between attentiveness and achievement? (d) Explain the method to someone who is familiar with correlation and prediction, but not with this method. (e) What statistical procedure would the psychologist use to test a prediction that age, gender, intelligence, and attentiveness cause achievement by examining the correlations between the variables? (f) Explain the method to someone who is familiar with multiple regression and partial correlation, but not with this method. (g) Finally, what statistical procedure would the psychologist use to obtain an overall measure of fit between the causal theory presented in (e) and the correlations among the scores? (h) Explain the method to someone who is familiar with multiple regression, but not with this method.

3. An educational psychologist has conducted a study to compare a computer-based course in introductory psychology with a traditional lecture course using the student scores on a comprehensive final examination as the dependent variable. Knowing that some students may have taken psychology courses in high school, the psychologist administered a pretest to determine the knowledge students brought to both courses. (a) What statistical procedure would the psychologist use to control for initial differences in knowledge of psychology identified by the pretest? (b) Explain the method to someone who is familiar with analysis of variance and partial correlation, but not with this method. (c) What statistical procedure could the psychologist use to control for the effects of different majors and class years (freshman, sophomore, junior, and senior) on examination performance? (d) Explain the method to someone who is familiar with regression procedures in general, but not with this procedure.

4. A sociologist has been hired to develop a brief (20 items or fewer) scale that employees of a large corporation can use to evaluate their supervisors. After published studies examining supervisory behavior, the sociologist has identified 60 statements that describe supervisory behavior. After administering a rating form including all 60 statements to a large number of employees in a variety of corporations and jobs, the sociologist is ready to begin reducing the number of statements. (a) What statistical procedure can the sociologist use to examine patterns of correlations between variables to see which variables are highly correlated and which are not correlated? (b) Explain the method to someone who is familiar with correlation, but not with this method. (c) After reducing the number of items to 20, what methods can the sociologist use to evaluate the consistency or stability of the rating scale? (d) Explain each method to someone who is familiar with correlation, but not with these methods.

5. (a) What statistical procedure would a behavioral scientist use to examine the effects of children's attentiveness in school (categorized as high, average, or low), teacher perceptions of children's coping skills (categorized as adequate or inadequate), and the children's parenting style (categorized as liberal or strict) on measures of the children's self-esteem and self-efficacy simultaneously? (b) What statistical procedure would the behavioral scientist use to partial out the effects of each child's level of achievement while comparing self-esteem and self-efficacy simultaneously? (c) Explain both methods to someone who is familiar with factorial analysis of variance, but not with either of these methods.

Additional Practice: Complete any Practice Problems in Set I that your instructor has not assigned and compare your responses to those provided by the authors. Pay particular attention to the problems that require you to explain your results to someone who has never taken a course in statistics.

Web Chapter W2 Key

Completion Items

1. stepwise multiple regression	12. hierarchical linear modeling	23. path coefficient
2. hierarchical multiple regression	13. factor analysis	24. mediational analysis
3. partial correlation	14. factor	25. structural equation modeling
4. holding constant	15. factor loading	26. fit index
5. partialing out*	16. reliability	27. latent variable
6. controlling for*	17. test–retest reliability	28. analysis of covariance
7. adjusting for*	18. split-half reliability	29. covariate
8. partial correlation coefficient	19. Cronbach's alpha	30. multivariate statistics
9. multilevel modeling	20. internal consistency reliability	31. multivariate analysis of variance
10. upper-level modeling	21. path analysis	32. multivariate analysis of covariance
11. lower-level modeling	22. path	

*in any order

Multiple-Choice Items

1. C	6. D	11. D	16. D	21. A
2. D	7. A	12. D	17. C	22. B
3. B	8. A	13. B	18. C	
4. A	9. D	14. A	19. B	
5. C	10. C	15. C	20. D	

Problems

1.
(a) Stepwise multiple regression.
(b) Hierarchical multiple regression.
(c) In stepwise multiple regression, statistically significant increases in R^2 are used to determine the variables that are included in the final regression equation. In hierarchical multiple regression, R^2 is used to determine how much each predictor contributes to the prediction of the criterion variable.
(d) Compare your explanations to the explanations provided for Problem 1 and Problem 2 in Set I of the Practice Problems in the text.

2.
(a) Partial correlation.
(b) Compare your explanation to the explanation provided for Problem 3 in Set I of the Practice Problems in the text.
(c) Mediational analysis.
(d) Compare your explanation to the explanation provided for Problem 7 in Set I of the Practice Problems in the text.
(e) Path analysis.
(f) Compare your explanation to the explanation provided for Problem 6 in Set I of the Practice Problems in the text.
(g) Structural equation modeling.
(h) Compare your explanation to the explanation provided for Problem 8 in Set I of the Practice Problems in the text.

3.
(a) Analysis of covariance.
(b) Compare your explanation to the explanation provided for Problem 10 in Set I of the Practice Problems in the text.
(c) Multilevel modeling.
(d) Multilevel modeling is an advanced type of regression analysis that handles a research situation in which people are grouped in some way that could affect a pattern of scores. In this situation, the experimenter might be concerned that students with different majors would have different patterns of scores, as might freshmen, sophomores, juniors, and seniors.

4.
(a) Factor analysis.
(b) Compare your explanation to the explanation provided for Problem 5 in Set I of the Practice Problems in the text.
(c) Test–retest, split-half, Cronbach's alpha.
(d) Compare your explanation to the explanation provided for Problem 4 in Set I of the Practice Problems in the text.

5.
(a) Multivariate analysis of variance.
(b) Multivariate analysis of covariance.
(c) Compare your explanation of MANOVA to the explanation provided for Problem 11 in Set I of the Practice Problems in the text. MANCOVA is an extension of ANCOVA to a situation in which an experimenter has data that includes two or more dependent variables and wants to control for one or more additional variables.

Appendix

How to Use SPSS

At the time of this writing, SPSS software is called IBM SPSS Statistics. Recent versions of SPSS were also called SPSS Statistics and PASW Statistics. The problem solutions and examples in this Study Guide were obtained using PASW Statistics Version 17.0.2. Your institution may have a different version of the software, but the versions available in most academic computing centers should be adequate to follow the problems in this Study Guide. In general, any differences in the procedural steps and output across different versions of the software will be very minor.

SPSS stands for Statistical Package for the Social Sciences and is just that—a package of programs for conducting statistical procedures like the ones presented in the text. A good way to learn SPSS is to arrange a tutoring session with someone who knows how to use the package. If your instructor does not provide introductory sessions, you may want to see if the computing center at your institution offers such sessions. If you need to learn to use the package on your own, manuals provided by SPSS are available, and the help function available when you are using the package is useful. You may also go to SPSS.com and register as a user, which will give you access to a compilation of frequently asked questions and their answers. Be aware that this manual will provide more information than you need to succeed in this course, so concentrate on learning the processes and procedures you need and avoid getting bogged down with information you do not need for this course. The purpose of this Appendix is to help you learn just what you need to open SPSS and begin using it.

The information presented in the text and in this Study Guide makes three assumptions, the first being that you are familiar with the fundamental operations of the computer system you will be using—how to turn it on, how to type in instructions, how to move between directories, and how to end a session. The second assumption is that you are familiar with basic computer terminology such as "file," "saving a file," and "cursor." The third assumption is that you have some experience working with computers and understand the necessity of following instructions.

Opening SPSS

You should communicate with your instructor or the computing center at your university to determine how you are to access SPSS. If a shortcut was installed on the computer you are using, ☜☜ the SPSS icon on the Desktop. (As in the text, ☜ indicates a left mouse click.) The screen will look like the one shown in Figure 1 except that the files listed in the two windows will be different because they will be your files. Next, you should ☜ *Type in data* and ☜ *OK*. The screen will change so that it looks like the one in Figure 2.

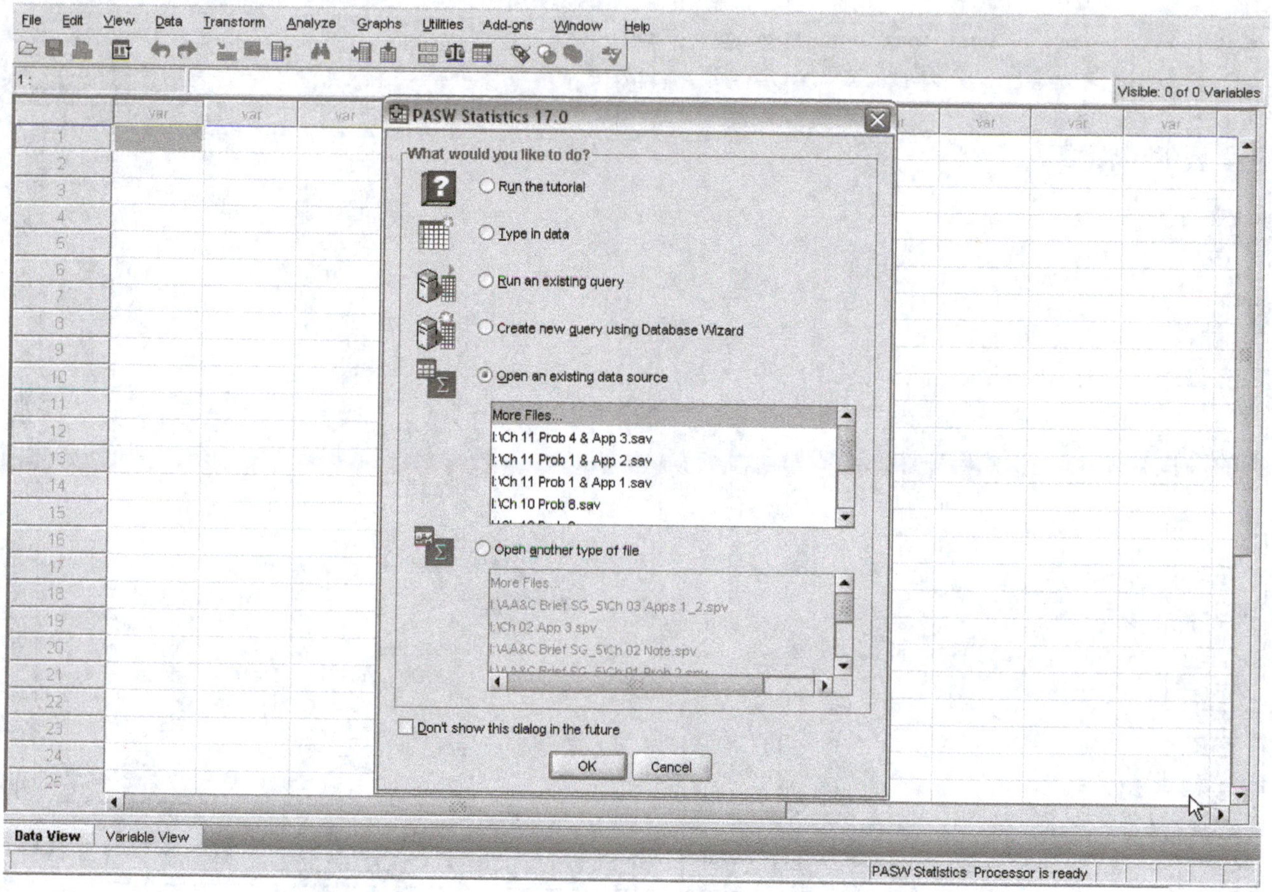

Figure 1

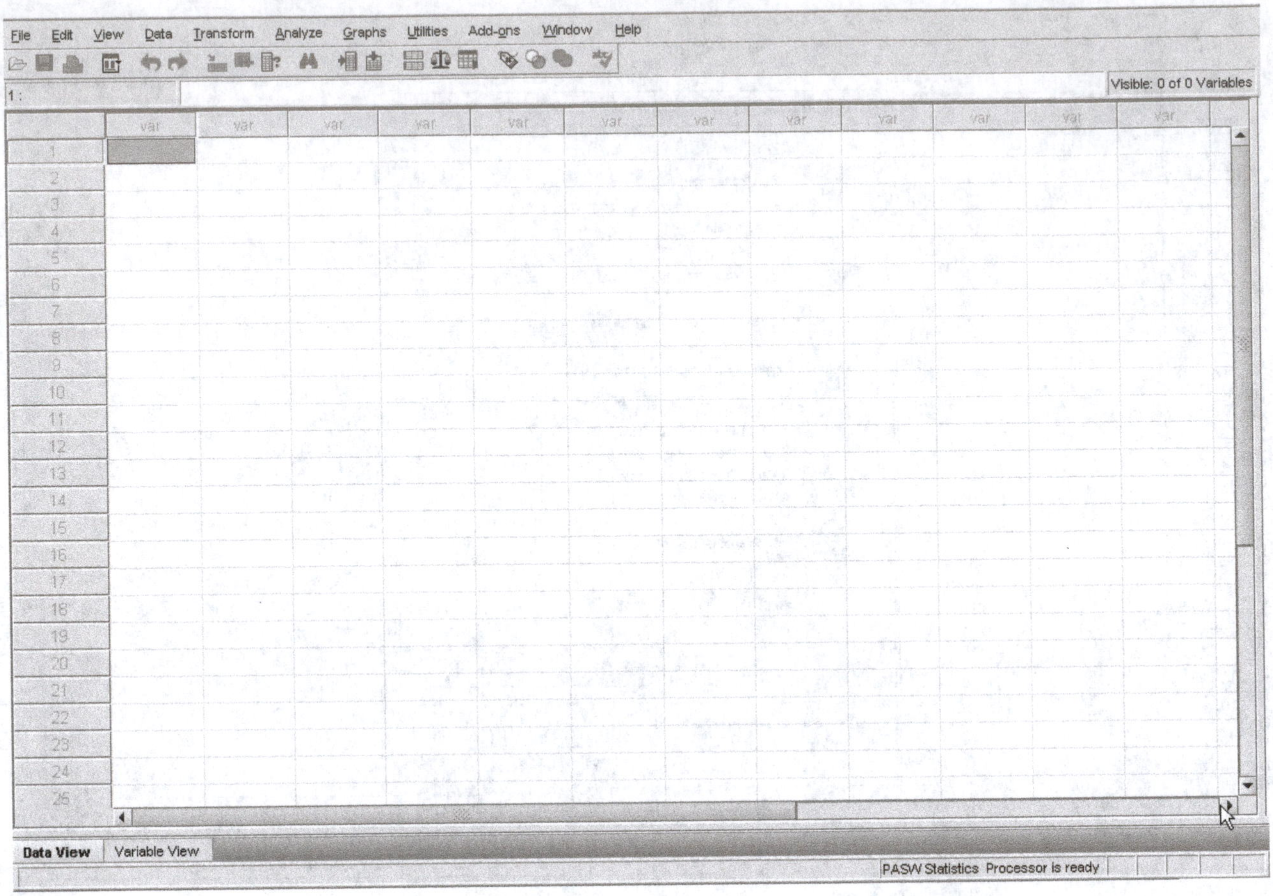

Figure 2

Entering Data

In behavioral and social science research, the data consist of scores on one or more variables measured for each individual enrolled in a study. For example, each of 10 students might have a score on a motivation inventory and on an examination. Thus, the dataset would contain two variables ("motiv" and "exam") with scores for each of the 10 students. To enter data in SPSS, begin by 🖱 in the upper left cell and type the motivation inventory score for the first individual. Then press the Enter key. Then type the motivation score for the second individual, and continue until the scores for all 10 students have been entered. Next, you should 🖱 in the top cell of the second column. Type the motivation inventory score for the first individual. Then press the Enter key. Then type the examination score for the first individual and press Enter. Continue until the scores for all 10 students have been entered. The screen should look like the one in Figure 3.

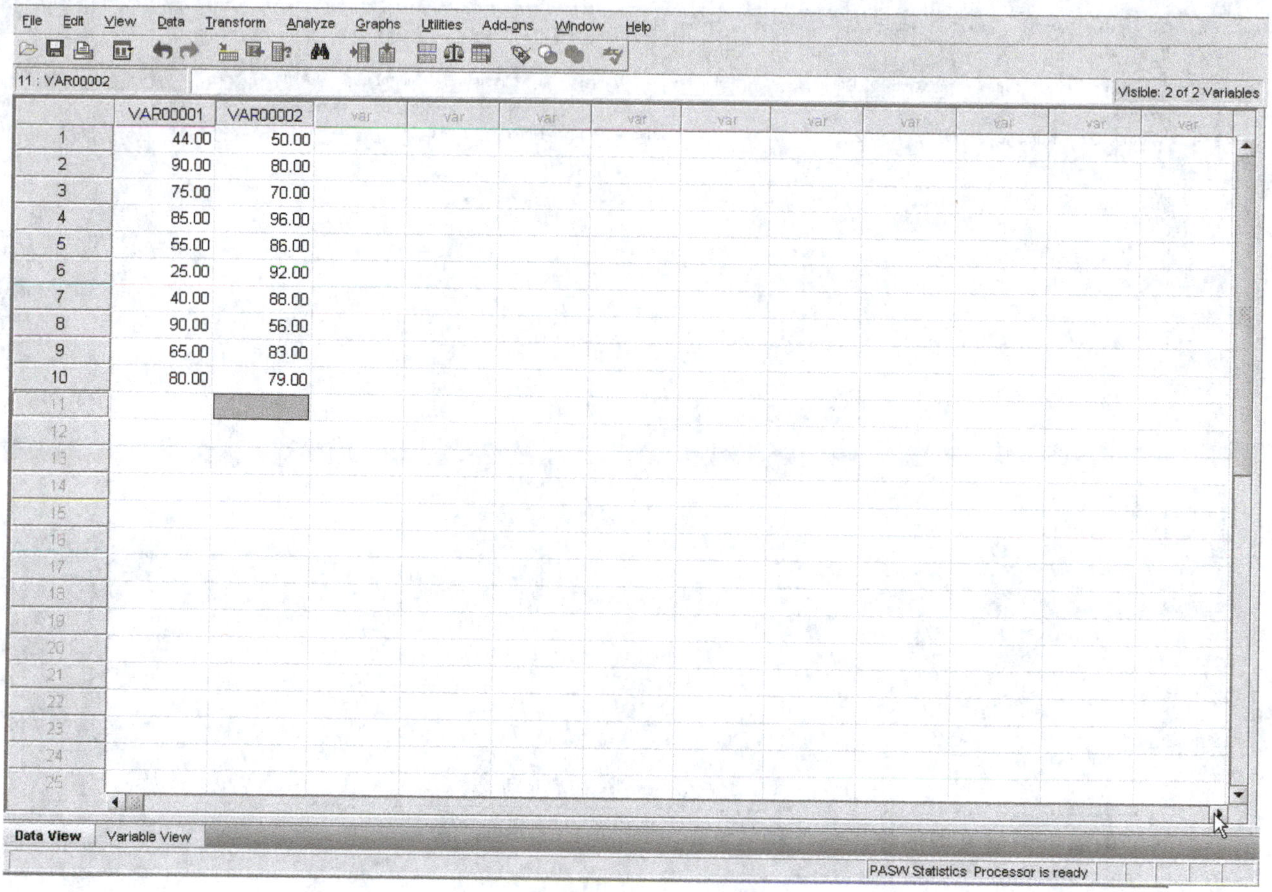

Figure 3

Naming Variables

🖰 the Variable View tab at the bottom of the screen to obtain the screen shown in Figure 4.

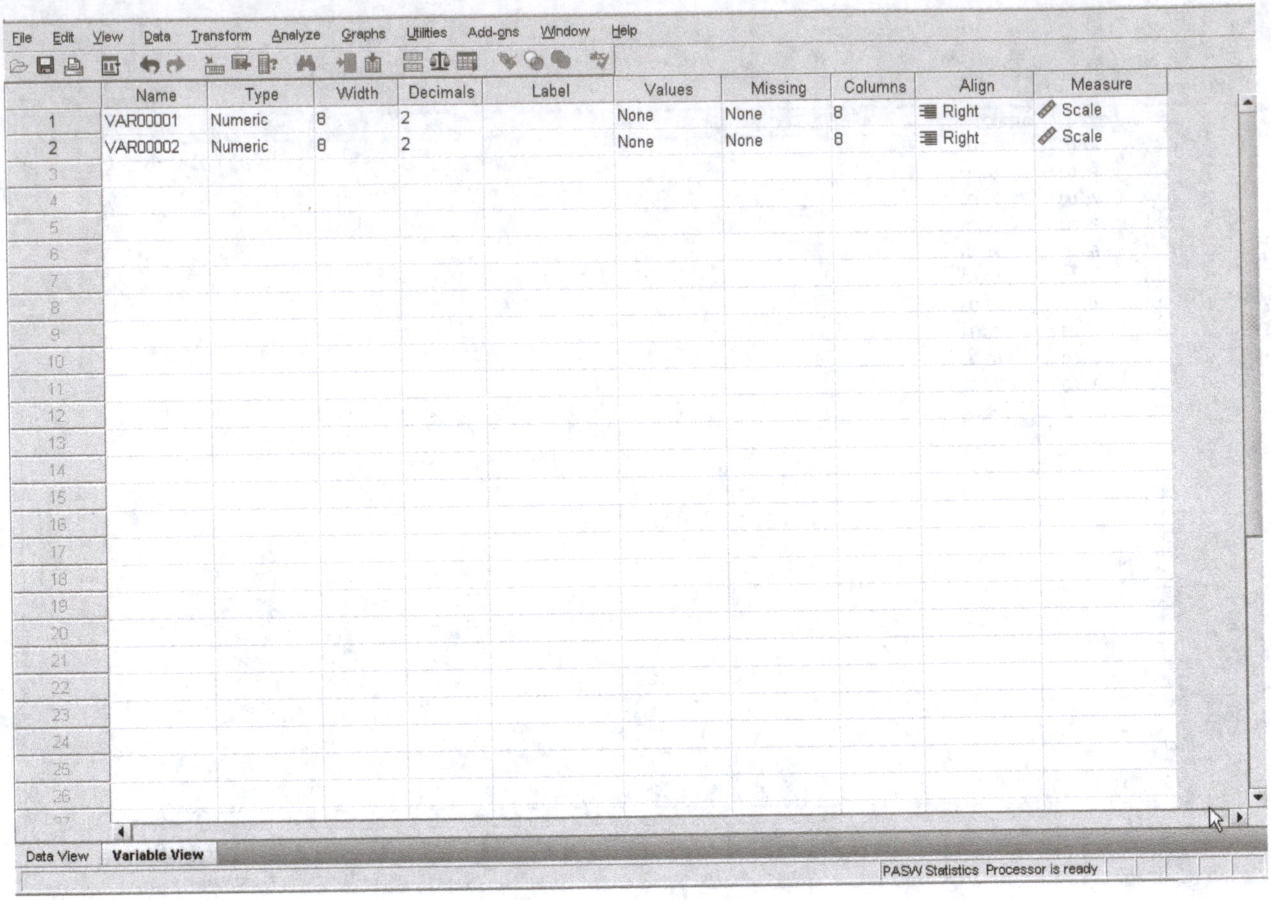

Figure 4

Place the cursor in front of the V in VAR0001 and 🖰. This action highlights the cell and permits you to name the variable "motiv," as is shown in Figure 5. Repeat this action with VAR0002 and name the variable "exam". In current versions of SPSS, variable names can be up to 64 characters long, but keeping variable names short (for example, 8–12 characters) will make the data view window more manageable—you will not have to scroll so much to see the different variables. Remember that some characters cannot be used in variable names, and others cannot be used to begin or end variable names. Keep your variable names simple and consult the manual or help function if you have problems.

If you click in the cells labeled "Decimals," up and down arrows will appear. These arrows can be used to change the number of decimals that appear in cells in the Data View screen. The number of variables has been changed to none for both variables, as in Figure 5. (Leaving the decimal and zeros will have no effect on your ability to follow the examples in this Study Guide.)

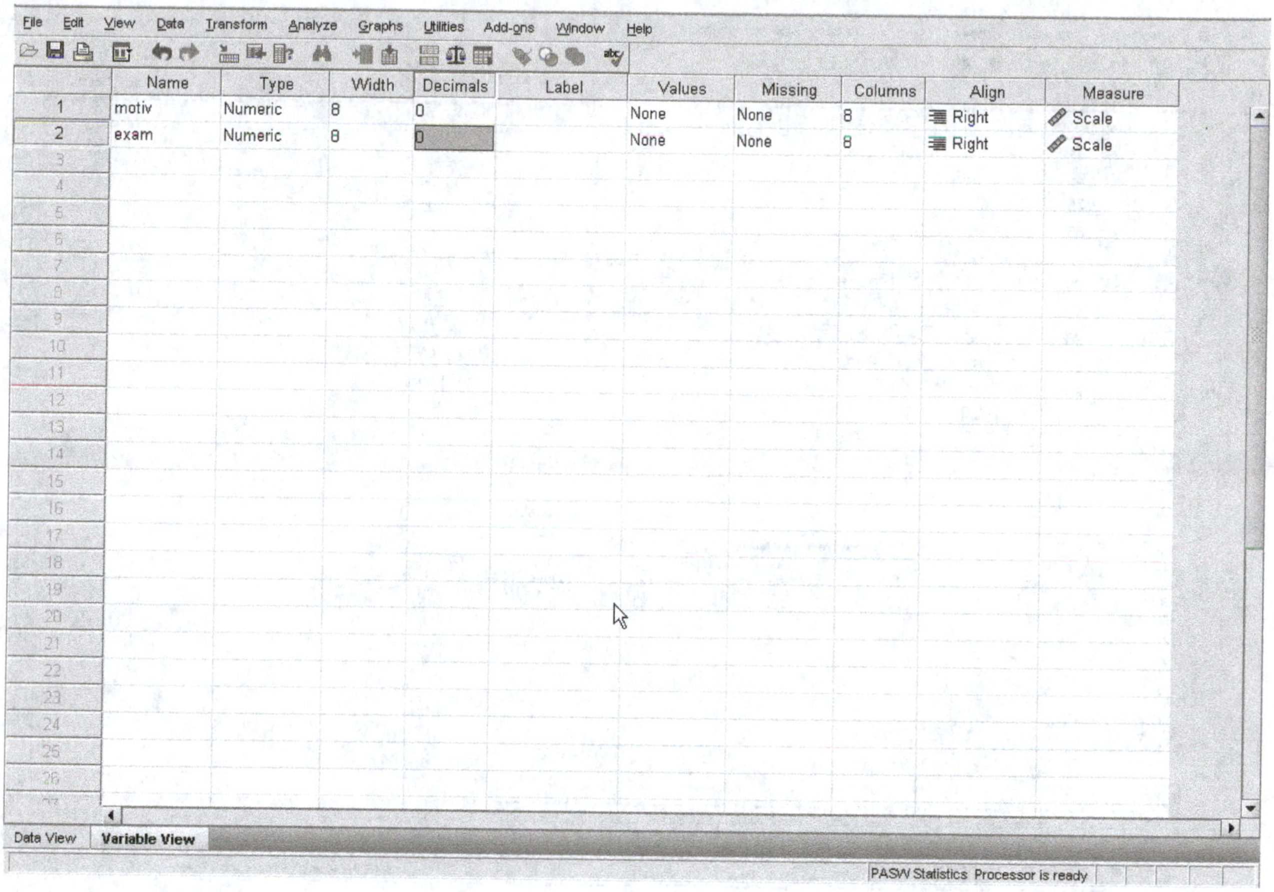

Figure 5

Thus, the rows represent data for students, and the columns represent the data for variables. You can enter the data by student or by variable, or you can use the mouse to select individual cells in which to enter data.

Conducting Analyses

All of the SPSS applications except the graphing applications will begin by having you ⌐ð Analyze on the SPSS toolbar. You can ⌐ð Analyze from either the Data View window or the Variable View window. You can either follow the steps below from the Variable view screen (Figure 5), or you can return to the Data View screen (Figure 3). The analyses in this Study Guide were done after returning to the Data View screen after you have named your variables and adjusted the decimals. For example, to obtain the average motivation and examination scores,
⌐ð Analyze.
⌐ð Descriptive Statistics.
⌐ð Frequencies.

These commands will give the screen shown in Figure 6.

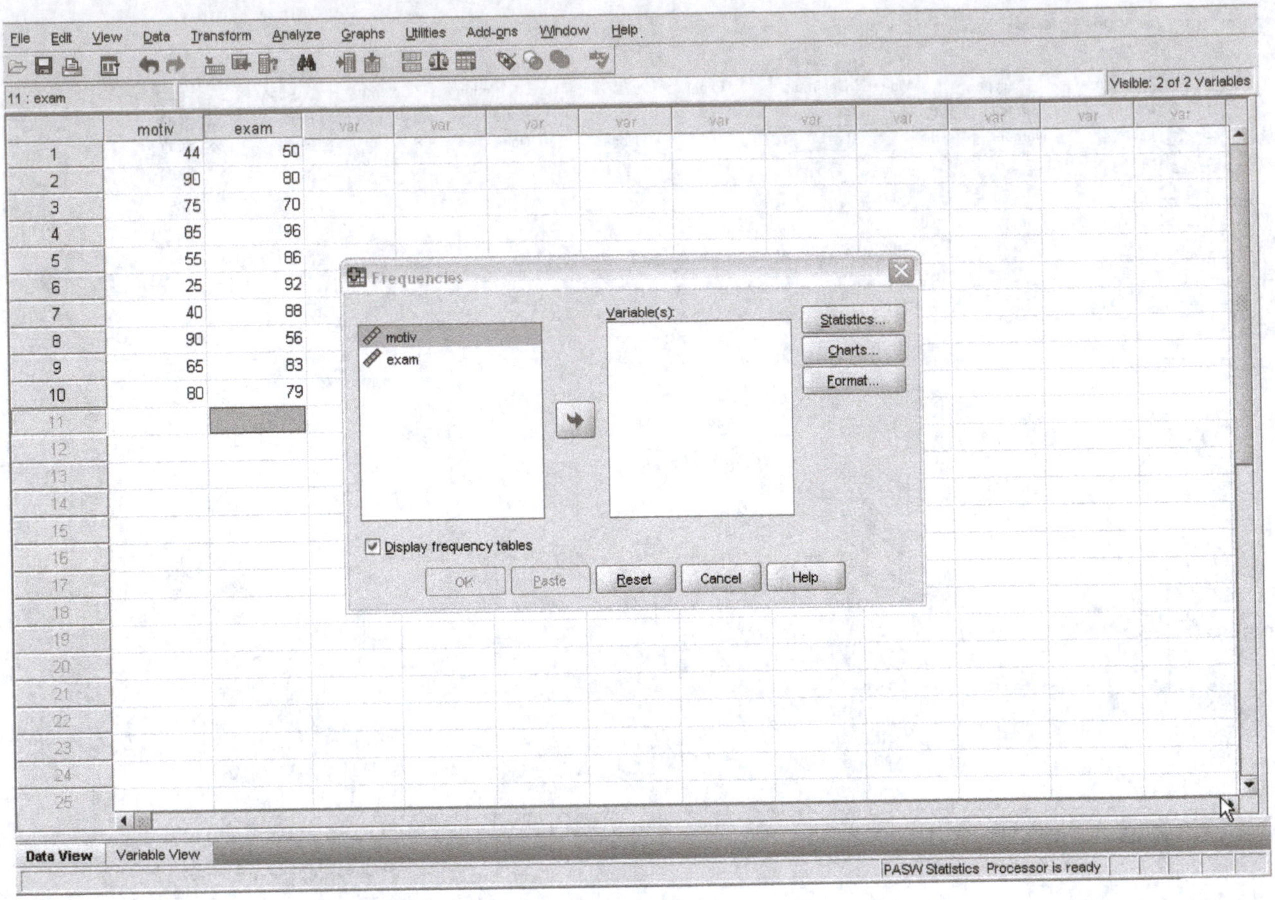

Figure 6

Since "motiv" is already selected, ✋ the arrow to move it into the Variable(s) box, and repeat for "exam." The screen should look like Figure 7.

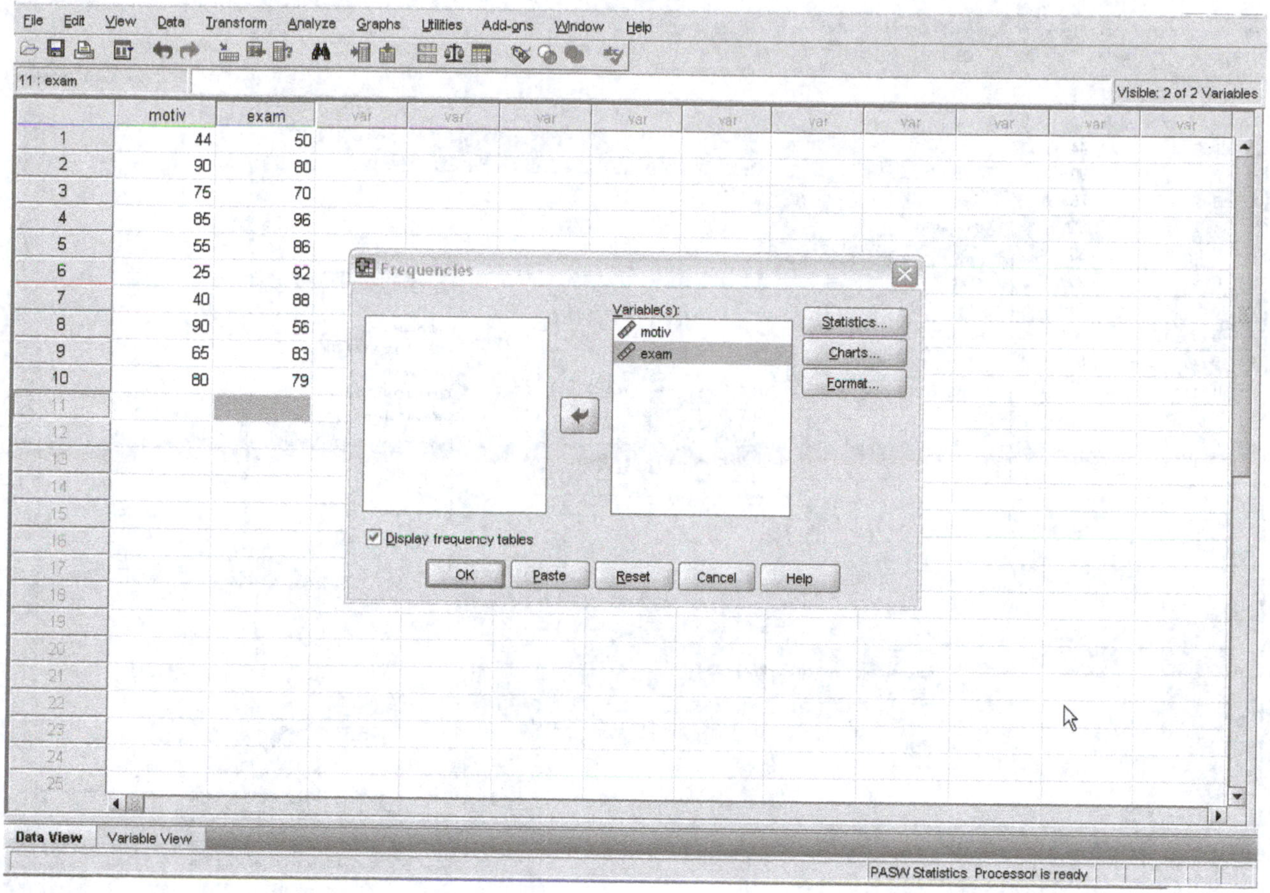

Figure 7

When you 🖱 OK, you will obtain output that includes the mean motivation and examination scores for the 10 students, and you will learn that the mean is the arithmetic average.

Creating New Variables

New variables can be created from existing variables. For example, suppose you wanted to weight the examination score so that its value is doubled.

🖱 Transform.
🖱 Compute Variable.
Enter the new variable name (for example, "exam2") in the Target Variable box.
Enter the computations using the name of any existing variables and the arithmetic symbols, in this case, exam*2, in the Numeric Expression window.
The screen will look like the one shown in Figure 8.

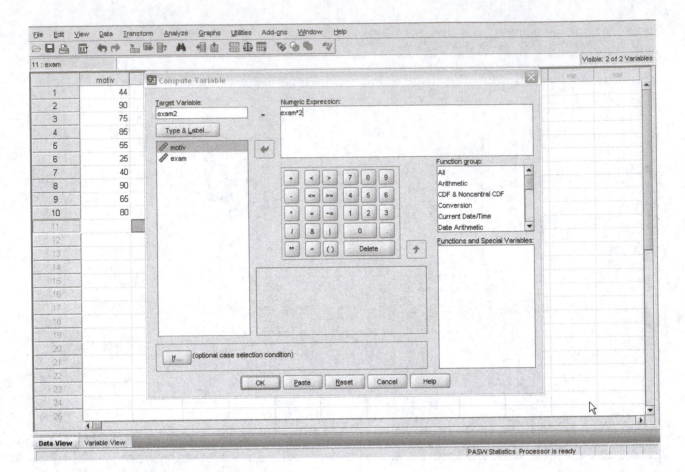

Figure 8

Note that many mathematical functions are listed in the lower right screen and that you can combine functions using parentheses to group computations following algebraic rules for operations like multiplication and division.

When you 🖱 OK, the new variable will appear in the Data Window, as is shown in Figure 9.

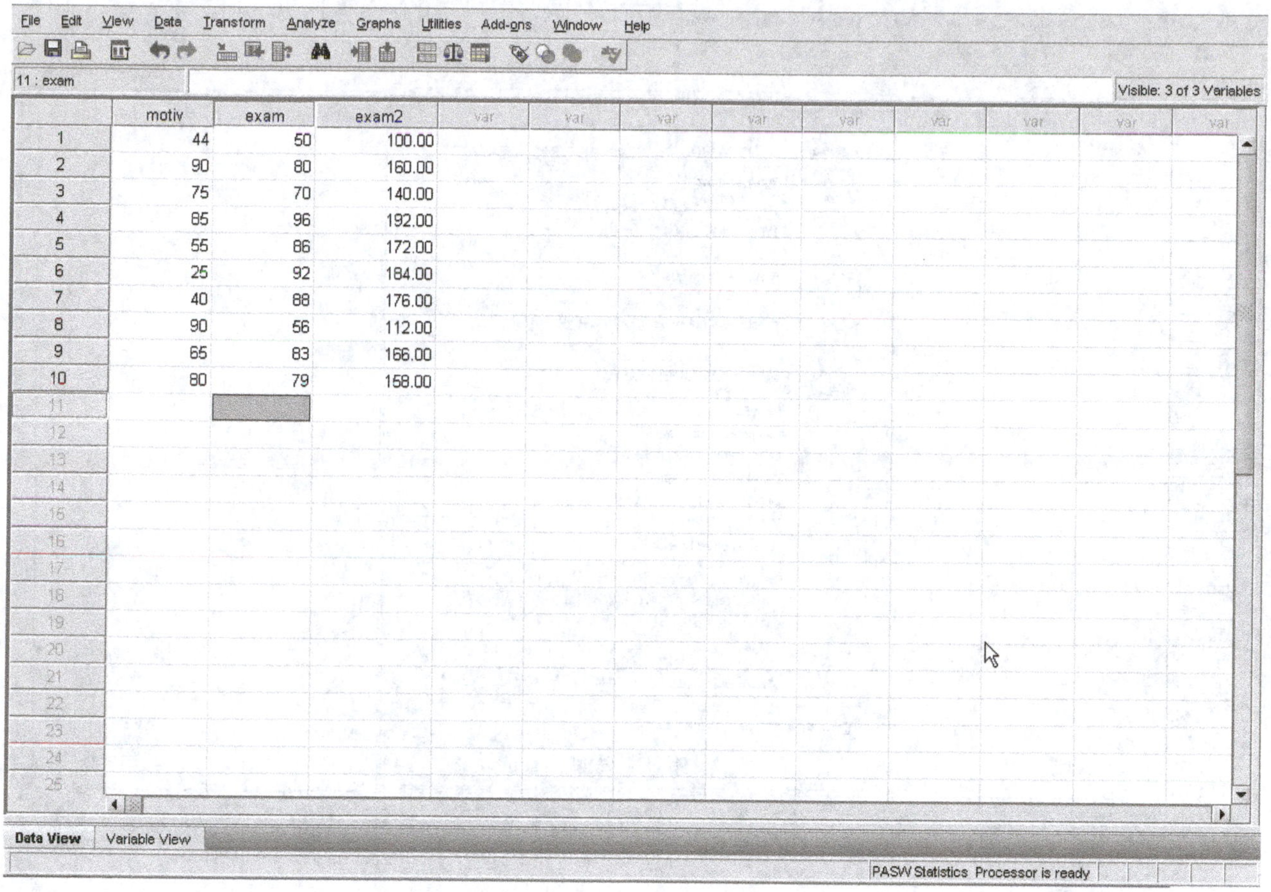

Figure 9

Saving the Data in Files

To save a dataset, on the toolbar,

⌒⊕ File.

⌒⊕ Save (or Save As).

Name your dataset (for example, Appendix Data) and designate the drive to which you would like the data to be saved.

⌒⊕ OK.

You may also save your output if you wish.

Ending an SPSS Session

After saving the dataset,

⌒⊕ the X in the box at the top right of the SPSS window, or

⌒⊕ File.

⌒⊕ Exit.

Recalling a Dataset

If a dataset already exists, you do not need to reenter all the data. Simply open SPSS, but instead of choosing "Type in data," choose "Open an existing data source." Then choose one of the SPSS datasets listed (for example, Appendix Data.sav), as shown in Figure 10.

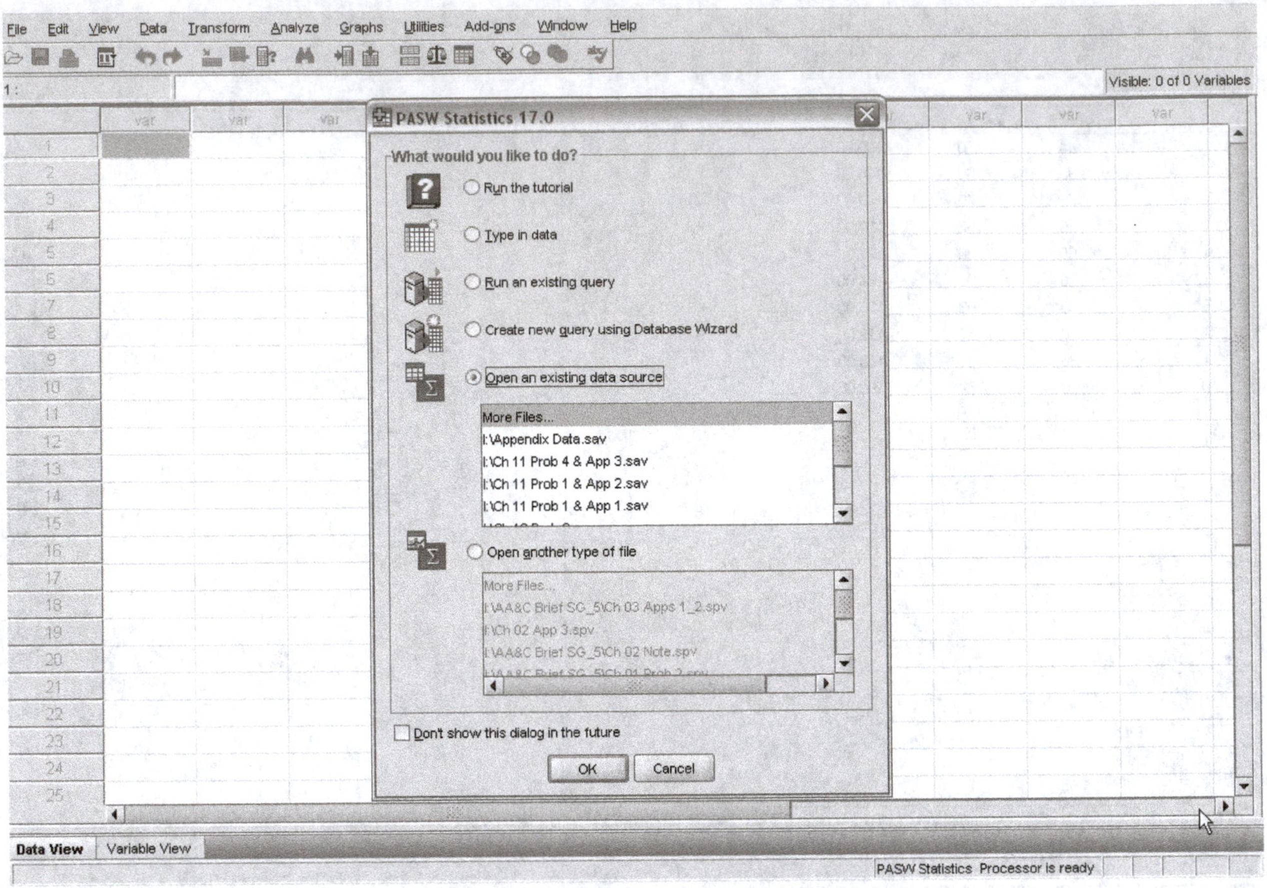

Figure 10

NOTES

NOTES

NOTES

NOTES

NOTES

NOTES